更快、更高、更强——更团结

Faster, Higher, Stronger—Together

CITIUS, ALTIUS, FORTIUS—COMMUNIS

每一个人，身上都拖带着一个世界，由他所见过、爱过的一切所组成的世界，即使他看起来是在另外一个不同的世界里旅行、生活，他仍然不停地回到他身上所拖带着的那个世界去。

——夏多布里昂

CITIES OF
SPORTING
EVENTS

周 澍 著
ZHOU SHU

赛事之城

浙江教育出版社·杭州

周　澍

浙江大学法学博士，美国伊利诺伊理工大学公共管理硕士；

浙江日报报业集团"潮新闻"、《浙江作家》及大公网专栏作者；

中国文艺评论家协会会员、中国美术学院访问学者；

杭州第19届亚运会会徽、吉祥物评委；亚奥理事会《亚洲体育》特约撰稿、美术设计。

主要作品有《窗》《城》《潮涌》和《不期而至》。

Zhou Shu holds a Ph.D. in Law from Zhejiang University and a Master in Public Administration from the Illinois Institute of Technology. She is an accomplished columnist for "Tide News"at Zhejiang Daily Press Group, *Zhejiang Writers,* and Ta Kung Pao. A member of China Literature and Art Critics Association, she has also served as a visiting scholar at the China Academy of Art.

Zhou Shu's diverse roles include judging emblem and mascot selections for the 19th Asian Games, as well as contributing as a special writer and graphic designer for the OCA *Sporting Asia* Newsletter. Notable among her works are *Window, City, Surging Tides* and *The Unexpected.*

推荐语

　　本书深入研究亚运会及其起源，以及多年来的演变发展，并对其进行全面概述。不仅深入探讨了亚运会的历史，还展望了奥林匹克运动的未来。与此同时，本书对这一亚洲多元体育赛事的文化和体育意义进行了引人入胜的探索。无论你是体育爱好者，抑或是对亚洲文化感兴趣，这本创新之书为你提供了了解亚运会内核与亚运世界富有价值的洞见。

——国际奥委会文化与奥林匹克遗产委员会主席　坤莹·帕塔玛

　　工作之余，伊依旧笔耕不辍，且时有佳作诞生，这便是热爱，便是才情。

——中国作家协会副主席、茅盾文学奖得主　麦家

我曾与作者一起参与第19届杭州亚运会会徽征集、吉祥物评选和主题口号发布，时隔许久，未见其人，已先读到《赛事之城》，只觉阳光下，人和城市都奋发奔跑。

　　——世界冠军、奥运冠军、杭州亚运会申办形象大使、杭州亚运会宣传形象大使　罗雪娟

　　亚洲人也掷铁饼。亚细亚古老悠久的文明史中，自然包含了体育这个章节。《赛事之城》描述的亚运之城回荡着一种古老而雄壮的声音，那是亚细亚奋起的呐喊声。

　　——作家，茅盾文学奖、鲁迅文学奖、英仕曼亚洲文学奖得主　苏童我是在"亚洲雄风"中成长的一代，北京亚运会第一次让我意识到亚洲之多元与活力。这本图文并茂的作品集，提醒我们多样、开放文化之重要。

　　　　　　　　　　　　　　——作家 、单向空间创始人　许知远

　　人类为什么喜欢涌向城市？因为城市繁华热闹，闪烁着文明的星光；人类为什么在遥远的古希腊就发明了体育运动？因为体育运动不断测量挑战人的能量和精神的极限。

　　《赛事之城》记述众多城市传接体育薪火的事实，又将人类、城市和体育三点连一线，揭示出像地下河一样默默流淌的文明史。

　　　　　　　　　　　　　　——大型文学期刊《收获》主编　程永新

《赛事之城》再次不期而至，每读一篇，就像观看一个关于城市的小型展览。记得作者来过巴塞罗那，这里既是奥运之城，也是艺术之都。期待她以独特的视角和笔触继续创作，将西班牙的美丽城市介绍给各地的朋友们。

——西班牙当代著名超现实主义画家　爱德华多·纳兰霍

德智体群美同是中华文化的根与源，各具感悟、各展莹泽。

作者以细腻颖敏的内蕴、不期而遇的潇洒、逸游文化瀚海的浪漫，通过观察、分析和笔触，用深邃的视角、文化的维度和心灵的感召，透释出文体共融、映衬出体育意度并剪影出拼搏人生的故事，为文体界带来耳目一新的妙悟和气息，促进文化与体育不期而至、传统与未来逐梦飞扬。

——亚奥理事会（东亚区）副会长、中国香港体育协会暨奥林匹克委员会会长　霍震霆

Recommendations

This well-researched book provides a comprehensive overview of the Asian Games, their origins, and their evolution over the years. It not only delves into the history of the Asian Games but also looks into the future of the Olympic Movement. The book is a fascinating exploration of the cultural and sporting significance of this multi-sport event in Asia. Whether you are a sports enthusiast or interested in Asian culture, this innovative book offers valuable insights into the world of the Asian Games.

— Khunying Patama Leeswadtrakul, Chairman of the International Olympic Committee on Culture and Olympic Heritage

In her spare time, she keeps writing, and from time to time produces outstanding articles which attract public attention. This is passion, this is talent.

— Mai Jia, Vice Chairman of China Writers Association, winner of the Mao Dun Literature Award

I once participated in the emblem collection, mascot selection, and theme slogan release of the 19th Hangzhou Asian Games with the author. After a long time, I didn't see her in person, but I had already read her book *Cities of Sporting Events*. I felt that under the sunshine, people and cities are running hard.

— Luo Xuejuan, World Champion, Olympic Champion, Hangzhou Asian Games Bid Ambassador, 19th Hangzhou Asian Games Promotion Ambassador

Among Asians there are also Discus Throwers. Sports is certainly an important chapter in ancient civilization history of Asia. In the book of *Cities of Sporting Events*, an ancient and majestic sound echoes in those cities which held the Asian Games. That is the yell for the rising of Asia.

— Su Tong, Author, winner of the Mao Dun Literature Award, Lu Xun Literature Award, and the Eastman Asian Literature Prize

As a member of the generation that grew up in "The Spirit of Asia", it was the Beijing Asian Games that made me realize for the first time the diversity and dynamism of Asia. This richly illustrated work reminds us of the importance of a diverse and open culture.

— Xu Zhiyuan, Writer, Founder of OWSpace

Why do humans like to flock to the city? Because the city is flourishing and lively, shining with the starlight of civilization. Why did humans create sports in distant ancient Greece? Because sports could continually measure and challenge the ultimate limits of people's energy and spirit.

Cities of Sporting Events narrates the stories that many cities inherit the flame of sports. It connects the relations among humanity, cities, and sports, and reveals the civilization history flowing silently like an underground river.

— Cheng Yongxin, Chief Editor of the famous Literary Journal *Harvest*

Once again, *Cities of Sporting Events* comes unexpectedly. Every story of this book makes you like a visitor of a small museum about the city. I remember that the author once visited Barcelona, which is both the city of the Olympics and the city of design and modernism. Looking forward to her continued creation with unique views and techniques, introducing the beautiful city of Spain to the world.

— Eduardo Naranjo, Renowned contemporary surrealist painter in Spain

The Chinese culture finds its roots in the Five Ways of Life (morality, intellect, physique, social skills, and aesthetics), each glittering with its own perceptions.

The author – with the delicacy and sensitivity in her sophistication, the insouciance towards the unexpected encounters, and the romance of swimming in the vast sea of culture – deciphers the harmony of culture and physique and reflects a physique intention. She silhouettes the stories of the struggling life through observation and analysis, with a profound perspective, cultural dimension, and spiritual appeal. She has brought a refreshing breath to this field and promoted the unexpected encounter between culture and sports, the soaring dreams of tradition and future.

— Timothy Tsun Ting FOK, Vice President of Olympic Council of Asia (East Asia), President of Sports Federation & Olympic Committee of Hong Kong, China

序 一
春华秋实

作者发来文稿的时候，通常在周末。阅读那些书写亚运城市的文字，唤起的不仅是回望，更有期待与向往。

再收到时已是媒体的推送版，其间间隔的时间并不长，表明她在"送审"的同时已着手公众号的制作。彼时再复读专栏文章，如同老胶片与新数码交织，又有了不一样的况味。加之图片精美，制作精良，强化了身临其境的代入感，让文章点击量不断刷新与进阶。

收到《东京"设计"》一文是在今年的3月底，同时发来的还有一篇《玫瑰花开》。春暖花开时对美术史上的重要花卉作品和奥林匹克运动的视觉设计进行梳理，恰逢其时。但那时我尚未意识到她的写作原本是一个完整的计划与体系。随着新德里、曼谷、广岛、德黑兰、雅加达、马尼拉等亚运城市一个个进入到潮新闻的"述说亚运"专栏，我鼓励她快马加鞭，争取在杭州亚运会举办前完成这个系列的写作。

压力与紧迫感一定是存在的，但她仍然按照不期而至的灵感与自己固有的节奏，又写了国际奥委会总部所在地洛桑，以及杭州成功申办亚运会的城市阿什哈巴德。到8月初完成关于多哈的文章时，正好经历了从"春分"到"立秋"的写作周期。

在她写到的一些城市，我曾与她相遇。对于她写的那些，譬如关于曼谷和帕塔玛女士的记忆，我感同身受，只是她的用心让她用文字留住了更多。而我也分明知道，有些城市是她未曾有缘去过的，但她总能找到办法，以别的方式接近，抵达，甚至深入。

读万卷书行万里路，转化与传达的前提，大抵如此。在极速的书写与从容的积累之间，她看似始终保持了一种合理的张力。当然这背后的付出与艰辛，非亲历者无从知晓。

她写运动员与竞技比赛，但只在璀璨的星河中汲取极具代表性的个体，以及与城市故事展开紧密相连的运动项目。她写冠军巅峰时的青春与光华，也写他们失利时的无助黯然，奋起重生后的"王者归来"。她自然也关注记录奖牌，但更写赛事历练与滔滔后浪！

她写赛事，但远远不止于赛事本身。笔触所及，画出城市的自然、人文景观，以及历史文化与经济社会的特色呈像，纵使涉及对现象与战略的表述，也力图以具象的实例作为支撑，那样的笔触，精准、概括而不浮夸。她写赛事之城，却每每在对他者的驻足与观察里，情难自已梦回故乡，写"双奥之城"的荣耀，"羊城"升腾的火焰，更写她心头永久的"江南忆"与明月光！

敲击键盘的手指，用不到5个月的业余时间，写遍亚洲奥林匹克运动史上所有举办过亚运会的海外城市，并且还准备了多语种的版本。这是一个人的孤独时光与搏击赛场，也是一个友谊团队合力献给广大读者的一场及时雨。期待不久的将来，《赛事之城》续篇能够再次注入时代的华章，给我们带来更多新的惊喜！

亚奥理事会副主席　宋鲁增

2023年8月6日

X

序二
留　痕

　　为《赛事之城》写上几句，内心首先泛起的该是一份羡慕。这是一个相当有诱惑力的题材，在我心里，曾计划过漫长的旅程，带上家人，最好能有充足的一年，从一座城到一座城，辗转着，找寻早已渗入城市深处的体育血脉。至今仍未上路，但已经读到了《赛事之城》的书稿。写作是件苦差事，作者的远行和坐地神游，终于让一座座城在我们面前立体起来。读着作者此前的作品，又厚又重，我深感她驾驭文字时的那份快乐、韧性与执着。将自己置身于那些遥远的城中，在她深爱的城市即将迎来一场期待已久的盛会之前，将见识与感受重新唤醒，落在键盘。读着书稿，那些城在我心中活了起来，自己当年置身其间的一幅幅画面与一丝丝气息，萦绕心头。时光远去，记忆仍鲜活生动。

　　因为出差，我是在南京捧着手机读的书稿，读了中文，再看英文。洛桑、多哈很遥远，新德里和广岛至今对我也依然神秘。不禁想起作者在本书附录文章所传达的——"移动"是一个当代的隐喻，我们对世界和未知的探索还远未完成。放下手机，融入南京的细小街巷，我渴望能找寻到近十年前青奥会在这座城里留下的痕迹。只是乍一看，人潮涌动的夫子庙似乎已优先给网红和热卖留下了更多闪耀的可能性。但那精心修过的城墙在提醒我，那个夏天我曾沿着它的指引快步绕圈，热汗奔流之后方能心安理得。在当年的国际奥委会官方酒店，我曾经与巴赫主席面对面聊着奥林匹克的青春话题，采访的细节在时间的沙漏中清晰如昨。我同时逼真记着的，还有国际奥委会前主席罗格在酒店大堂里坚持挺立走过的身影，老伴几步之后细心相随，随时做好搀扶的准备。那一刻，老人家深陷髋关节术后伤痛和身体每况愈下的传闻被无言证实，我的眼角变得湿润，心里满溢由衷的敬意！那一届空前的青奥会留下的难以抹除的痕迹，当然离不开新颖而接地气的开幕仪式。在解说里，我对巴赫主席掏出手机与青年人自拍的那个瞬间做了渲染和提亮，我想我会铭记长久，青年运动员们与观众也会铭记长久。因为世人眼中悠远的奥林匹克，在那一刻像老父亲般鼓舞取悦着自己的儿女。

青奥会给南京留下了什么？即便身旁的出租车司机对于眼前这座城翻天覆地的变化有更多期待，我一个外乡人只要花些心思，还是能在行走中找到那些承载了沉甸甸收获的奋斗者的场所与足迹。大赛固然在城市基因中留下日新月异的变化，另一种更刻骨深邃的留痕也许永存于人们的心灵。罗格，在奥林匹克运动艰难岁月中激流勇进，矢志于创建青奥会，尽管受病痛之苦，但仍会在清醒健朗之时，坚定地来到自己开创的青奥会场景之中，沉默中安享成果之乐，南京以此在老人记忆中留痕并刻下深深的烙印。六朝之都蝶变为现代奥林匹克之城，南京在国际化的路上又迈开了坚实步伐。

我生在北京，长在北京，因首都之尊，尽享中国大赛承办之先的荣耀。1990年的北京、2008年的北京和2022年的北京早被一一载入史册，每每重回那些年份，都会有最恰切的歌声相伴，《亚洲雄风》和《北京欢迎你》随时会掘开情感的闸门，猝不及防地泪流满面，徜徉在那遥远而美好的日子里。此种留痕无需去瞻仰超一流的体育场，无需去一次次确认闪耀的金牌总数，那是时代的温情与激荡。因为亚运，北京尽情展开怀抱；因为奥运，北京纵情拥抱世界。2008年，北京奥运会期间的某一个深夜，在台里完成直播后，我驾车奔驰在北四环上，行至鸟巢附近，那升腾的圣火映入眼帘。夜已深，四下无声，我将车速放到最慢，静静地陶醉于深夜里属于自己的这一奥林匹克时刻。这一留痕，至今在我记忆中色彩饱满，不断被自己诗化。

　　读《赛事之城》，你会得到一座座城中的赛事留痕，虽不相同，但个个生动。从第18届雅加达亚运会闭幕式叫响"中国新时代、杭州新亚运"已6个年头，中国江南城市浙江杭州将迎来举世瞩目的秋分盛典。一次次回望与再出发中，作者以悉心观察与诚挚笔触，涌流分享澎湃新作。征程无边，唯愿大家顺利抵达心中的每一座城！

中央电视台主持人、记者　张斌
于2023年立秋

Preface 1

Spring Blossoms Live on in Autumn's Harvest

The author would typically share sections of the draft manuscripts of this book with me on weekends. As I read those words that portray the host cities of the Asian Games, not only reflections, but also a sense of eager anticipation and longing arise within me.

Shortly after, I received news about the book through social media, indicating that the author had already begun preparations for its promotion while sharing its manuscripts with me to seek feedback. As I revisited those writings, I felt like a blend of vintage film photographs and contemporary digital images, providing a unique ambiance and taste. Moreover, the inclusion of beautifully crafted images and illustrations enhances the immersive experience for readers. The ever-increasing amount of reading on those social media posts stands as evidence of their popularity.

In late March of this year, I received two articles from the author: "Designing Tokyo" and "Rose Blossoms", both were sent around the same time. It was a vibrant spring, providing a perfect opportunity to reflect on significant artworks featuring flowers throughout the art history, while exploring various visual designs associated with the Olympic Movement. Little did I know at the time that she followed a rigorous schedule and had a systematic approach to her writing. As she gradually incorporated the narrative series of Asian Games host cities like New Delhi, Bangkok, Hiroshima, Tehran, Jakarta, Manila, and more, I encouraged her to pick up the pace and strive to complete this series before the opening of the

Hangzhou Asian Games.

Although there was an underlying sense of pressure and urgency, she remained patient, allowing inspiration to arrive unexpectedly and following her own rhythm to write more about Lausanne, the headquarters of the International Olympic Committee, and Ashgabat, the city where Hangzhou successfully secured the hosting rights for the upcoming Asian Games. As her article of Doha reached completion in early August, it coincided with the end of a writing cycle spanning from the Spring Equinox to the Beginning of Autumn.

Having met with the author in some of those cities, I was able to personally connect with what she wrote. Whether it was memories of Bangkok or encounters with Mme Khunying Patama Leeswadtrakul, I echoed the experiences that molded her perspective. However, it is through her keen observation and introspection that she is able to delve deeper and convey a broader understanding of those cities in her writings. Furthermore, I am aware that even for cities she has not yet to visit in person, she possesses the ability to approach, explore, and develop insights through her words.

Through reading thousands of books and walking thousands of miles, one acquires the capacity to translate and articulate their travel experiences through writing. Striking a delicate balance between swift composition and patient learning, the author consistently maintains a healthy tension. Undoubtedly, the author alone possesses an intimate knowledge of the tremendous exertion and steadfast dedication entailed in the entirety of her journey.

Her writings revolve around athletes and the realm of athletics, selectively highlighting prominent figures and sports intricately intertwined with each host city's narrative. She delves into the vibrancy and youthful allure of champions at their zenith, as well as the desolation and melancholy that accompany their defeats, followed by their triumphant resurgence after rising from the ashes. While she undoubtedly recognizes the importance of medals, the author also weaves captivating narratives that reveal the very essence of the events, and promising athletes of future generations who gained experience in the events.

She not only writes about the events themselves but goes far beyond them. Her brushstrokes encompass the natural and cultural landscapes of each host city, as well as its historical, cultural, economic, and societal characteristics. Even when exploring "phenomena"and "strategies", she strives to provide concrete examples, rendering her writings accurate, comprehensive, and devoid of ostentation. As she immerses herself in those host cities, every moment of pause and observation of the "other" stirs within her a deep yearning to return to her beloved home country. She eloquently captures the magnificence of Beijing, a city that has hosted both the Summer and Winter Olympic Games. She delves into the allure of Guangzhou, a city adorned with the legend of the Five Goats, and a noteworthy host of the Asian Games. And, of course, she beautifully depicts Hangzhou, representing an everlasting recollection of Jiangnan's charm and the eternal glow of moonlight that forever resides within her heart.

With deft fingers tapping on the keyboard, the author devoted her personal time, outside of work, to meticulously chronicling all the cities overseas that have hosted the Asian Games throughout the history of the Asian Olympic Movement, going the extra mile to create a bilingual version. It was a period marked by solitude and unwavering determination, akin to a battlefield of resilience. Yet, it was also a timely rain, a labor of love from a united team, with the aim of providing readers from all walks of life with an immersive experience. As a reader holding *Cities of Sporting Event*s in my hands, I eagerly anticipate its sequel, envisioning it as a gateway to unveil thrilling surprises for everyone's enjoyment in the future.

SONG Luzeng

Vice President of the Olympic Council of Asia

August 6, 2023

Lasting Imprints

As I sit down to write a few words about *Cities of Sporting Events*, a distinct feeling of envy wells up within me. This is a captivating subject, one that has ignited plans in my mind for an extensive journey with my family, preferably spanning an entire year, as we traverse from one city to another, seeking out the sporting elements that have long become intertwined with the very fabric of urban life. Although I have yet to embark on that adventure, having read the manuscript of this book, I now realize that by following in the author's footsteps, who has painstakingly crafted a mental landscape through words, readers will have the opportunity to perceive cities in a multidimensional manner, even without physically being there. Leafing through the author's previous works, which are substantial and weighty, I felt the joy, resilience, and determination she developed in mastering the art of words. On the brink of the eagerly anticipated Asian Games in her beloved home city, the author engrossed herself in those distant cities, reawakening her insights and feelings onto the keyboard. With each word I read, those cities came back to life in my heart. Images of my past visits flooded my mind, and their distinctive atmosphere enveloped me. These memories stay vibrant and alive, even as time goes by.

I first read the manuscript of this book on my mobile phone during a recent business trip to the city of Nanjing, flipping through both Chinese and English texts. While Lausanne and Doha seemed faraway, New Delhi and Hiroshima remained mysterious to me. It inevitably brings to mind what the author conveyed in the appendix of this book — "mobility"is a contemporary metaphor, and our exploration of the world and the unknown is far from complete. As I put down my phone and wandered through the narrow alleys of Nanjing, I yearned to discover traces of the Youth Olympic Games that took place in this city nearly a decade earlier. To my slight dismay, today's bustling Confucius Temple seemed to cater to the current wave of internet celebrities and trendy vendors, relinquishing the spotlight to let them shine even brighter. Nevertheless, as I took in the meticulously restored city walls, they served as a poignant reminder of that summer when I followed their guidance, navigating between various locations in the city on foot, perspiring profusely and seeking moments of tranquility, knowing that my diligent efforts as a reporter contributed to my inner peace. That year, at the official hotel of the International Olympic Committee, I engaged in a face-to-face conversation with President Bach about the significance of the Youth Olympic Games. The details of our interview are as fresh as if it happened just yesterday in the flow of time. Likewise, I can distinctly recall the determined presence of former President Rogge as he made his way through the hotel lobby, displaying tremendous effort and remarkable composure. His devoted spouse followed just a few steps behind, attentively accompanying him and always ready to extend a helping hand.

At that moment, whispers about the elderly gentleman's postoperative hip pain and deteriorating health were quietly validated, triggering a welling up of tears in my eyes and an overwhelming surge of respect in my heart. The indelible imprints left by that unprecedented Youth Olympic Games are intertwined with its innovative and down-to-earth opening ceremony. During my live commentary, I highlighted the memorable moment when President Bach took out his phone for a selfie with the young athletes — an image that will undoubtedly remain etched in my memory for years to come, as it will for the young athletes and spectators. The timeless Olympics, seen through the eyes of the world, took on the persona of a nurturing father figure, inspiring and bringing joy to his children.

What legacy did the Youth Olympic Games leave behind in Nanjing? The ambitious taxi driver I rode with on this trip envisioned even greater changes in the city's future, but as a visitor, I just needed to invest a little effort to discover the places and traces that bear the weighty achievements of those who fought for them. The Youth Olympic Games undeniably brought rapid transformations to the city's landscape, but its deeper imprints still resonate within the hearts of its people. Despite the challenges he faced, President Rogge, amidst the tumultuous years of the Olympic Movement, unwaveringly pursued the creation of the Youth Olympic Games. Despite his painful illness, he persevered and visited the very scene he helped to bring to life during moments of clarity and good health. In quiet contemplation, he found solace in the joyous realization of his efforts. Nanjing has thus left an enduring imprint in the memories of the esteemed gentleman. The city, once the capital of the Six Dynasties, has now evolved into a modern Olympic hub, exemplifying its resolute journey towards internationalization.

Born and raised in Beijing, I have witnessed the city's prestigious status as the nation's capital and the glory it enjoyed as the first host city in China of a range of international sporting events. The city in 1990, 2008, and 2022 has each left a mark in history, and whenever I revisit those moments, the melodic tunes of *Asian Mighty Winds* and *Beijing Welcomes You* effortlessly evoke a surge of emotions, bringing unexpected tears as I am transported back to those distant and beautiful days. I don't need to behold the grandeur of the best-in-class stadiums or repeatedly tally the sparkling gold medals; it is the warmth and exhilaration of that era that left a lasting imprint within me. Thanks to the Asian Games, Beijing opened its arms; thanks to the Olympics, Beijing embraced the world. One late night during the 2008 Olympics, after completing a live broadcast assignment at China Central Television, I drove along the North Fourth Ring Road. As I approached the National Stadium, the soaring Olympic flame came into view. The night was deep, and silence prevailed. I eased my car to its gentlest pace, immersing myself in the tranquil beauty of this personal Olympic moment — an imprint that remains vividly colorful in my memory, forever poeticized by my own reflection.

As you delve into the pages of *Cities of Sporting Events,* you will find vibrant and distinct impressions of the sporting events that unfolded in various host cities. It has been five years since the closing ceremony of the 18th Asian Games in Jakarta, where the resounding slogan "A New Era in China, A New Asian Games in Hangzhou" echoed through the air. Today, Hangzhou, Zhejiang, a city south of the Yangtze River in China, shall have an opening ceremony on Autumn Equinox Festival which will definitely be a remarkable spectacle to captivate global attention. With each reflection and departure, the author skillfully weaves these fresh narratives through keen observation and heartfelt prose. The literary journey knows no boundaries, and may everyone smoothly reach every city within their hearts!

ZHANG Bin

Presenter and Reporter, China Central Television

On the day of Beginning of Autumn in 2023

《夺冠之路》（常青作品）

目　录

新德里"起初"

2023年春天，傍晚的钱塘江畔，一位包着头巾的异域男士，看向江对岸蓝紫相融的灯光点亮"大小莲花"，似乎陷入了某种遐思。

杭州奥体中心场馆群

同一时刻，我正前往附近酒店的寄存处，取来自香港的朋友临走前给我留下的珍藏版印度畅销书作家奇坦·巴哈特的《三个傻瓜》。

商务茶室里有两位兄弟模样的先生，他们就正在进行的工作，以及某个日益临近和他们共同期待的时刻，展开了交流与对话。

几年以前，这里曾举办过"亚洲文明对话大会"的一场子活动，虽然是子活动，却也隆重盛大。因此当我翻到奇坦·巴哈特的签名时，不由自主地来到当时的展览区域。在那个瞬间，我的眼前重现了"相约杭州 相约亚运"的特展场景，那个特展精心展陈着杭州从第18届亚运会闭幕式接旗仪式上郑重接回的"三件宝贝"——首届亚运会火炬、首届亚运会会旗和亚奥理事会会旗。而这些宝贝正是从首届亚运会举办地，且曾两度举办亚运会的城市——印度首都新德里，通过一届又一届的亚运会在岁月绵延中传承而来的。犹记参加那次活动的亚奥理事会（东亚区）资深副会长、中国香港体育协会暨奥林匹克委员会会长霍震霆先生，在陈列的火炬和旗帜前深情注目、伫立良久。

首届亚运会会旗、首届亚运会火炬和亚奥理事会会旗

　　这时我看到那位包着头巾的男士不知什么时候已从外面回来，他似乎留意到了我手中的书，而我再次看了他特别的装束，心想他有没有可能来自新德里，然后我们礼节性地相视而笑。紧接着，像无数陌生人在初次相遇时会经历的那样，擦肩而过。

亚运会及其管理组织的"前世今生"

　　新德里之所以叫新德里，因为在它北边还有一个旧德里。有人曾戏说，新德里新得说不上历史，旧德里老得说不清历史。新德里在古老的德里城基础上扩建而成，两者之间隔着地标建筑"印度门"（又称"德里门"）。曾经，人们习惯于把"印度门"相隔的两个区域分别理解成现代与传统、理想与现实、富裕与贫穷，但随着时间的不断推移，它们正越来越不可避免地被连在一起。

新德里对于亚洲的奥林匹克运动，具有"起初""纪年"的意义，因为它见证了亚运会和亚洲运动会联合会的发展变迁，更孕育和开启了那些关于"起初"和"后来"的重要时刻与精彩故事。

亚洲最早的地区性综合运动会，由菲律宾、中国、日本三国在20世纪初发起，原名"远东奥林匹克运动会"，又称"远东运动会"。远东运动会从1913年至1934年共举办了十届。1934年，由于日本坚持把伪满洲国拉入远东运动会遭到中国的抗议并宣布退出，远东体育协会宣告解体，远东运动会随之消亡。作为世界上最早出现的洲际国际竞赛，远东运动会曾代表整个亚洲的运动水平，因此也被看作是后来亚运会的前身。

"二战"结束后，1949年的2月13日，来自亚洲各国体育组织的代表在新德里签署了亚洲运动会联合会宪章，亚洲运动会联合会正式成立。新德里获得了承办1950年首届亚运会的机会，新德里亚运会组委会也迅速成立。由于战争创伤、经济拮据、体育设施建设及器材供给跟不上等多方面的原因，亚洲运动会联合会同意将亚运会延迟到1951年举行。新德里首届亚运会有11个国家和地区的近500名运动员参加。比赛设6个大项57个小项，其中包括6个奥运项目。东道主印度和缅甸、伊朗参加了所有项目。

1951年新德里首届亚运会会徽

亚奥理事会会徽

1982年11月16日，亚洲运动会联合会改名为"亚洲奥林匹克理事会"（Olympic Council of Asia），简称亚奥理事会（OCA），其总部设在科威特。作为全面管理亚洲奥林匹克运动的组织，OCA是代表亚洲与国际奥委会和其他洲级体育组织联系的全权代表。

亚奥理事会总部内

"如果你要写新德里，这段亚洲奥林匹克运动史必然是浓墨重彩的部分。"后来，当我在茶室阅读《三个傻瓜》并见到兄弟模样的两人，他们给了我至关重要的建议。

"一个说得出历史的人，比一个单纯渴望未来的人更睿智。"我脑中闪过一位前辈的教导。

"但是，我想我需要提醒你们，新德里除了这个'起初'，还有'后来'。"包着头巾的男士应邀加入了我们的谈话，因为那时我们已经确认他是名副其实的、来自南亚的印度人。

1982年新德里第9届亚运会会徽、吉祥物

我们明白他的意思。他希望我们记住，新德里，除了首届亚运会，还举办过1982年第9届亚运会。而我们当然不会忘记，因为正是在那一届亚运会，中国以61枚金牌首度超越日本，从此成为亚洲体育第一强国。

《摔跤吧！爸爸》与女性运动员的崛起

《摔跤吧！爸爸》是由尼特什·提瓦瑞执导，根据真人真事改编的印度体育竞技主题电影。影片讲述曾经的摔跤冠军辛格培养两个女儿——大女儿吉塔、二女儿巴比塔成为女子全国摔跤冠军，大女儿吉塔获世界冠军从而打破印度传统的励志故事。2016年12月23日上映后获第62届印度电影观众奖，2017年5月5日在中国上映收获近13亿票房，并在观众中留下相当不错的口碑。

新德里街景

当两个年少的女儿被迫接受父亲给出的安排，即训练成女摔跤手，因而遭遇整个村庄人们嘲笑的时候，她们也曾痛苦、对抗和完全无法接受理解，直到另一个早早嫁为人妇的小女孩开导她们——

"我倒是希望上天能给我这样一个父亲，这样我的父亲会为我的未来考虑，否则女孩的命运，从出生开始，就是做饭打扫卫生，全身心地做家务，然后，等她成年，就会嫁出去。为了减轻家庭负担，把自己交给一个男人，而且跟这个男人一点都不熟悉，然后为他生孩子，抚养孩子，这就是一个女孩一生的宿命。再来看看你们和你们的父亲，他在和全世界对抗，他承受着所有人对他的嘲讽，为什么？为了你们有个好的未来。"

同龄女孩的现身说法，醍醐灌顶般的彻悟，从此两个女儿自觉接受父亲的训练，在通往女子摔跤项目冠军的道路上披荆斩棘，勇往直前。

中间的曲折不是没有，相反很多，且先按下快进键直接到女孩参加英联邦运动会决赛的前一天，看看父亲跟女儿说了什么——

"如果你得了金牌，你就会变成一个榜样，一个非常好的榜样，孩子们将永远记住你。明天如果你赢了，你将不再孤单，无数个女孩将跟你联合起来，反抗那些歧视女性的人，反抗只能做家务事，反抗从小就开始订婚。明天的比赛非常重要，因为明天，你的对手不是安吉丽娜·沃森（一名澳大利亚女摔跤手），你是在跟所有歧视女性的人战斗。"

最后的剧情是，2010年英联邦运动会女子55公斤级摔跤比赛，印度选手击败澳大利亚选手获得冠军，进而获得参加奥运会的资格。这在印度奥林匹克运动史上是前无古人的事。

电影呈现的是一种艺术真实。对于印度女性在自己国家的竞技体育，乃至社会和政治生活的其他方面究竟处于一个什么样的地位，也许只有她们自己才能做出最真切的回答。

"所以，如果我想知道，自新德里首届亚运会以来，印度女子运动员的地位和作用发生了什么变化，先生您会介意吗？"

"实际上，新德里首届亚运会，印度就有女运动员参加竞赛项目。"

随着谈话的深入，我们已经知道面前这位包着头巾的先生不是别人，正是杭州第19届亚运会印度体育代表团的团长布平德辛格·巴集瓦先生。

我的问题不仅没有对他构成任何冒犯，相反他微笑着，感谢我对印度电影和印度女运动员的关注。

"基本上，我可以预测在即将到来的杭州第19届亚运会，印度女运动员有望比她们的'另一半'获得更多的奖牌。"布平德辛格·巴集瓦以幽默而睿智的预判，回答了一个带有女性视角、富有挑战性的提问。

那些与新德里似有似无关联的"后来"

"除了女子摔跤，你还知道印度的其他运动强项吗？"兄弟模样的两人中，那个年长些的先生询问我。

我急中生智，指着《三个傻瓜》封面左侧那个穿红色T恤、右手高举板球拍的青年，脱口而出"板球"。因为就在先前我拿到奇坦·巴哈特的书时，我已经注意到在作家本人的签名后，忍痛送书给我的朋友补了一句"如果你看了这本书，你会明白印度人多么多么爱板球"。不排除送书给我的朋友如此刷一波存在感，是为了提醒我不要在写过新德里之后迅速忘记他的慷慨，他写下的话却拯救了我一时的贫乏。

奇坦·巴哈特畅销书《三个傻瓜》封面

"一本特别吸引年轻人的书。"兄弟模样中那位年少的先生说。唯其年轻，在这个关于年轻人的话题中，他无疑最有发言权。

"三个年轻人，一起开板球用品商店，他们各有志向。但是最后，为了保护一个非常具有板球运动天赋的孩子阿里，付出了沉重惨烈的代价，其中包括年轻的生命。"

他拿过书，只翻了几次，就翻到第184页，示意我看。

"要是我加入这个队的话，我是给哪一边打球？"阿里问道。

"澳大利亚。"卡特勒先生答道。

"但我是个印度人啊。"阿里说道。

"但你同时可以当一个澳大利亚人。我们社会的文化很多元的。"格林纳先生应道。

"不要。"阿里说道。

"什么？"

"我是印度人。我要为印度打球。我不给其他国家打。"

……

奇坦·巴哈特1974年4月出生于新德里，成年后先后获理学学士和工商管理硕士学位，毕业后投身银行业，曾在香港生活工作了11年。投身写作后他创造了印度英文小说的神话，成功将印度现代青年人的社会形象展现在世人面前。

出于直觉，我相信《三个傻瓜》写的不仅仅是板球，但板球给了奇坦·巴哈特一个拥有广泛国民度和共鸣度的叙事载体与情感取向。

回想起来，在认识面前这位包着头巾的印度先生之前，我曾与真正的新德里家庭有过接近一周时间的接触，不过那不是在新德里，而是在芝加哥留学时的一次"家庭寄宿"（Homestay）中。当时我与一个来自南京的女孩被安排到一户美籍印裔家庭，这多少让我们有些沮丧。他们说的英语带有明显的印度口音，特别是那个家庭没有女孩，这意味着我们要在兄弟俩住过的房间各自度过一周。当看到他们直接用手抓食物食用时，一时更不知所措。

后来的情形证明每一段"家庭寄宿"都不会白过。在那户家庭中，父亲是一位医术高明的医生，母亲承担全职太太的角色。感恩节清晨天刚亮，母亲就驾车带我们去逛商场，因为那天的折扣力度为全年最大。中午则把我们拜托给社区的另一户美国家庭吃火鸡，因为他们自己不做火鸡。临别的时候，母亲拿出儿子和儿媳参加总统招待会时的合照给我们看，脸上是自豪的笑容。

　　让我印象深刻的并不是那张照片，而是那家的"创二代"统统从事高精尖的IT行业，当时与我们在同一个学校留学的印度学生，有很多也攻读这个方向的专业。

　　"在新德里也有莲花建筑，你们的体育场让我想起了家乡。杭州亚运会的场馆设施非常好，比我看到的世界上很多城市的奥运场馆还要先进。未来这里完全可以举办奥运会。"布平德辛格·巴集瓦先生的声音打断了我的记忆，"当然印度也会第三次申办亚运会，我觉得必然会这样。"

　　"布平德辛格·巴集瓦先生，在您看来，以IT产业为代表的科技创新会对竞技体育，特别是大型体育赛事产生革命性的影响吗？"

"大小莲花"（翟莫梵作品）

这个问题很印度，同时又很共通，在ChatGPT被更多尝试使用、马斯克亲吻他自己研发的机器人时尤其如此。不知不觉中，时光也从傍晚转到入夜，我们再次相视而笑，在再次擦肩而过前握手道别，把问题和思索留给窗外的夜色。"大小莲花"的灯光依然闪亮照耀，"杭州之门"连接着偌大的城市，岁月静好，波澜不惊。

发于"潮新闻"，2023-05-23。大公网、《西湖》等转载。英文版发于杭州城市客户端Hangzhoufeel。

阿什哈巴德 "寻迹"

许久以后，我意识到如果不是因为体育，要进入中亚的土库曼斯坦并在其首都阿什哈巴德停留一段时间并非一件易事。因为土库曼斯坦签证办理的条件要求与境内停留时间的限制规定都相对严格。

阿什哈巴德对于杭州的非凡意义，在于那儿是杭州成功申办第19届亚运会的地方，这让人想起遥远而切近的2015年9月16日，仿佛一切仍历历在目。第34届亚奥理事会全体代表大会上，当亚奥理事会宣布"中国杭州获得2022年（第19届）亚运会举办权"，一切都是那么肯定那么水到渠成。

回望杭州亚运梦想与荣光的重大里程碑事件，也让我们得以走近并观看一个似乎神秘莫测、同时更具象立体的阿什哈巴德。

自然人文景观与历史的尘烟

倘若只能用极简的方式来描述土库曼斯坦及首都阿什哈巴德的独特景观，我们或许可以选择"火""水""石"三个字。

作为中亚五国的一员，土库曼斯坦属世界上最年轻的国家之列。"斯坦"这个后缀来自波斯语，意为"地方"或"土地"，因此土库曼斯坦的意思是"土库曼之地"。

"火"说的是沙漠中的"地狱之门"。

土库曼斯坦超过80%都是沙漠，"地狱之门"正是其大沙漠卡拉库姆沙漠（又称"黑沙漠"，曾被认为是丝绸之路上最为危险的路段之一）中一个燃烧的天然气坑。1971年，苏联地质学家前往阿什

"地狱之门"

哈巴德以北260公里处的卡拉库姆沙漠寻找自然资源，并发现了那里的天然气田。由于钻探使地面塌陷，导致形成一个约60米宽、20米深的巨型大坑，为防甲烷泄漏毒害周边村庄村民，科学家们点燃了那些气体，随之，成千上万条火苗融到一块，连成一片椭圆形的橙色大火。

但让他们始料不及的是，曾经预估几周就能熄灭的坑火，一烧竟烧了整整50多年。如今虽然火焰已不像以前那么大，却依旧持续燃烧着。即使是最高级别的行政扑火令，也未能"阻止"和"叫停"那从沙漠底下冒出的、源源不断的气体与火焰。

悖谬的是，尽管人们害怕"地狱"，这个当初为安全计让总统下令疏散整个村庄的天然气坑，之后却成了从远处看堪称"美景"的沙漠奇观，吸引着一批又一批去土库曼斯坦的旅人前往探究。

土库曼斯坦是地球上最干旱的地方之一，首都阿什哈巴德有"爱之城"的美称，阿什哈巴德城区到处可见如金子般珍贵的"水"。"水"以喷泉的曼妙姿态，占据和滋润着沙漠中的绿洲城市。水声潺潺，水流源源不断地奔涌、倾泻、循环，阿什哈巴德的居民自信他们的城市拥有世界上最多的喷泉。

就在那"火"与"水"的各自喷涌与交织中，2013年的阿什哈巴德又刷新了一项吉尼斯世界纪录。那就是，它成了世界上每平方公里拥有最多大理石建筑物的城市。

喷泉

"大理石之城"一角

且不说总统府、政府部门与清真寺用的是又好又贵的大理石，即使是拔地而起的公寓楼，也像一片片被积雪覆盖的大理石森林。因此在阿什哈巴德，无论你把头转向哪里，到处能看到闪亮、洁白的大理石，那广袤统一的白，没有任何多余的颜色。

传说中土库曼人对大理石如饥似渴的需求，简直要掏空意大利的卡拉拉山采石场。而为了用上好的卡拉拉石建构一个典雅华贵的现代城市，一些最主要的城市建筑通常请法国和土耳其的知名公司来进行设计与建造。

历史上，由于中亚地处东西方之间，使得一些地方与城镇得尝亚洲与欧洲间的丝路贸易红利而蓬勃发展，同时这种独特的地理位置，也曾让其遭受过包括波斯人、希腊人、蒙古人、阿拉伯人和土耳其人等诸多民族的攻占。

"这个国家夹在东西方之间，暴露无遗，能够用来自我保卫的除了环境恶劣的沙漠，别无他物。"挪威女记者、作家及社会人类学家埃丽卡·法特兰曾在《中亚行纪》中写道。这也许能部分解释为什么后来土库曼斯坦努力让自己成为一个中立国。

在沙皇治下，俄国人因关注经济利益而掌控中亚市场。后来，基于部族的传统社会（相对松散的组织）过渡到社会主义社会。苏联解体后，独立建国的土库曼斯坦选择了自己的发展方向与路径，其中重要的一条是坐上"一带一路"的快车。在中亚五国中，土库曼斯坦无论在经济还是体育方面，无疑是实力较强的一个。1995年，土库曼斯坦获联合国认可为中立国，随之也成为亚洲唯一的永久中立国。

在土库曼斯坦，石油、天然气等自然资源非常丰富，尤其天然气资源的探明储量居世界第四。在那里，居民用水、用电、用汽油都是免费或极度优惠的，那里还有世界上最便宜的国内航班。出于土库曼人对总统的爱戴与致敬，在首都阿什哈巴德，我们似乎常常有机会，与面带微笑的总统塑像和肖像互相凝望。

第 5 届亚洲室内与武道运动会及国宝汗血宝马

2017年杭州亚组委代表团出访土库曼斯坦时，正逢阿什哈巴德举办第五届亚洲室内与武道运动会。

亚洲室内与武道运动会是亚洲规模最大的室内综合性运动会，亚洲室内运动会起初为每两年举办一届，与亚洲武道运动会合并后每四年举办一届。

亚洲室内与武道运动会使体育运动的项目更趋多元与时尚（如电竞项目就首次列入在阿什哈巴德举办的这次运动会），能鼓励更多亚洲年轻人积极参与各类体育运动锻炼身体。主办该运动会标志着土库曼斯坦已跻身有能力承办世界级大型活动的国家之一，同时也成为中亚地区首个主办亚奥理事会运动会的国家。在更深远的意义上，赛会还将促进土库曼斯坦通过参与体育外交更有效融入世界奥林匹克大家庭。

运动会在阿什哈巴德新建的占地156公顷的多功能奥林匹克中心（位于阿什哈巴德四条主干道的交汇处）举行。此前，总统别尔德穆哈梅多夫亲自为运动会创作并演唱了主题歌。

奥林匹克中心

无限的空间等你我来展现。缤纷的世界是成功的条件，再高的山巅我们一样会跨越，时间的沉淀那是解放的瞬间，来创造我的梦想，释放我的力量，年轻的心要飞翔，飞进我的梦想，面对着蓝天与海洋的交界，希望的实现就在一刹那间，穿越地平线又是崭新的一天。

虽然不知道这个网上可查的中译版主题歌歌词，是否完美诠释了创作者的原意，但它看起来的确很"运动"很"通俗"，理论上也应该适合并便于传播。

关于亚洲室内与武道运动会设置的比赛项目，土库曼斯坦也像之前举办运动会的那些国家那样，除了赛会原有的通用项目，新增了土库曼斯坦的一些传统和特色项目，譬如摔跤运动，还有特别值得一提的马术项目。

起源于土库曼斯坦的汗血宝马，又称阿哈尔捷金马，由此理所当然地，成了该届运动会会徽的主体图案与符号。在"金马"右下方，亚奥理事会的太阳标志照耀着赛会举办国和城市之名，左边则环绕着一轮绿色的弯月和该届运动会的全称。极简的线条勾勒出汗血宝马的形象轮廓，黄色的丝带环宝马颈项敞开飘扬。现代主义风格的会徽，与融入土库曼斯坦传统图案的吉祥物阿拉拜（和汗血宝马一样同属于土库曼斯坦的国宝之一，曾是古丝绸之路上无数个商队的忠诚卫士）的设计既有呼应，又形成强烈的反差与对比。

据说，1960年的罗马奥运会上，一匹汗血宝马在"盛装舞步"项目上赢得金牌。这比土库曼斯坦运动员在最近一届（第32届）的东京夏季奥运会上取得其优势运动项目举重的第一枚奥运奖牌，要早很多很多年。

因此在土库曼斯坦，马是极其珍贵和备受呵护的生灵。如果马犯下错误，甚至可能比人更容易被原谅。虽然历史上，汗血宝马的经历也并非一帆风顺，一度被禁止私养甚至遭到屠杀。但土库曼人以惊人的毅力和艰苦卓绝的努力，证明宝马的独特价值，为他们的宝马迎来了安全存活和建功立业的好时代。之后，汗血宝马再度在土库曼斯坦国家外交和建设项目中发挥着重要作用。每个城镇都拥

汗血宝马

第 5 届亚洲室内与武道运动会吉祥物

有一个崭新的赛马场，国家有专门的"赛马部"，还设有"阿哈尔捷金马节"和"赛马日"，节会配套举办高级别的国际学术会议、相关展览和马拉松等形式丰富的活动。土库曼人坚决不吃马肉，特别是对汗血宝马几乎持一种虔诚的态度。

阿什哈巴德的网络信号与故乡的"明月"

除顺道观摩第5届亚洲室内与武道运动会，出访代表团更重要的任务是按亚奥理事会要求，参与第36届亚奥理事会全体代表大会以及第70次执委会，并作杭州亚运会筹办陈述。全体大会的主背景由黄绿两色组成，会议名称字体呈白色，绿色是土库曼斯坦国旗的底色，也是土库曼人喜欢的传统颜色。对于会议背景屏幕上对称式的传统图案，我没有时间做深入考证，如果考虑土库曼斯坦发达的地毯产业，或许可以理解为与地毯上的图案出自同一视觉资源系统，承袭着传统图案的一致脉络。

在土库曼斯坦的那次出访中，我们就已经遇到2026年爱知·名古屋亚运会（以及2020年东京奥运会）代表团的工作人员，在当时，我们惊奇于日本办一届亚运会竟然要花两倍于我们的时间去准备。我看着他们，与他们握手并交谈，脑子里却闪过那个一直在写作和长跑的日本畅销书作家村上春树。此后每次出访开会再遇到如影随形的他们，便也不再觉得奇怪。

全体大会期间还套开了体育委员会方面的专项会议。记得亚奥理事会副主席宋鲁增先生以及体育协调委员会的主管和一些专家参

第36届亚奥理事会全体代表大会

加了会议。相对于全体代表大会，专项会议聚焦于亚运会竞赛方面的事宜，其主要意义在于对杭州亚组委初步提出的竞赛项目规划进行了探讨、论证与引导。无论如

亚奥理事会第 70 次执委会

何，在汗血宝马故乡召开的这个专项会议，有力地影响了对场馆建设、检验检疫、后勤保障等方面均有特殊要求的马术项目最终能否列入杭州亚运会的比赛项目。

在完成出访的绝大部分工作任务后，我们有间隙到宾馆外透个气，并路过一座造型奇特的建筑。有一瞬间，在那个像极了迪拜七星级酒店的建筑前，我感到有些神思恍惚。后来，车辆把我们扔在一处离某个古城遗址较近的地方停留了约15分钟。那里没有"地狱之门"，更没有挪威女记者埃丽卡·法特兰遇到的意为"少女的城堡"的吉兹卡拉。能够想象沙漠中的人很早就开始一起生活在防御性城墙的后面，但无法知道远处遗址的城墙之内和土壤之下究竟埋藏着什么。

我用手机朝远处拍了几张照片，想要发给正处在求知欲特别旺盛阶段的女儿，在数次发送未能成功后，才想起我们离开杭州前就在支付宝上另建了一个代表团小群作为替代交流方式。紧张的工作中，我忘了在阿什哈巴德已经有几天没有用微信，即使在宾馆住地网络也并没有那么通畅。但相比于未引进和使用互联网的"从前"的土库曼斯坦，彼时的阿什哈巴德已经有了超越自身的突飞猛进。

不知名的古城遗址

记忆让我回到2015年的9月，中国奥委会、杭州市政府和亚奥理事会在阿什哈巴德共同签订了《主办城市合同》。时隔两年，合同中的条款已逐条有序被研究并转化成执行中的"鱼骨图"。与此同时，在遥远的家园，中国良渚古城申请世界文化遗产的步伐在加紧加快，数字经济也在时代的巨轮驱动中飞速发展。

　　资料显示，在土库曼斯坦的经济中心和第二大城市马雷以北的数十公里，有着青铜时代的遗址贡努尔德佩。考古学家告诉我们，早在4000年前，那里就有一个组织良好的大城市，居住在那里的人们还开发了复杂的灌溉系统，甚至已有污水处理的功能。历史的相似与神奇似乎既解释了阿什哈巴德当代曼妙飞舞的"水之歌"，更勾连起心头对青铜时代世界上几个主要文明——以及更为远古的良渚文明的溯源与遐想。

　　"杭州亚运会，预计土库曼斯坦将有超100人组成的体育代表团前来参加。"土库曼斯坦奥委会代表、体育部负责人马克萨特·戈科夫介绍说。

　　过去以尚未完成的字句向我们倾诉讲述，而我们注定要成为"未来"的人。

发于"潮新闻"，2023-06-05。搜狐网、大公网、《西湖》等转载。

东京 "设计"

东京是新冠疫情全球蔓延前我最后抵达的城市之一。

对于东京，我所知不多，因而在很长一段时间里，对于日本的总体印象草草代替了对东京的印象。

对日本体育的认知，也一度选择性地停留在曾有"东洋魔女"之称的排球女将上。小鹿纯子那绝无仅有的笑容，以及伴随一声清脆的"晴空霹雳"跃上空中翻腾数圈再振臂扣住的球——恐怕是我们那个年代人们关于"大球"的一场集体记忆。

当然对于东京，以及与东京相关的那些事，我也与时间一起慢慢知道得更多。譬如《菊与刀》（首次出版于1946年）、二次元（90年代世界范围内形成的动漫热潮）和《日本沉没》（2006年上映），譬如胜见胜（1964年东京奥运会设计委员会核心人物）与安藤忠雄（2020年东京奥运会新国立竞技场评委会主席），又譬如山本耀司、三宅一生与草间弥生……

东京街景

21

东京街景

而真正走进东京并感知真实的东京，却是许久以后筹办杭州第19届亚运会时的事。

史上"最贵"的奥运会会徽

"接近"东京，始于对2020年东京奥运会（第32届夏季奥运会）宣传传播和公众参与的考察——更具体地说，始于对东京奥运会视觉系统尤其是重要视觉标志会徽的关注。

2020年东京奥运会的第一版会徽，发布于2015年7月24日，奥运会会徽从整体上看像字母"T"，残奥会会徽则为竖立的等号。发布伊始，由于这一对会徽与比利时列日剧场的标志颇相似，一时在设计界和全球媒体中引起不小的波澜，甚至被指控涉嫌抄袭。这对于以设计闻名全球的日本，断然是不小的刺激。

也许因为这个插曲，2019年3月，当我随杭州亚运会组委会代表团赴日本东京学习交流，在东京奥组委大楼入口处看到发布的新版会徽与吉祥物时，一时竟心生感慨，无法移开脚步。

追溯1964年东京奥运会，设计界会记起那个名叫龟仓雄策、后来被称为"日本现代平面设计之父"的设计师。那一年，奥林匹克的光芒首次普照亚细亚大地。龟仓雄策用奥林匹克五环和日本国旗的大胆叠加设计了亚洲历史上的第一个奥运会会徽。

处在日本平面设计的黄金时代（20世纪50至70年代），1964年东京奥运会举办时，以"日本宣传美术会"（简称JAAC）为中心的日本平面设计师，已着手对奥运会标志、海报、奖牌、奖状、赛事日程、会场引导、门票、纪念币和邮票等一系列项目进行了整体、系统的视觉识别设计，并形成一个中心元素与整体间协同的设计系统——这一设计方法开创了现代奥运设计史上系统设计的新时代。

可以想象，一个有着如此深厚设计传统的国家与城市，是无法接受一个明显有缺陷的会徽的。因此，东京奥组委于2015年9月1日对已经发布的2020年东京奥运会会徽果断宣布停用。

新版会徽由野老朝雄设计。1969年生于东京、毕业于东京造形大学建筑设计科系的野老朝雄，后来获英国建筑联盟学院硕士，他创有"朝雄工作室"，还兼任武藏野美术大学的讲师。

源自日本江户时代颇为流行的市松图案（一种日本传统纹样，也称为格子纹）是会徽的重要设计灵感。会徽选择了抽象形态，强化"连接环"的意识，以设计成一种强有力的形状，三种不同的长方形代表了不同的国家、文化和思维方式。奥运会和残奥会会徽用

2020 年东京奥运会、残奥会会徽

同样的形状连接在一起，传达了东京奥运会将成为一个多元化的平台，连接全世界。因为赛事在夏天举行，野老朝雄选定了呈现清爽、纯净感的蓝色。设计师努力让会徽既凝聚着厚重的东方历史文化，也融入西方文化元素，以收到"和""素""寂"的多重美学效果。

在东京奥组委大楼看到的会徽，让我忆起到东京前，我在中国美术学院国际设计博物馆看到的1972年札幌（第11届）冬奥会会徽。那是一场日本当代著名设计师作品的联展，由G20杭州峰会会徽和杭州第19届亚运会会徽及运动图标设计师、中国美术学院国际设计博物馆馆长袁由敏教授策展。札幌冬奥会会徽设计师永井一正延续了1964年东京奥运会会徽设计师龟仓雄策的设计理念，在象征日本的旭日东升和奥运五环中间加了象征冬天的雪花（古时日本家庭纹章图案的素描），同时在奥运五环下标注了"Sapporo'72"（意为"札幌1972年"）字样。

不得不说，日本对申办综合性国际体育赛事，一直抱有极大的热情。这也是为什么，日本至今已成功举办了两届夏奥会、两届冬奥会，同时还办过两届亚运会，并且乐此不疲，继续申办和筹备将在爱知·名古屋举办的第20届亚运会。

视觉系统"设计"是大型体育赛事不可或缺也是重要的组成部分。因为亲身参与执行过2022年杭州亚运会、亚残运会主要视觉标志和"杭州国际日""杭州国际友城市长论坛"等一系列视觉内容设计的具体组织和国际传播工作，我深深地理解——即使对于最优秀的设计师，要在一个二维的世界创造出众人一看便会觉得"对了，就是它"的作品，是多么难乎其难的事情。甚至于，如果愿意相信，哪怕功力深厚的设计师，在没有任何抄袭意图的情况下，也可能设计出"英雄所见略同"的作品。

"查重"由此与时俱进，并变得十分重要，而日益进步的互联网技术使海量的图形比对成为可能。为了一个尽可能完美的会徽，在新会徽的投票过程中，东京奥组委慎之又慎，先后花费了不菲的调查经费来排查是否有与候选作品明显相似的作品。当野老朝雄的作品被选中后，前车之鉴让东京奥组委又花了10天面向社会进行调查和公示，最后才正式将其选定为2020年东京奥运会会徽。因此不妨大胆地推测一下，在日本的奥林匹克运动史上，2020年东京奥运会会徽无疑是特别"昂贵"的。除了花费上可能的史无前例，这种"贵"，同时体现了对真正原创设计的渴望与尊重，以及正视现实和纠错的勇气。

小朋友"挑选"的奥运会吉祥物

在听取东京奥组委国际局负责人小仓文雄关于东京奥运会筹备工作的有关介绍后，我再次被立在会议室门口的吉祥物吸引，并与它们展开了一场无声的回望与对话。

东京奥运会组委会总部内

奥运会最早的吉祥物名叫"瓦尔迪"，是一只短腿长身的德国猎犬，它诞生于1972年慕尼黑（第20届）奥运会。因此举办于1964年的东京奥运会，实际上还没有吉祥物。不过后来还是有热心的网友为之杜撰出虚拟的"樱花娃娃"，网友们大抵是觉得：与旭日东升的意象相对，1964年东京奥运会的吉祥物，非日本民间非常喜欢的樱花莫属了吧？

"花"真正以独立的形象作为日本大型赛事的主要视觉标识，出现于1998年在日本长野举办的第18届冬奥会。它不是网友们臆想的"花宝宝"，而是由篠塚正典设计的作为会徽的花。该会徽由富有动感的运动员形象与雪花图案组成，整体像一朵雪莲，名为"五彩的雪花"。而长野冬奥会的吉祥物，实际上是4只小猫头鹰，由兰德公司设计，这也是奥运会历史上首次以4只动物作为吉祥物。

4只吉祥物分别取名为寸喜、能城、家喜和部木（Sukki, Nokki, Lekki, Tsukki），代表着火、风、地和水4个不同的森林生命组成要素。四个名字的英文字头加起来，再组合成"Snowlets"就成了4只猫头鹰共同的名字，其中"snow"代表冬季，"lets"是"让我们"，"Owlets"则意为小猫头鹰。

长野冬残奥会的吉祥物是一只名叫"Parabbit"的兔子，其名称"Parabbit"由残奥会的英文"Paralympic"前缀与兔子的英文"rabbit"组成。该吉祥物的形象据说来源于英国画家沃茨的画作。

按照国际性大型体育赛事筹备的一般规律，吉祥物的发布通常在会徽之后，因为会徽必须在吉祥物中得到使用。在亚洲奥林匹克运动史上，亚奥理事会对亚运会吉祥物的普遍要求，包括在吉祥物的明显位置，必须有该届亚运会的会徽呈现。2020年东京奥运会吉祥物令人刮目相看之处，是会徽的主体和基本元素，巧妙而内在地融合于奥运会和残奥会吉祥物整体中。

东京奥组委于2018年2月28日发布了东京奥运会吉祥物。当年7月22日，东京奥组委在官方网站上正式公布了吉祥物的名字"Miraitowa"。"Miraitowa"是日语单词"mirai"（未来）和"towa"（永恒）的组合，它寄寓了在世界各地的人们心中对促进充满永恒希望未来的期盼。

"Miraitowa"以蓝白两色为主色调，有猫一样的耳朵，动漫风格的黑色眼睛以及一个运动型框架。前额上是2020年东京奥运会会徽，脸上的图案回溯到古代武士戴的头盔。Miraitowa性格活泼，热爱运动且运动能力惊人，同时正直无私，富有诚信，被设定为生活在数字世界里的人物，可使用互联网在数字世界与现实世界之间自由往来。Miraitowa的特技为瞬间移动，拥有超能力的它可自如移动到自己想要去的地方。东京奥运会吉祥物既具有尊重传统的意义，又具有与尖端信息相协调的创新。

与之相对应，2020年东京残奥会的吉祥物名叫"Someity"，它来自日语单词"Someiyoshino"（染井吉野，一个樱花品种）和英语词组"so mighty"（无所不能）的组合。Someity拥有樱花触觉传感器，呈现红（玫瑰色）白相间的色彩，它拥有强大的心理和身体力量，代表着那些排除万难，重新定义可能性的残奥会运动员。

2020 年东京奥运会、残奥会吉祥物

吉祥物出自设计师谷口亮之手。谷口亮是一位居住在福冈县的自由设计师，从事原创角色的创作与插画设计，也会做些搪胶玩具。设计师采用传统和未来主义的风格，呼应"每个人拿出自己最佳状态""多样性和协调性""面向未来的继承"的东京奥运会理念。

明显可见可感的是，Someity和Miraitowa不仅色彩互为对比映照，形体神情相互匹配，更是要好可爱的朋友。

这对以日本传统市松图案为元素、颇具未来感的机器人吉祥物，最终在日本小学生投票中高票获选。

　　吉祥物选取的这一方式与途径，无疑是2020年东京奥运会最饶有趣味的事情。

办一场哪怕没有现场观众的奥运会

　　在奥林匹克运动史上，除非不可抗力，国际奥委会一般不会轻易更改关于重大赛事的既定计划。

东京街景

2020年东京奥运会无疑是个例外。

早在2013年9月7日，国际奥委会第125次全体会议上，国际奥委会主席雅克·罗格宣布东京成为2020年奥运会的主办城市。

由于新冠疫情的影响，国际奥委会同意东京奥运会延期一年举办。

之后依然存在于世界各地的一波波疫情，让人们一度猜测东京奥运会最终会不会被取消。直到2020年3月30日，国际奥委会主席巴赫宣布，推迟后的东京奥运会举办时间是2021年7月23日至8月8日，东京残奥会也将于2021年8月24日至9月5日举办，而届时举办的东京奥运会仍将使用"东京2020年奥运会和残奥会"名称。这事才算尘埃落定。

其间，我们还在媒体上看到，即使没有现场观众，东京奥运会也不会停办。换句话说，没有什么能够阻挡国际奥委会特别是东京奥组委的办赛决心。

因为奥运会对于举办国和承办城市的意义，从来就不限于体育本身。

以1964年东京奥运会为例，日本新干线的第一条线路，即连结东京与大阪之间的东海道新干线于开幕前的1964年10月1日通车运营，新干线的开通，标志着日本高速铁路时代的到来。同时为了观赏奥运，当时尚未发展起互联网的日本掀起了购买彩电的热潮，家庭电视持有比例激增，催生出松下、东芝等品牌彩电产业的发展。丹下健三设计的代代木国立综合体育馆、内藤多仲设计的东京塔等日本地标性建筑及其他一些城市基础设施得以新建，并形成鲜明的建筑设计风格。毫无疑问，1964年东京奥运会不仅带动了战后日本经济的崛起，还将日本重新介绍给了世界。2020年东京奥运会在2013年申奥成功时曾带来约3万亿日元的经济估值，这也让这一届奥运会，一开始就同样承载了再次为日本经济插上腾飞翅膀的梦想与热望。不过从2020年东京奥运会主体育场东京新国立竞技场设计师易主，以及日本本土著名建筑师隈研吾（亦为中国美术学院民艺博物馆设计师）设计的"木与绿色的体育场"，我们看到设计师以自然材料回应"经济与生态挑战并存"的努力，也可以瞥见2020年东京奥运会与1964年东京奥运会会有的差异。

新干线站内

事实上，奥运会的溢出效应，贯穿了赛事筹办的全过程。在这个过程中，仅以国际传播为例，东京就进行了精心的"设计"。

继申奥宣传片之后，东京城市宣传片《东京 东京》（*Tokyo Tokyo*）亮丽出圈。宣传片采用分屏镜头，展示了东京这座城市传统与现代的对比。榻榻米与席梦思、纸伞与现代伞、剑道与电

东京城市宣传片《东京 东京》封面截屏

竞、传统和服与现代和服、浮世绘与"初音未来"（音源库）、手写书法与机械泼墨……所有这一切形象地讲述沧海桑田的东京，日新月异的城市。尽管这种分屏拍摄的方式最早其实并非源自日本，而可能是美国波普艺术大师、流行文化之父、电影制片人安迪·沃霍尔的首创，但正如安迪·沃霍尔一开始设计这种拍摄方式时所预期的那样，分屏的方式意味着更抓观者的眼球，同时意味着同样片长传输更多的信息量，并由此达成"专注"和"看到更多"的效果。

最大的"设计"往往隐藏在开幕式中，但或许是文化差异的因素，疫情的影响和闭环办赛的冷清，也或者由于别的什么道不明的理由，多数观众对于2016年里约奥运会闭幕式上"接棒仪式"中的"东京8分钟"怀有更深刻的记忆。

在那8分钟里，Hello Kitty、足球小将、马里奥、哆啦A梦等闪亮登场，将体育场带进二次元世界，既怀旧又激发想象。最后，日本首相身着动漫形象马里奥的装束登场，将二次元与现实的连接推向高潮。

诚如东京奥委会曾经表示的那样：那场秀的目的就是要把日本与东京展现出去，而ACG（动画、漫画、游戏）就是日本所拥有的强有力的内容之一，这也是全球的共识。

我未曾想过，"东京8分钟"里的动漫形象，背后藏着多少经济价值；我同样并不确定，动漫科技是否再次成功成为2020年东京奥运会的焦点。因为在时尚产业中，三宅一生征服世界的"褶皱"，山本耀司低调耀眼的"黑色"，以及带有鲜明草间弥生印记的"波点"与"南瓜"，给了我远超过动漫的吸引与占据。我所知道的是，2020年东京奥运会历经波折跌宕，极不容易，但最后总还是办了的，以一种"前无古人"的方式办了。而且在办赛最为艰难的时刻，国际奥委会给了东京难能可贵的责任"豁免"——"没有政府和卫生部门能够保证对疫情绝对管控，所有人都有被感染的可能，这是我们都要承担的风险"。因此，国际奥委会通知奥运会运动员必须签署一份"豁免书"，免除东京奥组委对新冠疫情的责任。

然而，仅仅一年之隔，一些有"常青树"美誉的运动员就青春不再；一些原本要夺冠的抱负遭遇了霜打；许多相约去东京看奥运的愿望破碎了，像飘散的樱花……

"设计"的都市，"遥远"的东京。

人算不如天算。

发于"潮新闻"，2023-03-31。人民日报新媒体平台、大公网等转载。英文版发表于杭州城市客户端Hangzhoufeel。

德黑兰"影艺"

"去德黑兰，你随身携带的书会是哪一本？"

"金庸的《倚天屠龙记》。"

我的回答半认真半开玩笑，除了自小背下的世界历史，古老帝国和它的"王"们，大侠笔下的"小昭"，大概是我最早知晓的"波斯"人，而且还是个武功高强的美丽"教主"。

"德黑兰举办第7届亚运会时，你还小。"

1974年的我，的确还小，大概就只认得卡片上乒乓球之类的文字与图样。

"看看《小鞋子》。电影里有一场赛事，一个男孩的内心角逐，一场男孩与自己的极限较量。"

关于德黑兰，我平日关注的重点，是它在"丝绸之路"和"海上丝绸之路"的独特位置，通过电影了解这个城市，倒是观看的另一个视角。

德黑兰有非常优秀的电影人群体。不同于好莱坞的电影，德黑兰影片没有大投入大制作，它们以温暖、真实和力量打动观众，在国际影坛为伊朗电影赢得一个又一个高光时刻。

"他们塑造女人，刻画小孩，直面成年男人的痛苦，讲述生与死的意义。"

更重要的是，他们中有一位名叫阿巴斯·基亚罗斯塔米（下称"阿巴斯"）的著名导演，曾数次来到杭州，准备拍摄一部名叫《杭州之恋》的电影。

奔跑吧，小鞋子

有那么一场绝无仅有的跑步比赛，男主角不要冠军，不要亚军，所有的努力就奔着得季军。因为季军的奖品是一双球鞋，他承诺要送给妹妹的奖品。为此，当他遥遥领先时，他回头放慢让一名参赛者先跑一步，紧接着再让出一名。谁知却冷不防被后面的一名男孩使坏绊倒，终点临近，重新爬起的他不顾一切，慌乱中拼命向前冲去……

与影片中站上冠军领奖台却噙满绝望泪水的男孩互相凝视，我的泪水和着他的泪水，打湿了屏幕，打湿了心情。那一刻，我明白为什么这部名叫《小鞋子》的电影获得了第72届奥斯卡金像奖最佳外语片提名，为什么几十万人给这部低成本的电影打出了9.2的高分。

1974年德黑兰（第7届）亚运会时，伊朗的富裕发达，已让不少国家的人们震惊。

1959年出生于德黑兰的导演马基德·马基迪，却在1997年拍摄这部《小鞋子》时，把情节的展开设置在一个穷得交不起房租，兄妹俩只能轮换着穿同一双旧球鞋飞奔去上学的穷苦人家。导演说，是美和诗性表达的需要，是他对那个阶层和那种生活的理解，加上导演本人童年经历的一些融入，形成了影片这样一个叙述语境。

《小鞋子》并非一部典型的体育电影，影片以性格塑造和人性美的诗性展示为主。年少的哥哥阿里和妹妹莎拉明理、仗义，有担当，把所有艰难和委屈往自己身上扛。

电影《小鞋子》剧照

电影《小鞋子》海报

第 7 届德黑兰亚运会会徽　　　　　　第 7 届德黑兰亚运会主体育场

　　《小鞋子》的环境局促而逼仄，那条往来家与学校之间的小巷，几乎就是年幼兄妹童年生活的"主场"。错时上学，在隐秘的角落仓促换鞋，分秒不敢停留地拼命奔跑。生活如此艰难，但当他们好不容易发现妹妹失落的小红鞋穿在一个盲人家的小女孩脚上时，他们放弃了索回，怀抱深深的失望回家。

　　日思夜想的鞋子，毫无盼头的日常，经由一场孩子间的体育长跑比赛，将情节推向高潮并打开一个不一样的世界。比赛前，还出现了老师向小选手们交代"体育精神比名次更重要"这样的场面。影片的最后，阿里把磨满水泡的脚伸进水池，一群红色的鱼游弋在他的脚边。家门外，阿里父亲捎着给兄妹买的新鞋，正往家里赶来。

电影《小鞋子》剧照

奔跑着的小男孩的身影，也出现在前辈大师级导演阿巴斯的《何处是我朋友的家》，不过这一次，男主角巴比·艾哈迈德·波是为了寻找同桌，亲手把其作业本送回到他那里，以免因再次未完成作业第二天被老师责罚甚至开除。

阿里在奔跑，巴比·艾哈迈德·波在奔跑，许许多多的男孩在奔跑。小鞋子变成了大鞋子，再变成专业的跑鞋，镜头从鞋子的特写往上移，那些奔跑着长大的孩子，不少变成了田径场上的名将，他们不会忘记，曾在第一届亚运会获得男子5000米金牌和3000米障碍赛跑银牌的伊朗选手巴邦巴希，将1974年德黑兰亚运会的圣火点燃。

尽管体育电影在伊朗并不多见，导演还是对这一领域的题材和元素抱有充分热情。《小鞋子》的导演，就曾在2008年北京奥运会时，执导了透过孩子视角展现北京的宣传短片《飞扬的五环》。作为伊朗优势体育项目的足球，更以这样那样的方式出现在伊朗影片中。

如果获柏林国际电影节银熊奖的《越位》讲述了女性足球球迷沉重的故事，2019年终究还是迎来了500名伊朗女性入场观赛的权利。而在阿巴斯的电影《生生长流》中出现不多却贯穿始终的足球元素，几乎是人们困顿疲惫生活中的英雄梦想。

"你知道球赛几点直播吗？"
"7点开始9点结束。但已经知道谁会赢了。"
……
"地震造成这么严重的伤害，大家都在悲痛中，你们还要看比赛吗？"
……
"世界杯4年一届，生活还是要继续。地震40年一次……"

除此之外，关于足球的对白，也在《生生长流》中的父与子、小朋友与小朋友间进行。

如导演马基德·马基迪所希冀的，他的电影所表达的生活世界，应当是和平、安宁与美好的。

伊朗阿萨迪体育场

　　"足球运动员在主场踢得更好，尽管比赛规则到处都一样。我最好的作品很可能就是我在家做的。"阿巴斯用这样一个比喻，表达了与后辈导演马基德·马基迪同样的对自己家园的深情。

获戛纳影后的德黑兰女演员

　　呼声归呼声，奖项花落谁家由不得影迷。

　　当韩国导演朴赞郁以《分手的决心》获戛纳国际电影节最佳导演奖时，来自伊朗德黑兰的女演员扎拉·阿布拉希米凭出演《圣蛛》女主角"封后"。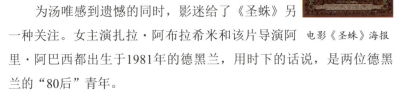

　　那已是2022年，巴黎时间5月28日晚，第75届戛纳国际电影节上的往事。

　　为汤唯感到遗憾的同时，影迷给了《圣蛛》另　电影《圣蛛》海报一种关注。女主演扎拉·阿布拉希米和该片导演阿里·阿巴西都出生于1981年的德黑兰，用时下的话说，是两位德黑兰的"80后"青年。

　　"你说你爱我时，你的爱结束了；当你的爱结束时，我的爱开始了。"看过《分手的决心》的观众，应该很难忘记，宋瑞莱（汤唯饰）决绝奔向大海前，车窗内那段美得心碎的经典演绎。

制作上的精良、悬疑片情节的一波三折，以及影片整体的审美与悲剧性……所有《分手的决心》拥有的这些，让汤唯在之后不久横扫韩国春史电影节、釜日电影节、青龙电影奖、百想艺术大赏和亚洲电影大奖等多个影后。这也算填补了影迷对汤唯错失戛纳影后的"意难平"。

与《分手的决心》不同，甚至也与很多描述连环杀人案的片子不同，《圣蛛》的重点不在追捕杀手"圣蛛"的过程，且凶手的身份也不是到后面、而是在剧情过半时就已揭开。尽管如此，作为女主角的女记者，在推动连环杀人案真相的调查中，依然遭遇了包括来自民众等多个层面的重重阻挠。

悖谬和意味深长的是，评审几乎总要对原本如此不同的作品进行比较，并最终选出"最佳"的那个——因为规则就是如此。

我走了很长一段路才站在今晚的台上……
但我最终还是带着奖项站在了这里……

扎拉·阿布拉希米的获奖感言，说的既是女演员本人，也是拍摄《圣蛛》的不凡历程。前者暗合了女演员从家园流落到异国重新摸爬滚打的演艺成长之路，后者包括这部影片最终不是在伊朗而是在约旦拍摄而成，并且即使在获奖后影片依然遭遇一些抵制。

客观说，《圣蛛》的观影感受压抑而沉重，基于20多年前真实案件改编的情节，亦无法规避暴力与血腥。但在那样一个影片设定的背景、基调与氛围中，同样潜藏和生长着"根深蒂固的传统与现代精神之间"的一种张力。女主角无畏的勇敢与真实的恐惧，她的韧劲，以及最终取得的有限度的胜利，就是影片仅有和全部的光亮。

也许，当导演将那样一个犯罪惊悚片主题——片中底层女人的生存窘境，以及女主角的锲而不舍，甚至不惜以身犯险最终让罪犯落网的努力与抗争过程呈现出来时，那份勇气首先就已经打动人了。

影片情节展开的地点并非德黑兰,而是在伊朗第二大城市马什哈德。导演选择在"圣城"马什哈德讲《圣蛛》这样一个故事,应当是基于他对影片事件真实土壤与文化的考量。此外,早在影片获奖之前,无论导演还是女主角都已离开德黑兰多年。扎拉·阿布拉希米是伊朗演员,她多年前的"出走"与其说是"出走",更像一场向死而生的"亡命天涯"。阿里·阿巴西则是丹麦籍导演与编剧,移居他国既因学业深造所起,或还有他后来做出选择的其他理由。鉴于他们长期处于米兰·昆德拉所说的"生活在别处"的境遇,观众是否会对影片的"伊朗性"产生疑问甚至提出质询?

一些具有全球影响力的"节""展"中,会有一些起初在本国未被引起充分重视,或者带有强烈批评意味的作品,在国际上反而容易获奖。不能排除在一些情况下,话语霸权和价值输出会直接或间接影响评审的结果,但对于权威和公认度相对高的奖项,受众尊重它专业判断的那些部分,内容创造者珍视评审委员会赋予的荣誉。

我在这里,但我的心与伊朗的男女同胞在一起……

当扎拉·阿布拉希米以戛纳影后的身份如此发表感言,至少有不少观众,会只从电影艺术本身出发,相信她的勇敢与真诚。

阿巴斯和他未完成的《杭州之恋》

在尝试开启德黑兰的认知之门时,我有幸认识了阿巴斯。这位天才的德黑兰导演给我的更多惊喜与遗憾,是他已经开始却终未完成的《杭州之恋》。

循着阿巴斯的电影地图,我们进入《樱桃的滋味》。一个名叫巴迪的中年男人,计划吞下安眠药,然后躺在德黑兰郊外路旁的一条沟里。他在寻找某人帮他自杀,一个能在次日早晨用土把他盖住的人。"求死"的线索,让人想起瑞典电影《一个叫欧维的男人决定去死》,还有巴西作家保罗·柯艾略的小说《维罗妮卡决定去死》。通常，以"决定去死"命名的作品，主人公最后都不会死。因为在他们决定去死的过程中，很多"意外"会发生，他们不是死不成，就是不想死了。

"死"在本质上是极其个人化的事，若不是飞来横祸毫无防备，则有可能处心积虑计划周详（因疾病而逝不在此列）。"死"不动声色，它不声张，亦不告别，去了就去了，随风而逝。

《樱桃的滋味》的结构取自一首关于蝴蝶的波斯诗歌，蝴蝶绕着烛火飞，离火焰越来越近，直到被烧毁。主人公巴迪驾车四处跑，直到掉进他为自己掘的坟墓。影片故事的灵感来自一个男人被狮子追逐的传说：跳下悬崖的男人被山腰上的根茎接住，而两只老鼠却正在啃咬接住他的植物根茎。在如此提心吊胆的情况下，男人看见山腰上长着一颗草莓，他小心翼翼地伸出手去摘草莓，并把它吃了。

作为一部成功的心理剧情片，《樱桃的滋味》曾获第50届戛纳国际电影节主竞赛单元最佳影片金棕榈奖，但阿巴斯这部电影的意义，也许更在于对此后同类主题作品的启示。

与"死"相对，阿巴斯另一部为他赢得世界声誉的影片叫《生生长流》。片中讲述一位电影导演驾车回到伊朗的一个地区，几年前他曾在那里拍摄《何处是我朋友的家》，而最近那儿遭遇了地震，他要去那里寻找曾在他电影里扮演主要角色的两个孩子，确认他们是否安全。

电影《樱桃的滋味》海报

电影《生生长流》海报

与王家卫的《蓝莓之夜》类似，《生生长流》属明显的公路片类型。阿巴斯让一位演员驾驶着他本人的路虎，边走边停，向沿途路人展开灾难情境下对"生"之理解的追问。

影片设置在地震发生的3天后，实际的拍摄却在几个月后才得以进行。地震中，各有各的不幸。大片房子受损或倒塌，无数家庭的亲人遇难，满眼疮痍荒凉，生活依旧在持续。该结婚的不等各种各样耗时长久的祷丧，不管怎样都会结婚。山坡上竖起了天线，毕竟世界杯4年才举办一次。世界会比任何个体的命运更长久，"我们"是短暂的。重建家园，供养家庭，生还者本当如此，其他一切都是浮华。

"当我要求经历了灾难的人们把他们抢回的少数财产放得杂乱些，很多人拒绝了……有些人为了拍电影还借了新衣服来穿。他们的生存本能是强大的，一如他们在如此恶劣的环境中维持自尊的渴望。"

"旅途的想法，从一点挪动到下一点，在伊朗文化中很重要"，在阿巴斯看来，"路表达了人们寻找必需品，寻找永远不安的灵魂，寻找不结束的探索"。

曾计划第5次来杭州的阿巴斯，于2016年巴黎当地时间7月4日逝世，他酝酿并筹备了许久的《杭州之恋》，由此停留在深长的"未完成态"。

从对应"死""生"主题的《樱桃的滋味》和《生生长流》出发，途径阿巴斯乡村三部曲中的《何处是我朋友的家》与《橄榄树下的情人》，再到阿巴斯分别拍摄于欧洲和日本的《原样复制》与《如沐爱河》——当阿巴斯像他在工作坊的实践课中那样把未竟之作交到我们手上，我们该如何对着他早已确定的主题"接着说"？

回望阿巴斯生前的4次杭州之旅，2014年12月的那次，他曾经去过书店买关于中国的书。相信那些书中，至少有一本关于东方的诗歌，因为诗，向来是他电影灵感的源泉。入乡随俗，他会读杭州"老市长"苏东坡的诗吗？当然未必，但他的《杭州之恋》一定是诗性的。

2014年6月，阿巴斯的首次杭州之旅，他戴着墨镜、手持DV随时拍摄行走的姿态，似乎再次跟自己也是他面前的中国朋友说：

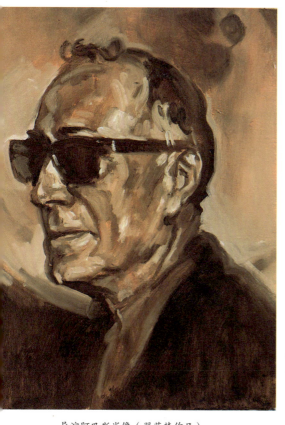

导演阿巴斯肖像（瞿莫梵作品）　　　　　德黑兰女演员阿莎妮肖像（任志忠作品）

"为什么导演不能够直接以影像开始呢？""不用词语的思想、感觉和表达不仅可能还应该被鼓励。"在充分领略过人间天堂的美景后，阿巴斯的《杭州之恋》，要更多让影像本身来传达吗？

2015年5月，阿巴斯第三次来到杭州，但那次他还带来了一名德黑兰的女演员阿莎妮，阿巴斯带她去了中国美术学院象山校区、凤凰国际创意园，还去了元谷创意园和LOFT49创意产业园。阿莎妮能说简单的中文，那是她专门花两个月特意学的。导演是要她用中文向陌生人发问吗？因为"向陌生人问路"曾多次出现在阿巴斯过往的电影里，它将一如既往成为导演对杭州兼具诗意及哲学意味的探寻与打开方式？

阿巴斯的最后一次杭州行，停留在2015年的9月，数次与杭州的接近、熟悉与对话，让他确定将上天竺的法喜寺和小河直街作为电影的取景地。同年10月10日，北京的798艺术区，阿巴斯与新闻媒体的见面会，预告了电影会讲述一个伊朗女学生在杭州的一段历程。

想象阿巴斯的《杭州之恋》是一种异乎寻常的奇特经历，因为只有在无数次地走进他的电影后，这种想象才有了依据与方向。阿巴斯说他喜欢半完成的电影模糊的样子，因为他是一个要求观众比平时看电影做更多努力的导演。在某些瞬间，我想让那个从法喜寺往小河直街走的德黑兰女孩，经过杭州亚运会的电竞场馆体验电竞。因为阿巴斯的电影，原本就是一场永不结束的游戏。就像他自己躲起来玩失踪不再见我们，不过是朝向一种把更多责任交给演员和观众而导演最终可以被摒弃的情形的旅程。

阿巴斯之后，伊朗导演与杭州的互相选择在继续。

中国美术学院院长高世名（右2）聘请马基德·马基迪（左2）为客座教授

发于"潮新闻"，2023-05-03。大公网转载。

广岛"叙事"

"就算是成为废墟，甚或坍塌得只剩下一部分楼宇，却仍然充满着叙事力量的，那才叫建筑。"

日本著名建筑设计师安藤忠雄对建筑的定义和建筑精神的理解，在某个瞬间，也许会让人浮想起广岛原子弹爆炸圆顶屋残骸（位于广岛市中部，原广岛县产业奖励馆遭原子弹轰炸后的废墟，是永久保存的原子弹受害纪念物），废墟中的城市，以及重生的广岛。

而诺贝尔文学奖获得者大江健三郎的《广岛札记》，法国女作家玛格丽特·杜拉斯的电影剧本《广岛之恋》，似乎又恰好成为这种"叙事力量"的具体承载与不同版本。

"你在广岛看见了什么?"

广岛原子弹爆炸圆顶屋残骸

我没有去过广岛，所以，我向每一个可能去过广岛的人们询问——你在广岛看见了什么？

出乎意料的是，很多人和我一样没有去过广岛，尽管他们去过东京，去过京都，去过大阪，去过奈良，或在K歌时投入歌唱《广岛之恋》，他们并没有去过广岛。

后来，我总算找到3个与广岛有过真实关联或短暂邂逅的人，他们分别是画家、体育工作者和留学生。他们说，关于我想探寻的广岛，他们知道的其实也不多，但是他们的确曾经身处其中。

广岛·爱

"我到广岛，起初是想调整状态，"画家说，"但后来发生了一些别的事。"

俄乌冲突爆发以来，画家根据他能获得的资讯，每天画一幅画，结果他画了400幅后，冲突还未结束，他迷茫了，不知道要不要继续画下去。

多年以前去广岛时，画家已完成了有关南京历史的巨幅作品。战争的主题，悲愤惨烈的氛围，无辜的平民和凶残的刽子手——让他感到长时间的沉重，同时由于长期以来的劳作，那件作品完成时，画家也落下了严重的"画后综合征"。他一度发誓，他不画那样的画了。他要去画画世界各地的美女、风情，结果他去了广岛。

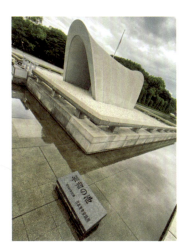
广岛和平纪念公园

"一个矛盾的地方。一方面，军国主义咎由自取的后果重重落在那里；另一方面，城市和平民遭受了空前浩劫与灭顶之灾。"

因此在广岛，画家是画不成美女的。无论他走到哪里，都无法规避曾经的残骸与废墟，灾难与伤痛。

"广岛重新遍地鲜花。到处是矢车菊和菖兰，还有牵牛花和三色旋花，这些花以花卉中迄今未见的非凡活力从灰烬中复燃。"

这是玛格丽特·杜拉斯剧本中的句子，杜拉斯在书中为它做了这样的注解——这句话几乎只字不漏地从约翰·赫西那篇关于广岛的出色报道中抄来的。

起初画家只想画夹竹桃，作为广岛市市花的夹竹桃，画杜拉斯引用句子中那些和夹竹桃一样强韧的花草树木。当它们最初从废墟的罅隙顽强生长，它们无疑成了广岛人心头的慰藉（当时流传着"这地方75年里，草木不生，人也住不得"的魔咒）。但后来的发展"可预期"地超出了画家的"预期"。

废墟中重生的赤松

"在广岛，你是不由自主的。"

于是画家疯狂地画了一些他曾信誓旦旦不会再画的作品，他如此疯狂，以至于无论他走到哪里，都带着他的便携画箱（支起来就是个简易画架）和速写稿册，手、眼和脑都进入一种快速旋转的状态。直到有一天，他住进了广岛的医院。

画家经历了一段时间的恍惚与空白，当医生告诉他必须做心脏支架手术时，他不敢相信那竟是发生在自己身上的事。他想他曾经多么年富力强，他那些不同时期的肖像，逼真记录了从儿童到少年，再从青年到壮年的成长轨迹。像多数油画家最终都会把主题性绘画视为创作的最高境界，那些对历史的回望与艺术再现也成了他的青春记忆与"光辉岁月"。

医生递给画家一份文件，跟他说需要他的亲人签字。画家摇摇头，说如果必须要签，那就只能他自己签了。到广岛的行程，他孤身而来，亦未做周详的计划，即使有，他依然得独自一人，面对已轰然倒塌的爱情废墟。但是医生说根据惯例，必须有家属来签字。

"我签吧！"

这个声音，从医生身边一名护士的口中发出。画家和医生同时看向她，像看着一个梦。

"我看过前辈那些画广岛的画，画得真好。"女护士说。

画家注意到，那是一张亚洲女人的脸，看不出具体国籍，但她的眼神与声音一样肯定。那一瞬间，时间和空间都仿佛静止凝固了。

后来，画家画了那个画面，取名《广岛·爱》。后来，护士成了画家的妻子。再后来，他们有了一个儿子。

个人的体验

"谈论广岛是不可能的。人们所能做的，就是谈谈不可能谈论广岛这件事。"

这同样是玛格丽特·杜拉斯的句子。

时隔多年，《广岛之恋》依然是它该有的样子，经典恒流传。"无人之城"广岛，也不再是满纸荒凉。

"谈论广岛不仅可能，而且现实。体育加强了这种可能。"一名资深的体育界前辈说。

玛格丽特·杜拉斯著作《广岛之恋》

大江健三郎著作《广岛札记》

他碰巧去过广岛，还亲历了1994年广岛亚运会。

经由"你在广岛看见了什么"的对话展开与反复回旋，杜拉斯最终用"可陈述"的方式，将女主人公的眼前经验与过去经历叠加，讲述了战争阴影下"不可能"的爱情。

希望以广岛和真正的广岛人为锉刀来检验自己内心硬度的大江健三郎，则在1963年、1964年两次寻访广岛后，把即将宣告死亡的"悲惨与威严"的形象一个个记录下来，提出人类应如何避免悲剧再次发生的严肃命题。

艺术的反思，文学的批判，以及——在更为普遍的意义和更为普遍的表达中，"和平"都是"广岛叙事"的主题。

这个主题也体现在1994年广岛（第12届）亚运会中。

1984年，在韩国召开的第3届亚奥理事会会员大会上，广岛被亚奥理事会授予1994年（第12届）亚运会主办权。广岛争取了首次在首都以外城市举办亚运会的难得机遇。

承载亚奥理事会"亚洲人的融合"愿景，从战争阴影中慢慢苏醒的广岛，没有忘记赛事的文化表达。

广岛亚运会会徽带有明显的城市精神气质，上部是象征亚奥理事会的太阳光芒，主体部分为两只白鸽构成的英文字母"H"，象征主办城市广岛（Hiroshima）。

"鸽"的具象也出现在广岛亚运会的吉祥物中，雄鸽"波波"（Poppo）和雌鸽"咕咕"（Coccu）是亚运会历史上吉祥物首次以"对"的卡通形式出现。作为广岛亚运会的代言，白鸽寄寓着世界和平的愿望与反战精神。

1994 年广岛亚运会会徽、吉祥物

47

"除了这既抽象又具体的符号，在广岛您还看到了什么？"

他沉默。他没有说那一年伊拉克被剥夺了参赛资格，也没有说那一年中亚五国首度参加亚运会。他没有说这一切，而只是沉默。

他没有说这一切，还因为，1994年广岛亚运会，中国中央电视台派出了由54人组成的记者团，那一年，央视首次在国外建立演播室，直接向国内播出电视节目，中国电视史上的这一壮举，使得对广岛亚运会的清晰记忆成为现实。

"怎么看邓亚萍与小山智丽的那场球？"我转移了话题。

"在广岛，邓亚萍开启了另一种完成。"这一次，他不再沉默。

邓亚萍要战胜的，无非是她自己。她战胜了，所以，她在之后不久的1996年亚特兰大奥运会一举夺得女单、女双两枚奥运金牌。所以，她依然是世界乒坛最闪亮的星。

"你知道1964年东京奥运会传递圣火最后一棒的运动员是谁吗？"轮到他来考我。

"一名在投下原子弹当日出生的广岛青年？"他似乎并没有难住我。

"那正是一个以人类自身的强韧令人震撼的肉体。他面带从一切不安中解脱出来的微笑，飞奔在巨大的运动场上。"大江健三郎这样写道。

"在广岛，我看到体育释放出的人的潜能，以及这种潜能与力量对于伤痛的愈合。"

离开广岛前，他再次去了广岛和平纪念公园。登机后，他的手上多了两本书，大江健三郎日文版的《广岛札记》，以及另一位日本作家原民喜的著作《夏天的花》。

"广岛式"的人们

如果不是因为在日本留学的宇潇，我唯一"认识"的广岛人，大概就只有三宅一生了。

2022年8月5日，84岁的日本著名服装设计师三宅一生因癌症去世。巨匠陨落，喜欢他的人们惋惜感怀。

三宅一生生于1938年的日本广岛，原子弹落向广岛时，他约7周岁，母亲及大部分亲人受伤、去世，他也体弱多病。移居东京后，21岁考入多摩美术大学。他曾先后前往巴黎和纽约学习，师从著名高定设计师——奥斯卡"影后"赫本的终身好友纪梵希。

作为战争幸存者，三宅一生曾吐露心声："我努力将这段记忆深藏起来，选择服装设计的部分原因也正是源于它象征着创造与重生。"

三宅一生用独属于他的褶皱征服了世界，他打破西方追求夸张身体曲线的传统，设计出方便女性行动工作的服装。他为苹果前CEO乔布斯设计的黑色高领套头衫及蕴涵其中的理念，为乔布斯喜爱，更被人们传为美谈。

在了解广岛的过程中，我认识了一个叫"原子弹爆炸后遗症"的词。所谓"后遗症"其实包括了至少两个方面：直接的毁灭与伤痛，以及由于这种毁灭和伤痛带来的心理创伤，进而合并成一种新的甚至可能更严重的病症。

从三宅一生所取得的成就看，他或许与这个词没有关联。又或者，他设计里传达的"解放"的信号，原本就是对这种病症的有力抗衡与疗愈。我不知道在这个意义上，他是否是大江健三郎所说的"广岛式"的人。但当他走向更宽广的世界，"广岛"也早已成为他的一个背景。

"在广岛，有一位名叫'信太郎'的导游。"宇潇说。

就读于九州立命馆亚洲太平洋大学的宇潇，曾两次寻访广岛，第一次是他20岁生日的新年前后，第二次在广岛住了近一个月。他与好朋友"菜菜花"结伴而行，想去看看原子弹爆炸许久以后，广岛和广岛人真实的生活。

"我们叫他信酱，'信太郎'是他祖父给他取的名字，意寓'相信能够从战火的阴霾中走出来'。"

宇潇的20岁生日，在广岛一家不大不小的居酒屋短暂度过，老板在烙铁板烧时，从旁人口中知道那天是他的生日，烙得愈发卖力。那一晚，除了广岛烧，他还吃到了发祥于广岛的"年轮蛋糕"。

对于自己为什么选择在广岛过生日这件事，宇潇也说不出个所以然，也许在潜意识的深处，他觉得广岛是个适合思考生命的城市。

宇潇是在第二次去广岛绕和平纪念公园骑行时遇到的信酱。当天信酱带着几名游客，看出宇潇的中国留学生身份后，尝试用中文和他交流。

信酱带游客到红十字会侧门的弄堂时，宇潇才知道，原来除了举世闻名的原子弹爆炸圆顶屋残骸，那里也修复了一墙断壁残垣。

《广岛札记》中，以原子弹爆炸一周前刚到日本红十字会医院赴任的重藤文夫博士为代表，大江健三郎写了具有"广岛人"特质的人们，有着人类"威严"的——"不屈的人们"，他们在任何情况下都不屈服，坚持着艰苦卓绝的工作。

日本红十字会医院残垣

一路上每逢故址，信酱都会讲解由来和原子弹落下时的惨状。这些故事也许所有的导游都说得差不多，但宇潇无法忘记信酱父祖三代的遭遇与因缘。

关于信酱祖母的故事，大意是原子弹爆炸那天，身怀六甲的祖母顾不上多想，对伤者展开送水和包扎，因劳累过度，加上伤者的惨状，令她深感骇然，渐渐不支又反过来被众人所救。后来，祖母生完信酱父亲没过几个月就过世了。

第二个故事说的是信酱的祖父。从电车上被甩出、没受太大伤的祖父看到被房梁压住的小孩，与几个人合力搬挪，没有成功，人们垂头散去后，祖父不死心又一人试了许久，不得不放弃。小孩歇斯底里大喊："救救我！救救我！"祖父只觉无力，捂住耳朵逃了。此后天天念叨"我终于没能救出那个小孩""我终于没能救出那个小孩"……

讲到父亲时，信酱说，父亲常教他："在世界里交很多很多的朋友，把大家都变成朋友就能太平了。"这也是为什么信酱选择了做广岛的一名导游。

不觉来到骑行的终点大喷泉前，全日本喷吐量最大、倾泻高度最高的喷泉之所以在广岛，据说是为了告慰原子弹爆炸中渴死的受难者。

环公园有路面电车。据说广岛电车虽然在原子弹爆炸当天停运了，但拓清路障后，第二天就复工了。即使根本没什么人乘坐，也不停运行着，免费亏本运行着。当时奔驰在轨道上而直到今天也没

广岛和平纪念公园内的大喷泉

广岛的电车

　　"退役"的电车有一辆——651号。恰巧它在广岛电铁株式会社总部"调休"，于是信酱不失时机地让游客与它合了影。

　　广岛地面电车的数量、班次、线路都让人眼花缭乱，马路也特别宽。

　　"有时间的话，你们还可以去看看广岛市环境局中工场。明明是一个垃圾处理厂，谷口吉生却把它设计得像个美术馆。"

　　看着欣然露出门牙的信酱，宇潇像是突然意识到，信太郎不只想让他们看过往沉重的悲剧。穿梭在历史的废墟与重建的城市，这个想要在世界里多多交朋友的广岛导游，此时已有意让自己对伤痛多些钝感，从而让他的游客看到"和平之城"生机勃勃的气象。

发于"潮新闻"，2023-04-16。大公网转载。

洛桑"大脑"

　　火车从巴黎抵达瑞士西南的洛桑时，女孩才发现使用欧盟手机卡的手机在中立国没有现成流量。她来得匆忙，也只有半天的时间可以停留，她的行程简单，目的地明确。但在互联网时代连不上地图，一时竟有些不知如何是好。

　　"路是长在嘴巴上的！"女孩想起童年时就受到的教导，将眼睛瞄向四周，人来人往，她却还是把目光投向一根集中了四个路标的柱子。

　　路标显示，她的目的地与一个就近的博物馆是同一个方向，于是她设法先进到那个博物馆，再搜索抵达目的地的准确路径。

　　女孩身穿印有古代东方"天书"的红色套头衫，那是她在韩美林艺术馆做志愿者时得到的员工同等奖励。在她到法国留学前，韩美林老师还曾亲切地把他获得的顾拜旦奖章在她脖子上挂了几分钟。她的双肩包里有一本"现代奥林匹克运动创始人"皮埃

路标　　　　　　　　　　寻访国际奥委会总部

尔·德·顾拜旦的著作《奥林匹克回忆录》，她此刻要去寻访的地方，正是国际奥委会总部和奥林匹克博物馆。

向未来：伟大的构想

国际奥委会总部设在瑞士洛桑，始于1915年的4月10日。

历史上，在国际奥委会成立后相当长的一段时间内，顾拜旦在巴黎的住所也就是国际奥委会的总部。1915年为避免第一次世界大战的干扰，总部迁址，称为"现代奥林匹克主义世界管理中心和档案中心"。在1915年至1922年间，国际奥委会秘书处直接设在顾拜旦在洛桑的住处。随着国际奥委会先后宣布洛桑为"奥林匹克之城""奥林匹克之都"，国际奥委会总部及国际奥林匹克公园最终发展成今天的气势与规模。

在顾拜旦前，还有一位国际奥委会主席，即该组织的首任主席德米特留斯·维凯拉斯，他积极支持希腊主办雅典奥运会（首届现代奥运会），根据当时"国际奥委会主席应该是奥运会举办国公民"的"轮值制"规定，维凯拉斯被选为第一任主席，他终生为奥林匹克运动积极努力。

国际奥委会总部

由于女孩对奥运会的认知与记忆，基本始于她8岁时去"鸟巢"和"水立方"观看过比赛的2008年北京奥运会，因此在相当长的一段时间，她对顾拜旦之后的四任奥委会主席了解不多，即使对父母一代经常会提起的胡安·安东尼奥·萨马兰奇，也停留在"听说萨马兰奇很欣赏邓亚萍""他非常支持中国申办奥运会"等有限的认知。对于雅克·罗格和现任国际奥委会主席托马斯·巴赫与她的家乡杭州的紧密联系，则大多来源于媒体的报道和父母的转述。

但是顾拜旦就有些不同了，这跟顾拜旦是法国公民而她正在法国求学有关，但并非全部缘由。最先把女孩和顾拜旦联系起来的情感纽带与其说是巴黎，不如说是希腊。

女孩曾经把她人生中第一场说走就走的旅行锁定在希腊的奥林匹亚。无论是那个为了将胜利消息传给同胞而跑了40多公里最终累得倒下的勇士菲迪皮德斯，还是奥林匹亚充满年代感的奥运会旧址，那里的

顾拜旦著作《奥林匹克回忆录》

荣光与废墟——她所学习的一切希腊哲学、历史和文学艺术都驱使她将目标指向那里。

而在1894年，即奥林匹克运动会宣告恢复的那一年，顾拜旦就曾带着怀古之幽情，孤独地去那里朝圣。在历经此后33年漫长的努力后，1927年4月16日顾拜旦再次去了那里。17日上午10点，现代奥林匹克运动史迎来了一个重要的时刻：奥林匹克运动会恢复纪念碑落成典礼在奥林匹亚以简单而庄重的仪式举行，当天通过无线电波传出《致各国体育青年》的信中，有这样一段文字——

……我们恢复了一个拥有两千五百年历史的活动，是希望你

们能够成为祖先所设计的体育信仰的弟子，在这充满巨大的可能性，同时也受到危险的堕落所威胁的现代世界里，奥林匹克主义可以是一所既培育高尚精神和美好情操的学校，也是培养身体耐力和力量的学校，但条件是你们必须不断地将你们的体育荣誉观念和非功利观念提高到与你们的身体力量相称的高度。未来寄托在你们身上。

如顾拜旦本人所说，当他完全从国际的角度构想奥运会并赋予它一个世界框架时，他不仅采取了唯一可以使之永恒的实际手段（其中包括让"独立"成为奥委会组织最基本的武器并保持自行选举的特权），并以符合其真正利益的最佳方式支持了古希腊的文化。因为，他并非把那历史悠久的运动会及文化精神表现为值得敬重和深思的"过去的事物"，而努力把它表现为与我们的信念和忠诚相称的"未来的事物"。

现代奥林匹克运动的这一"未来性"指向和特质，经由国际奥委会一任任核心人物和奥委会大家庭成员的共同努力，使奥运会在全球的可持续发展成为可能，算上2024年巴黎奥运会，将共有33届现代奥运会遍布全球。

他乡见家国

由于寻访的那天是星期天，女孩只能在国际奥委会总部的门外，留下对总部外观的记录。她拍了空镜，又拍了一些人们骑自行车经过总部的场景。在洛桑，到处是骑车跑步的人们，运动成为城市和生活的一部分。

更多的时间，女孩在奥林匹克公园特别是公园内的国际奥林匹克博物馆度过。公园里设置了一些有意思的运动体验项目。女孩憋足劲掂量了铅球，脸涨得通红。目之所及，与做了世界纪录标记的界标相比，感觉到汪峰歌中"霓虹灯与月亮的距离"。于是女孩用她那简直无缚鸡之力的双手，带着她的相机转战奥林匹克博物馆。

奥林匹克公园的雕塑   从外面看国际奥委会总部内

       国际奥林匹克博物馆同国际奥委会总部一样，由国际奥委会委员、墨西哥建筑设计师佩德罗·拉米雷斯·巴斯克斯和瑞士设计师皮埃尔·卡昂共同设计并主持施工，建成于1993年6月23日，国际奥委会终身名誉主席（2018年获"中国改革友谊奖章"）萨马兰奇出席开馆仪式并为博物馆剪彩。该博物馆是迄今为止世界上收藏最完整、最著名、最有活力的体育博物馆，馆前的广场有奥林匹克之火终年点燃。

国际奥林匹克博物馆

通常，女孩会把她不同寻常的寻访与观看视作"一场宏伟的朝向他者的旅程"，但在洛桑，在那样一个特殊的场景，女孩还是不由自主地，在众多雕刻和陈列之物中寻找她的心中之物，在远离家国时迫切寻找家国的文化符号、记忆象征。

女孩先在博物馆的石阶上发现2022年北京冬奥会两位主火炬手赵嘉文和迪妮格尔·衣拉木江的名字，接着又在馆内拍下了2008年北京奥运会和2022年北京冬奥会的火炬。在陈列历届奥运会和冬奥会吉祥物的专区，当她看到

刻有火炬手名字的台阶

2008年北京奥运会吉祥物福娃组合，以及2022年北京冬奥会吉祥物冰墩墩与雪容融时，内心泛起了阵阵涟漪。

智享冬奥（邬大勇、王子岩作品）

她的眼前掠过在北京韩美林艺术馆观看韩老师设计福娃的有关整体介绍、过程草图及吉祥物展陈的情景，还想起自己不止一次买过冰墩墩——那个与1990年北京亚运会吉祥物熊猫盼盼有着"亲缘"关系，但显然已迭

博物馆内的吉祥物陈列

代进化了的新一代智能宝贝。在表彰全体北京人民作出贡献的奖碑前，她停留了许久，还为自己作为高校学生拥有的临时北京户口感到自豪。

2008年北京奥运会时期，担任国际奥委会主席的是来自比利时的雅克·罗格，罗格是国际奥委会第8任主席，也是青年奥林匹克运动会的创始人。上任伊始就支持北京申办奥运会，当一位美国记者问他为何将2008年奥运会交给北京举办时，他的回答十分巧妙："国际奥委会就是想要让世界人口最多的国家举办奥运会。"在闭幕式致辞中，罗格盛赞北京奥运会是一届真正"无与伦比的奥运会"。

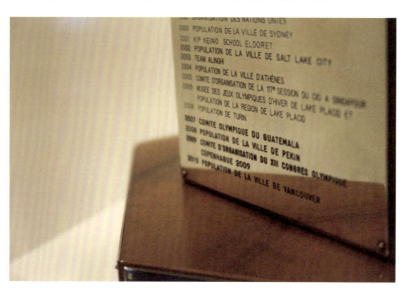

刻有"2008，全体北京人民"和"2022，全体北京人民"字样的奖碑
意在表彰北京人民在奥运会和冬奥会期间作出的贡献

2017年，已经担任国际奥委会名誉主席的罗格到访浙江杭州，对浙江体育事业和筹办杭州亚运会给予指导。他还提出廉洁办会、反兴奋剂、赛事瘦身等一系列重要的赛事改革观点和思想。

罗格之后，2013年9月，巴赫当选第9任国际奥委会主席，成为历史上首位当选国际奥委会主席的奥运冠军。巴赫曾是德国击剑运动员，在1976年蒙特利尔奥运会上获得男子花剑团体冠军，以及多次世锦赛冠军。早在南京青奥会开幕式上，巴赫在现场与运动员一起自拍的照片广为流传，富有亲和力的形象为世界各地青年所喜爱。

以巴赫为灵魂人物的国际奥委会对北京举办2022年冬奥会的支持，使北京通过非凡的努力书写历史，实现带动3亿人参与冰雪运动的承诺，成为世界上第一个既举办过夏季奥运会，也举办过冬季奥运会的"双奥"之城。

与此同时，由于北京冬奥会所处的特殊时期，奥委会和主办城市共同探索了艰难情况下圆满办会的经验。"北京冬奥会表明即使在非常困难的情况下，也可以组织一届成功的奥运会。可以向全人类传递希望和信心。"在历经卓越的北京冬奥会体验后，巴赫更盛赞北京冬

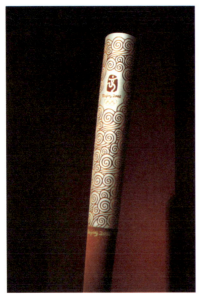

2008 年北京奥运会火炬　　　　　　2022 年北京冬奥会火炬

奥会"精彩非凡""无与伦比"。闭幕式上，巴赫用字正腔圆的中文说："谢谢！中国！"北京冬奥会一周年庆祝活动时，巴赫发视频致辞，高度评价北京冬奥会"开启全球冰雪运动新时代"。

2023年5月9日，第3次来到杭州的巴赫坚信，杭州亚运会一定会非常成功！

文化的交流与互译

快要离开的时候，女孩来到国际奥林匹克博物馆正前方的大理石圆柱旁，走过镌刻着历届奥运会、冬奥会举办年份及主办城市名字的两根柱子后，再去看另一根柱子上刻着的奥委会历任主席的名字。"他们是现代国际奥林匹克运动的'大脑'啊！"女孩心想。与此同时，她注意到广场前燃烧的火炬台边，伫立着一位女士，干练的短发，似曾相识的面容，正是传说中的林小发老师。

国际奥林匹克博物馆

林老师是从瑞士德语区的比尔家里赶过来的，女孩从一个书友会上了解到她在名著译介和文化交流上的成就，抱着试试看的心情给她写了邮件，没想到还真让她给见到了。

林老师的经历，就像她翻译的古典名著《西游记》一样，几乎带着神话般的色彩与光晕。她14岁开始学中文，在杭州生活了25年，其间完成中国美术学院版画系本科和浙江大学中文系硕士研究生学业。后又用10多年时间，讲学研究之余完成首部《西游记》德文全译本，经德国知名出版社雷克拉姆出版社推出，深受欢迎，多次重印，在第13届莱比锡图书奖一举获得翻译类大奖。

　　"看得怎么样？"

　　"史诗般辉煌！"

　　林老师和女孩默契地用中文开始交谈，两位初见者间的对话，没有多余的铺垫，甚至无需必要的界定，语境就自我生成了。天色渐渐暗下去时，燃烧的火炬愈加明亮，照耀着博物馆白色的大理石护墙，也映照着一张睿智迷人、轮廓清晰的脸和一双稚气未脱却充满神采的眼睛。

　　女孩说，自己的法语还需要修炼，这样她才能把法国女作家安妮·埃尔诺获诺贝尔文学奖的《悠悠岁月》阐释给

德文版《西游记》封面

看不懂的中文读者，也才有可能努力成为一名合格的2024年巴黎奥运会志愿者。林老师说，既是修炼，就急不得，西游途中"唐僧天团"的一切磨难，凡人也要经历，坚持做，相信自己就好。

　　林老师对《西游记》丰富性和多样性的呈现，赢得莱比锡书展主办方的盛赞——她不仅仅是把一种语言译成另一种，更在不同时代、不同思维方式的峭壁中搭起了一座桥。这正是世界文学的真意——一种来自全世界、面向全世界的文学。

　　奥运会宣布恢复以降，从体育思想中获得灵感的文学与艺术创作，正越来越融入四年一届的奥运会，虽然前期也历经了曲折与延宕。建筑、雕塑、音乐、绘画和文学——以及以人工智能为代表的新技术，让四年一届的世界性盛会更丰富、更美丽、更青春。

国际奥林匹克博物馆后的雕塑

国际奥林匹克博物馆前广场上燃烧的火炬

63

这大地上的所有造物，向上追求至高的善；从中生长出的事物，最终将实现美德。如果你们想要了解哪种力量，它决定了存在的循环……

女孩背出这段话时，没有谁比林老师更懂得，那正是她以史诗的方式翻译的《西游记》的开头——此时此刻，应和着她们身处其中的场域，竟特别贴切。其实在林老师的心里，她一直觉得，她固然翻译了《西游记》，而《西游记》也翻译和成就了她。

"邮件，你随时发，我不总在那里，但会定时看。"女孩最初找到林老师的方式，依然被鼓励沿用。

"惟愿更多的人、事、物流经我，让我成为桥、河流、纪念册和熔炉。"

女孩拥抱过林老师，把洛桑留在身后。

发于"潮新闻"，2023-06-13。大公网、《西湖》转载。

雅加达"不眠夜"

迄今为止，没有哪一个异域城市可以像印度尼西亚首都雅加达那样，让我在短时间里往返多次。且每一次的靠近与抵达，只为一个纯粹而盛大的事件。

除了棕榈树和热带灌木的气息，漫上镜片的水雾，永远塞满道路的机动车，起初眼前并没有更多的风景。第18届雅加达·巨港亚运会闭幕式总导演的约定点，杭州亚运会"接旗仪式"演出团队的代用场，还有印尼亚组委办公楼，构成了我们活动半径所能抵达的整个扇面。

沟通碰撞中，一些脉络延展过那个扇面；雅加达的晨曦与星空交替时，那个扇面，也沉积了一点又一点的重量。

后来，更多的人们前往雅加达，在朋加诺体育场汇聚成激情的巨流。我们融入那欢乐，像水滴融入海洋。

第 18 届亚运会开幕式展示的雅加达城

开闭幕式："椰壳碗外"的华美盛宴

无论你在现场，或者不在，总统的入场方式，都有点超乎想象。

第 18 届亚运会开幕式开场宣传片

　　屏幕点亮、开启，映入观众眼帘的是——总统佐科·维多多从总统府出发，乘坐轿车来到雅加达市中心，因堵车改骑单人摩托。他走街串巷，行云流水，路过学校时不忘礼让，与孩子们亲切互动。然后，宣传片切换到现场，追光亮起，紧随驾驶摩托车进场的总统。当灯光再次聚焦到总统的专属座位，只见他起立，向现场和电视机前的观众致意，一时嗨爆全场。

　　导演秀了一把总统的摩托特技，总统本人好像也并不介意，那别具一格的入场方式，同时把首都交通拥堵的实况展露无遗，一些网友更把它称为总统对"堵城"雅加达的"自黑式调侃"。

　　雅加达之"堵"，非亲见无从体会。早有不完全数据显示：1000多万人口的雅加达，拥有摩托车900多万部，汽车300多万辆，加上外地牌照进城的车辆特别是外来摩托，保守估计也有超过1300万辆机动车。某天的下班时段即塞车"高峰期"，快崩溃的我干脆就在路边垫张纸坐了下来。慢慢地我发现，那看不到尽头的滚滚车流中，没有交警，少有车变道，听不到抱怨声，仿佛开天辟地起就是那样，尽管行进缓慢，人和车都富有耐心，最后也总会一点点挪动的。

东南亚问题专家本尼迪克特·安德森在他的著作《椰壳碗外的人生》中，写到20世纪60年代他在雅加达做田野调查时，就曾弄到一辆黄峰牌小型摩托车，当时雅加达还是一个相当小的前殖民地首府城市，街区泾渭分明，凭借那辆小摩托车，安德森很快熟悉了首府各地，雅加达也成了"他的城镇"。半个多世纪过去后，摩托车看来依然是雅加达人的出行神器。

"椰壳碗外"的华美盛宴

"椰壳碗"三字，简单地说就是那口束缚青蛙只能看到它头上那片天的"井"。在安德森那里，"椰壳碗外的人生"既是他打开东南亚国家的方式，也是他的学术研究与思想心路历程。因此当我们借用安德森的"椰壳碗外"来回望2018年9月雅加达亚运会的"盛宴"，我们首先要传达的，是一个"打开"的舞台。

雅加达·巨港亚运会主题歌《心比天高》无疑是"椰壳碗外"盛宴的非凡亮点。其风靡的程度，席卷了亚细亚。

那一晚，印度尼西亚青年歌唱家薇娅·瓦伦以一身点缀着鲜花与孔雀图案的白色套装登台之时，体育场的气氛立即被点燃。

仰慕许久 梦寐以求的一切
满怀希望 摘下耀眼的金牌
灌注心血 努力追寻的目标
就是现在 要让美梦成真

薇娅·瓦伦身后的舞台呈现金属质地的第18届亚运会巨大会徽，而她面对入场式后印尼运动员集聚的区域，同时面向全场观众激情演唱。当穿插印尼语言的段落唱响，薇娅·瓦伦一开嗓就唤起的观众的情绪进一步催化发酵，歌者与运动员间擦出强烈的火花与共鸣。

紧张时刻 战况激烈 全神贯注 激起斗志
心无旁骛 唯一念头 告诉自己 我是赢家
不轻易放弃 要燃烧自信 登峰造极
哦 追求崇高的理想

而歌者最煽情的时候，也是主题歌最简单、且不管每一位观众此前是否会唱这首歌，此刻都能迅速跟唱并融入的部分——

来吧 来吧 来吧 来吧
来吧 来吧

来吧　来吧

来吧　来吧　来吧

……

别让任何人　动摇了你的决心

即使难如登天　也不妄自菲薄

摘下胜利之星

　　只见运动员们挥舞起小旗帜，几乎全场的观众情不自禁被带入歌中，包括刚刚还在炫车技的总统，彼时也在自己的座位上开始随着节奏舞动双臂，先往左旋转几圈，再惬意地向右摇摆，映在屏幕上的总统实时特写再次加强了现场的氛围——这不禁让人想起许久以前皇后乐队在伦敦温布利体育场演唱《波西米亚狂想曲》和《我们是冠军》时的盛况，虽然两场演出的属性或许完全不同。

　　开闭幕式的看点很多，"爪哇风情"的部分，以及巽他族、马都拉族、马来族的不同文化符号，尽显"千岛之国"的绚烂活力。飞流直下的瀑布，燃烧的火山，水与火在某个视点相交融，生猛诠释了第18届亚运会的主题口号——亚洲能量！

"爪哇风情"文艺节目

"天堂的影像"与"杭州8分钟"

　　根据惯例，作为下一届亚运会的承办城市，杭州在闭幕式上有一段简短的文艺演出并举行"接旗仪式"。自从北京冬奥会在韩国平昌的演出被称为"北京8分钟"，雅加达"杭州时间"文艺演出理所当然地也成了"杭州8分钟"。没有人掐着表去核对分与秒，媒体也并不在意，那一夜与第二天，几乎所有的媒体都报道了"杭州8分钟"在雅加达惊艳呈现。

表达是时间的艺术，多数时候，我们渴望恰到好处，限制性的规定，又激起更充盈的表达欲。历史的影像显示，并不是所有的接旗城市宣传片都能得到实时全球传播，而杭州要这个，非常笃定。那争取与延展的3分钟，给人间天堂故事的讲述，带来了无穷的空间与可能。

"那是窗，"我们思忖，"是天堂的影像。"

而我们首先要找到一种叙述方式，使得这个宣传片不只是图像与视频的简单堆叠。于是我们想到了编剧，还有电影，竭力在小成本投入中通过一个好的构思与后期制作呈现出大片的感觉。

然后，我们有了从良渚文明时戴玉佩搭弓射箭、穿越数千年光阴来到今日杭州的女孩，途经的一切令她感到清新好奇，她天马行空地，链接起了我们想要她链接的一切，最后在跑进杭州亚运会主体育场时，遇到另一个与自己长得一模一样的当代女孩，四目交汇处，人物隐去，"大莲花"及照耀着它的太阳与第19届亚运会会徽图案闪出，最后定格。

短片同时被赋予绘画的审美与感觉，水墨是流淌于其机体的血脉，东方的线性与空灵写意，每一帧影像都取向唯美；扎实的造型，强劲真实的刻画，唯美的同时渲染力量。

"要瘦身，不必试图去传达一切。内容包袱会让你们和片子都不够从容。"成片过程中，那是执行者最想听的"智者"的话语。

杭州城市形象外宣片画面

桥（常青作品）

荷（常青作品）

"外宣片，画面与音乐就是语言，个别瞬间即过的陌生形象，心里也有数就行了。"犹记片子在雅加达终审时，国家体育总局的领导一锤定音时的场景与叮咛。

比宣传片更早开始筹划的文艺演出，宛如一个硕大的平行工场，集聚了陈维亚等一批有着2008年北京奥运会、2010年广州亚运会开闭幕式丰富经验的各领域专家。除了极富江南辨识度的歌舞，北京奥运会总美术陈岩老师策划启用的可平移可升降"智能屏"，以及此前从未在大型国际体育赛事演出舞台现过身的易烊千玺，可谓导演团队的秘密武器与精妙手笔。

"杭州8分钟"文艺演出的"智能屏"（策划：陈岩）

易烊千玺在演唱《向往》（词：朱海，曲：孟可）

为了创作贴切"接旗仪式"文艺演出、同时也适合年轻人演唱的歌曲,作曲家孟可一遍遍研究了第18届亚运会的主题曲。在他看来,主题曲之所以能被亚洲青年热捧和喜爱,是因为它节奏灵动、旋律时尚,主题曲用了雷鬼乐的那种感觉,很好地把巴西音乐与印度音乐的节奏结合了起来,很像欧美的时尚流行乐,但又有浓郁的亚洲风,尤其在B段。因此在朱海老师为歌曲《向往》作词在先的情况下,孟可老师有意识地在交响乐的基础上融入电子乐的手法及音色,突出传统与现代时尚相存并蓄,既有回眸更有展望,从而传达出从美好今日迈向更加生机勃勃之未来的精神面貌。

　　升起于高台的女孩从良渚的陶罐中缓缓倒出一壶水,那一瞬间,整个朋加诺体育场演绎成江南的西湖。那一刻,雅加达和全亚洲在欢呼。文艺演出的最后,杭州向亚洲与世界发出了参加杭州第19届亚运

"杭州8分钟"文艺演出

会的邀约。紧接着，庄严的中华人民共和国国歌奏响，"接旗仪式"按既定的程序有条不紊进行。随后，首届亚运会火炬、首届亚运会会旗和亚奥理事会会旗千里迢迢抵达杭州！

在闭幕式现场的中国运动员

想象与现实的"共同体"

早在1962年，雅加达就已经承办过第4届亚运会。第18届亚运会，原本由越南计划于2019年11月在首都河内举办、2014年中途宣布放弃的。2014年9月，亚奥理事会全体代表大会通过了印尼申办第18届亚运会的申请。因此印尼雅加达·巨港亚运会的承办工作，时间就相对紧张得多，这自然也影响到牵涉面特别广的开闭幕式。

由于东道主对下一届举办城市的文艺演出场地，通常会做出严格的限制，下届举办城市的导演团队，难免会生出跨国"客场"工作，施展和发挥余地太过局促的感叹。

"接旗仪式"迫近的最后数天前，我们的演出团队依然只能在距主体育场较远的代用场演练。在那之前，尽管两个导演团队和工作人员定期碰面，彼此询问，但都语焉不详，有所保留，唯恐各自的创意提前被泄露。所以双方基本就是我想着你可能的样子，你猜测我会有的呈现。但终究都适可而止，有所为有所不为，只想着把自己的那部分做到极致。

直到宣传片流畅播放，"杭州8分钟"预期呈现，朋加诺体育场经久不息的掌声，雄辩地提示这原本就是"我们"共同的派对啊！

时间距离雅加达"不眠夜"已经过去太久太久，斗转星移，万象更新，杭州将迎来新时代的又一场辉煌盛典。这时突然好想雅加达——想那里满街的运动海报，想无处不在的三个卡通小动物极乐鸟、独角犀牛和梅花鹿，在雅加达最后的那些日子里，它们环绕和簇拥着我，构成了雅加达地方特区（印尼有雅加达首都、日惹、亚齐3个地方特区）的新风景。我还想让人民币看上去特别强劲的印尼卢比，虽然在雅加达我根本无暇消费，想没有告别也没有拥抱只有笔尖在极速行走的夜晚，想盘旋在主体育场头顶的浩瀚星空，想那趟没有停息更不会懈怠的孤身长途飞行。

18届亚运会吉祥物及应用

滚滚车流中，雅加达是否还是那么"堵"那么"从容"？

曾经，有位留学于中国河南的印尼混血姑娘翁玄孝，想要把高铁像"打包"的行李那样带回家，而当"全球海洋支点"遇上"一带一路"，翁玄孝的梦想竟然成真了！2017年2月，翁玄孝通过应聘，成了中国与印尼合作的"雅万（雅加达至万隆）高铁"1号隧道的现场翻译。2023年4月，"雅万高铁"的土建已完成超90%，全线13条隧道全部贯通，全线轨道铺设完成……

耳畔再次响起雅加达第18届亚运会的主题歌——

快与我牵手 共襄盛举
传奇事迹 将不断被记下……

发于"潮新闻"，2023-06-25。大公网、腾讯网、《西湖》等转载。英文版发表于杭州城市客户端Hangzhoufeel。

曼谷"消息"

　　给新一期（2023年6月号，总第61期）的《亚洲体育》做美术设计时，我见到了久违的帕塔玛女士。

　　帕塔玛女士是国际奥委会文化与奥林匹克遗产委员会主席，同时也是亚奥理事会文化委员会主席。2023年2月25日，她参加了泰国奥委会在清莱府（泰国北部地区的一个小城镇）举办的一场"奥林匹克日"活动，手举发令枪、一身运动装的她，眼神俏皮，像快活的孩子。3月8日，《曼谷邮报》报道了她被评为泰国年度影响力女性的消息，以表彰其卓越的商业神勇和为扩大泰国国际影响力所做的贡献。不一样的图片，一样的是洋溢在她脸上的微笑，她一贯的优雅与活力。

帕塔玛女士出席"奥林匹克日"活动

记忆

独自处在月光下

我可以笑对旧日时光

　　自从2019年3月在曼谷听过帕塔玛女士演唱的百老汇歌剧《猫》的主题曲"Memory"，我似乎能看到她无限可能的那一切，随着她的歌声飞扬播撒。此刻，她的形象与歌声相交织，把我带回2019年的曼谷春天，带回到更悠长的泰国奥林匹克运动史。

曼谷春天

　　说起曼谷，人们首先想起的也许是泰式按摩、国宝大象以及善于制造新闻的王室。

　　而当走进真实的曼谷，哪怕只一星半点的时光，也会有一些别的市井风情，闪过眼前。

曼谷街景

商业中心扑面而来现代化的气息，商场间的连廊，有种梦回杭州武林商圈的感觉。滚滚车流伴着滚滚红尘，BTS（空中轻轨）站点大都有大型商场，可以让人们任性释放心情释放购买力。

　　曼谷同时是个充满烟火味的城市。夜间的大排档，人流熙熙攘攘，一些叫得出名或叫不出名的海鲜，一种和数种不同颜色不同浓度的酒，更多相识与不相识的人，挨挨挤挤地，为热闹或孤独，短暂相逢胡吃海喝。

　　烟火，当然还萦绕在寺庙里，萦绕在精神性的修炼与俗世功利的祈祷里，畅通无阻。尽管人们被劝说感官世界皆为幻象，却又求取实现"生意兴隆""职务升迁""金榜题名""鸿运当头"等非幻象的愿望。

　　泰国，历史上称"暹罗"，是东南亚唯一没有沦为殖民地的国家，19世纪末开始实行对外开放，并进行社会改革，1932年6月改君主专制为君主立宪制，1949年正式定名泰国。首都曼谷是泰国5个地区77个府中唯一的府级直辖市，位于湄南河东岸，南临暹罗湾，军队、王室、大财团和大量的中产阶级（华裔占据了很高的比例）集聚于此。

大皇宫一角

第38届亚奥理事会全体代表大会在曼谷举行时，杭州亚组委进行了杭州亚运会筹办工作的陈述。一系列涉及场馆建设、竞赛项目、新闻宣传、公众参与、市场开发的构想，成为被热议的话题。

会议室外，热带季风吹过，棕榈树摇曳着这座东南亚大城市的独特风情。

第38届亚奥理事会全体代表大会

棕榈树

虽是春天，会后去拉加曼加拉国家体育场观摩一场大型体育活动时，即使身着短袖，仍觉得阳光猛烈。

而在苏帕查拉赛国家体育场（又称泰国国家体育场），"奥林匹克日"等公众参与活动的持续规划与举办，让古老的体育场依然散发出春天的魅力。

拉加曼加拉国家体育场

苏帕查拉赛国家体育场

81

情有独钟

亚运城市列表中，曼谷出现的次数至今依然占据榜首。

从1966年到1998年，曼谷先后承办了4届亚运会，且前3届均集中于亚运会诞生后的早期阶段。

1966年，首次申办亚运会（第5届亚运会）的曼谷没有遇到任何竞争对手，此前由政府投入带动的基础设施兴建，从硬件上保障了亚运会的顺利举办。之后，曼谷先后两次接办韩国与巴基斯坦因财政问题放弃的1970年第6届亚运会和1978年第8届亚运会。1998年，已积累了丰富办赛经验的曼谷，又举办了第13届亚运会。

亚运会历史上，中途接办比赛的情况，后来还曾发生于印度尼西亚的雅加达。曼谷的贡献显而易见——因为它的敢于承担，避免了亚运会在成长之初可能会遭遇的中断——而且曼谷把每一届亚运会都办成功了，其中最简单而直接的证明，就是曼谷举办的4届亚运会上，都有泰国国王的身影。

通常，若一个国家多次获得亚运会的举办权，从带动基础设施建设和经济发展等诸多因素出发，会考虑把赛事落在不同的城市，如后来的韩国，就先后将汉城（后中文译名改为"首尔"）、釜山、仁川作为亚运会举办城市。印度尼西亚则在第二次举办亚运会（第18届亚运会）时，增加了巨港作为首都雅加达的协办城市。曼谷的情况之所以是个例外，或许是因为在早期，主办方既没有时间也没有条件想那么多，又或许亚奥理事会和泰国政府原本就对曼谷情有独钟。

建成于1935年的苏帕查拉赛体育场是曼谷前三届亚运会的主赛场。到1998年第13届亚运会时，新的拉加曼加拉国家体育场建成并投入使用。

曼谷在亚运美学方面也有较大的贡献。以主要视觉标志的设计为例，第5届和第6届亚运会会徽标注了举办地、举办届数，并融合了亚奥理事会的太阳图案和口号"永远向前"。第8届亚运会会徽有了更多的泰国元素，两个既似手臂、又似泰国国鸟火背鹇的图案，拱卫着太阳，在展现泰国文化精神的同时，凸显了亚运会的茁壮成长、欣欣向荣。第13届亚运会会徽则直接运用泰国佛教文化的符号尖顶佛塔进行设计，形成代表亚洲的"A"字，与上方的太阳标志共同表达了"亚洲一家亲"愿景。

第5届亚运会会徽　　　　　第6届亚运会会徽　　　　　第8届亚运会会徽

　　吉祥物选择了颇有代表性的大象。有趣的是，其命名"猜裕"，恰好是泰国人表示快乐、幸福和庆祝胜利时常用的语气词。四届亚运会的主题口号，从"光"的主题，演进到"体育精神"以及"不分国界的友谊"，寄寓着泰国对不断发展着的亚运会的美好祝福。

　　第13届亚运会，无可避免地，遭遇了1997年席卷亚洲的金融危机，但也许由于有猜裕的护佑，有如同猜裕的乐观豁达，当然还有——亚运会带来的红利，泰国经济于1999年开始复苏，并于2003年7月提前还清危机期间国际货币基金组织提供的贷款。

第13届亚运会会徽、吉祥物

风华绝代

那时，我风华绝代

我仍记得

那时我曾知晓幸福的意义

就让回忆 重新苏醒

　　2019年春天的那个夜晚，帕塔玛女士的歌声依然萦绕。虽然做了降调处理，帕塔玛女士还是以恰如其分的情感投入与歌唱技巧，把这首高难度的主题歌成功演唱。一样精彩的是泰国皇家乐队的演奏，除了帕塔玛女士，还有另外两名青年女歌唱家活跃在临时舞台，她们在泰语与英语间自由切换，伴随着轻快的旋律边歌边舞。

　　除了帕塔玛女士的服饰（我们或许可以理解为她有意识地为"泰丝"代言），整个场景是近乎完全西式的。

　　历史上，泰国经历过文化的"美国化"影响。随着国家实力的增强，泰国在追求国际化的同时，也强调文化的民族特性。2023年，华裔王后苏提达出席英国国王查尔斯的加冕礼时，穿的就是极具泰国民族特质的服装（做了融合现代时装元素的改良设计），平时一些场合还会穿中式旗袍。

　　首都曼谷，正是异质文化的汇流处。

　　以泰国知名独立导演、编剧、制片人阿彼察邦的电影《热带疾病》为例，这种异质文化的交汇碰撞，就反应得特别强烈。阿彼察邦曾凭《能召回前世的布米叔叔》获第63届戛纳国际电影节主竞赛单元金棕榈奖。从时间上，《热带疾病》比李安的《断背山》还要略早；而在内容展开方面，导演借助了"化身虎"形象与"丛林之虎"的隐喻，来讲述灵魂之爱与宿命分离，表达更为含蓄曲折。但《热带疾病》这部讲述同性相爱的电影，只在曼谷的三家影院上映了一周。电影在国际上获得的巨大声望，与在曼谷的冷遇形成强烈反差，甚至在曼谷和外府农村与小镇的反应，也完全不同。

王室理论上代表了泰国文化的"正统"。关于泰国王室的各路传闻与消息，也最易于被社交媒体所津津乐道。但不管那些消息如何千奇百怪，泰国公主诗琳通的形象总是受人喜欢和尊敬。她精通多国语言，尤爱东方文化，曾先后50次访问中国，为促进两国文化交流身体力行。

诗琳通公主是著名艺术家韩美林和夫人周建萍的老朋友。2018年4月出访中国期间，曾专门参观北京韩美林艺术馆。被韩老师绚烂丰厚的艺术作品及植根于其中的深厚文化传统所感动，她欣然在工作室写下"扎根沃土"四个大字，并兴致勃勃地看韩老师用中国印将她的书法作品补充完整。她还送了一本自己写的中文著作给周建萍女士。2020年1月，韩老师在泰国办展时，诗琳通公主前往观展，亲切与韩老师团队合影。时值新冠疫情暴发，韩老师回国前，泰国旅游局局长送上"比黄金更可贵"的300多个口罩作为礼物。

据媒体消息，诗琳通公主还曾于2018年4月前往四川眉山市三苏纪念馆和三苏祠，用中文写下"苏门出才子"，以此来"对话"宋代大文豪苏轼。如此，公主与杭州"老市长"苏东坡的文化缘，又让此前已数次来访浙江的她，与杭州的缘分更多了一层。

我没有想过诗琳通公主的确切年纪，但我知道，80多岁的韩美林老师，从来都说自己是"80后"青年。"一代人的芳华已逝，面目全非，虽然他们谈笑如故，可还是不难看出岁月给每个人带来的改变。"记得这是电影《芳华》中的台词，透彻、富有哲理，同时夹杂了淡淡的忧伤。

而他们，以及那个歌唱中的女士，许许多多像他们那样的人们，也许也曾历尽沧桑，但依然风华绝代。

当那黎明到来
今夜，也将成为回忆
新的一天，即将开启

第 42 届亚奥理事会全体代表大会

　　2023年7月8日，在曼谷召开的第42届亚奥理事会全体代表大会上，杭州亚运会组委会作报告，哈尔滨市获得2025年第9届亚洲冬季运动会举办权，亚奥理事会杰出贡献奖颁发。

发于"潮新闻"，2023-07-08。大公网、腾讯网转载。

马尼拉"胶片"

　　马尼拉很远，远得宛如王家卫《阿飞正传》中一代影星的青葱岁月；马尼拉又很近，近得就像从菲律宾"生命之树"上刚采摘的椰子。

　　马尼拉的色彩单纯，缤纷。由日本放送协会（NHK）摄制保留的1954年第2届亚运会黑白视频、新加坡国家博物馆陈列的男子水球团体金牌，映照铺展出"椰城"（马尼拉有"椰城"之称）自远东运动会以来的体育历程。

马尼拉街景

海边

　　风物纷繁，"斗鸡"翻新传统，广告传达时尚，古迹与海岸将沧桑浪漫交错绵延。

　　有人奔马尼拉而去，就有更多的人从马尼拉突围。譬如《阿飞正传》中的旭仔与超仔，跑船或者寻母；又譬如出走世界各地的菲律宾女人，一不小心闯出了未曾预料的人生。

《阿飞正传》外景与马尼拉"风物"

　　1989年11月28日至12月5日，始终戴着墨镜、经常折腾演员的香港天才导演王家卫，带着张国荣、刘德华等一众明星以及《阿飞正传》摄制团队，在马尼拉度过了他们的外景疯狂八日。

　　《阿飞正传》并不存在一个名叫"阿飞"的人，但王家卫却让男主角张国荣讲了一个"无脚鸟"的故事。"世界上有一种鸟是没有脚的，它只可以一直地飞啊飞，飞得累了便在风中睡觉"——纵使遭遇激情真爱，还是无法驻足停留，不论他遇到的女子，是张曼玉饰演的温柔女子苏丽珍，还是刘嘉玲饰演的泼辣舞女梁凤英。因为命运的魔咒早已预示，"这种鸟一辈子只能落地一次"，停止飞翔

马尼拉俯瞰图

漂泊之日，便也是他的死亡之日。

电影镜像与真实情境相交织，映现出似梦似真的马尼拉。

"马尼拉的空气比香港郁结，使人容易疲倦。"

但这只是电影团队落地之初的感受，并不符合马尼拉和影片外景地的情况。演员和拍摄团队的到来，围观雀跃的人群，时时组合成一场热闹非凡的嘉年华。

据说在菲律宾，看戏曾是最便宜的休闲娱乐，菲律宾人因此养成看戏的习惯，戏院林立。时光向前，俊男靓女代言的消费品广告和房地产广告成为马尼拉街头的新风景。KTV、酒吧等新娱乐方式延续了"看戏""演戏"的基因与传统，酒吧乐队不仅是重要的文化输出产物，也成了部分群体的生活与生存方式。

电影中，张国荣饰演的旭仔是一名菲律宾贵妇的私生子，旭仔由身为舞女的养母带大，养母因为害怕失去他，直到很久以后才告知亲生母亲是谁，因而旭仔实际上是一个精神上的孤儿。从香港到菲律宾，王家卫让历经"寻母"艰难的旭仔，一直追寻到埃斯库德罗庄园，但抵达即终结，生母碍于身份，没有与旭仔相认。

大片的椰林，旭仔走在一条似乎没有尽头的林中之路，留给观众无奈而决绝的背影，"我只不过想看看她的样子，既然她没有给我机会，我也不会给她这个机会"。独白过后，电影给出了一个全景的画面，配合升格的慢镜头，预示了旭仔的自我救赎并没有成功，而是走向彻底的迷失。

菲律宾有"椰子之国"的美誉，马尼拉放眼望去随处可见散发着热带气息的椰子树。椰子是生存之果，可营养机体，还能修复伤口。而在影片中，旭仔的心在流血，伤口被无情撕裂，他二十多年的希望，不过是一场虚无缥缈的梦。王家卫把旭仔的"梦碎"与"心死"设置在一个常识中的"希望之境"，但它不属于"无脚鸟"般存在的旭仔。

树与果

之后，由刘德华饰演、先一步到菲律宾跑船的超仔，在一幢19世纪的古旧建筑旁与落魄潦倒的旭仔再次重逢。导演并没有给出古建筑的全貌，而是呈现了一系列马车、楼梯以及有些晃动的欧美风铁艺窗口的特写。

在马尼拉，有不少那样的历史建筑，教堂尤其多。那些"别人"种下的东西，暗合了菲律宾长期被西班牙和美国殖民的历史。

而那次重逢，也让超仔见证了旭仔被改写的命运。为了一本假护照，旭仔打架还拿刀捅了人，在当过警察的超仔的奋力帮助下，两人逃脱，跳上一列火车。车上，受伤的超仔责怪旭仔鲁莽，旭仔却不以为意，两人于是发生争执，超仔一气之下离开，等他回到车厢，遭遇枪杀的旭仔已身处血泊之中。

旭仔忧郁苍白的脸，超仔爱莫能助的痛，车窗外茂密的雨林和大片的椰林，在雨雾中迷蒙，快闪中推移。如果我们不愿面对旭仔的死亡，导演却不得不斩断这个孤儿与世间最后的执念与羁绊，那是解脱，也许还有重生的意味。尽管影片中的每个人都有可能是阿飞，尽管还会有新的无脚鸟。

《阿飞正传》的情节设定和王家卫独特的美学风格，使得电影不可能对马尼拉风情做全面的铺陈。建于1832年的杜杜曼火车站，在当年拍摄《阿飞正传》时已日趋荒凉，但随着2022年菲律宾克拉克线路段一期工程完工，又开始恢复了原初的生机。凭借更加便捷的交通，人们也许可以在高速行走中看到水牛节、高脚屋、吕宋烟叶等菲律宾的特有风物，并发现那古老、堪称全民运动的"斗鸡"风俗，已迭代升级成"马尼拉国际斗鸡邀请赛"。只要一只斗鸡足够优秀强悍，也可以漂洋过海，成为马尼拉的超级嘉宾。

大事记

在梳理菲律宾体育发展史上的大事记前，有一个需要被提起的时间，它既是世界航海史的新纪元，也关乎菲律宾的国家命运和历史文脉。

1521年3月，麦哲伦率领西班牙远征队（摩鹿加舰队）到达菲律宾群岛，成为首个将航海纪录从美洲延伸到亚洲的"冲锋舰队"。在群岛南部贸易枢纽宿务（现菲律宾第二大城市），麦哲伦和船员停留了一段时间，船员以玻璃珠子和小镜子等物品做"贸易"，换取当地人的黄金，他自己则与宿务国王胡马邦交往，同时不遗余力地传播天主教。4月27日进攻麦克坦岛时，麦哲伦被刺身亡，就此终结了他雄心勃勃的冒险与征服生涯。

之后西班牙逐步侵占菲律宾，开始长达300多年的统治。1898年菲律宾宣告独立并成立共和国，但很快又相继被美国和日本占领，直到1946年7月4日重新独立。

早在麦哲伦开始他的冒险远航前，1913年首届远东运动会在马尼拉举办，这个区域性的国际比赛，由菲律宾、中国和日本一道发起。作为亚运会的前身，远东运动会是世界上最早出现的洲际国际竞赛，从1913到1934年间共举办了10届。而在那10届运动会中，中国男子在足球项目上曾9次获得冠军。

1954年5月1日至9日，第2届亚运会开幕式在马尼拉黎刹纪念体育场举办。18个国家约千名运动员参加了8个大项76个小项的角逐。

黎刹纪念体育场位于马尼拉狂欢节场地旧址，又称菲律宾国家体育场，为纪念菲律宾民族英雄何塞·黎刹而命名。始建于1927年，1934年远东锦标赛时落成，能容纳3万人次。体育场此后经历了向市民开放、用于演唱会等通用做法，也一度面临拟被售卖改建的命运，因人们的剧烈反对得以保留，并被宣布为国家历史地标。体育场在东南亚运动会举办前得到翻新完善，后用于本地和多种国际体育赛事。新冠疫情流行期间，体育场被改建为隔离设施，收容来自菲律宾总医院症状轻微的病人。

1954年的马尼拉亚运会，视角系统的设计还相对有限，会徽沿用了新德里首届亚运会的风格，吉祥物尚未提上日程。但马尼拉亚运会已经有自己的专属邮票与明信片，邮票有5分、18分和30分三种币值的款式，一一对应铁饼、游泳、拳击三个不同运动项目和湖蓝、浅绿、粉红三种底色。三枚邮票同时被设计进明信片的右上方；明信片左侧图案的设计相对复杂，高扬和密集排列的旗帜、跳水运动员以及建筑背景，有限的空间承载了充盈的信息；明信片的中下方伫立着一名男运动员，他的右手将火炬高高举起。

马尼拉亚运会会徽、邮票及明信片

马尼拉亚运会的金牌，可以在新加坡国家博物馆看到。那枚金牌也是新加坡在该届亚运会上取得的唯一金牌，由新加坡男子水球团体获得。

马尼拉亚运会金牌

马尼拉亚运会上，作为东道主的菲律宾凭借天时地利，从首届的奖牌榜第四跃居1954年亚运会时的第二。年仅16岁的菲律宾女运动员海迪·科洛索·埃斯皮诺击败两名日本竞争对手获得100米自由泳冠军，一举成名。以此为好开局，她后来在国际性比赛中取得多枚奖牌，一度有"亚洲游泳皇后"之称。

马尼拉亚运会备受关注的运动员中，有一位来自日本的南部敦子，是女子100米冠军的获得者，留下了跟当地粉丝虚心互动的画面，被菲律宾人称为"运动会的甜心"。

日本放送协会的开幕视频，有中国香港队入场时的情景。王家卫在拍摄《阿飞正传》续篇《花样年华》和《2046》时曾谈到，电影中反复出现的音乐，深受西班牙或拉美音乐的影响，因为那时香港的大多数音乐人来自菲律宾。

与香港有传奇关联的，还有被尊称为菲律宾"国父"的何塞·黎刹。移居菲律宾前，他曾在香港中环开设眼科医院。直到今天，还可以看到竖立在黎刹故居的纪念牌匾。

黎刹（厘沙路）医生在香港使用的名片

黎刹医生故居的纪念牌匾

东京第32届奥运会上，女选手迪亚兹在举重55公斤级决赛中夺冠，为菲律宾赢得奥运会历史上的首枚金牌，同时结束了该国97年来的"金牌荒"。

城里女人和乡下男人

"你需要一个假期，一个难得的好假期进入世界，你曾经有过这样的梦想，而我们可以快速地让它实现。"

一则马尼拉杂志上的广告词，用来招募菲律宾女性去日本做工。广告将海外工作经验染上玫瑰色的浪漫与梦想。

来自马尼拉或菲律宾其他地方的女人，无论已婚，或依然单身，正不断走出家门开启她们的跨国旅程，然后源源不断地把辛苦赚到的钱寄回家。应对失业、赚更多钱、摆脱困境或谋求发展，也许还有对海外生活的文化想象，让远走高飞成为可能与必须。她们说流利的英语，不少还受过大学教育，她们在不同的国度从事不同或大抵相同的工作，常常被统称为"菲佣"，不过社会学学者赋予她们"女性移工"的称谓。

经由这条路，不知道菲律宾女人是否已经占领了世界上尽可能多的城市。但菲佣对本国经济的贡献，已然使她们无意间成了国家的无冕"英雄"。

命运交错的码头

挪威剧作家易卜生在他的《玩偶之家》中，辛辣披露了男权社会与妇女解放之间的矛盾冲突，全剧以女主人公娜拉的觉醒和愤然离家告终。如果易卜生的重心是激励妇女为争取自由平等而斗争，那么鲁迅先生紧接着提出了"娜拉出走以后"这一更为深刻的社会命题。

"英雄"是怎样炼成的？在跨越国界与性别藩篱的路上，她们究竟能够走多远？

成长千差万别

问询使用过菲佣的家庭，大多对其专业性与职业操守评价积极，与此同时，支付给菲佣的薪水也比本地保姆或其他外籍保姆相对更高些。

　　与雇主在薪资和休假等事宜上的讨价还价能力，离不开菲佣的组织化服务。这类权益的实现反过来又培育了属于她们的"团聚"文化。

　　脱下工作服，涂上口红，从雇主家的工作前台穿越到城市的公共场域，与其他姐妹短暂相聚，吃家乡菜，高兴时适度消费，放飞自我，那样的时光与场景，或许就是菲佣给自己颁发的"奖牌"，是她们城市边缘生活中的亮色与慰藉。

　　她们出走，她们变得富有，然后她们回家。易卜生和鲁迅，好像都只预言对了一半。

　　从养家到持家，劳动让她们完成了身份角色的重要转变。使她们有能力孝敬父母、资助阿弟阿妹的教育，或舍得用自己赚的钱，为家人购买同样的雇佣服务，以便更安心长久地延续在别国城市的生活与工作。走得更远的，直接从外籍女佣变成了外籍新娘。

　　假定有一个理想的家庭模式，很难判断这是否算成功，因为路上的辛苦，如鱼饮水，冷暖自知。但改变是确定的，走走停停也好，义无反顾也罢，总之是她们令自己身上"有事情发生!"

　　《老爸的笑声》是菲律宾作家卡洛斯·布洛桑以家乡农村为题材写的小说。故事发生在吕宋岛一个灾害不断的村子，作者以第一人称的视角，写了家族的9位成员。老爸是斗鸡高手，满嘴大男子主义；老妈是职业哭丧师，生气就拿老爸练拳；大哥从战场回来后，变成酗酒的忧郁男；二哥专偷自家的东西；三哥是个书呆子；四哥12岁就想结婚生小孩……而"我"，在5岁时就爱上喝烈酒。"我们家的人都有点怪怪的，不过幸好我们仍有

《老爸的笑声》封面

彼此。每天，我们全家都会笑成一团"，卡洛斯·布洛桑进一步得出——"笑声，是我们家仅有的财富"。

《老爸的笑声》通篇诙谐，有时甚至略带戏谑，被《纽约客》杂志认证为爆笑动人的"菲律宾物语"。它虽然写的是作者故乡的故事，但也呈现了菲律宾农民普遍的生活样貌。

出国寻求更好生活的梦想深植于菲律宾的文化及历史脉络。小说中，日渐长大的"我"一边被动"相亲"，一边被老爸悄悄安排出国。"我们人只能活一次。"老爸说。所以老爸希望"我""去看看世界上其他人在做什么"。

在菲律宾，父权逻辑一方面限制女性参与当地劳动市场下的席位，另一方面却保留了她们在全球劳力市场上的席位，她们甚至比丈夫有更多机会得到海外的工作。

这是吊诡的现实，还是梦想的土壤？

海之梦

发于"潮新闻"，2023-07-20。大公网转载。英文版发于杭州城市客户端 Hangzhoufeel。

三城记

1981年对于韩国首都汉城（2005年中文译名改为"首尔"）来说是个不平凡的年份，继9月被国际奥委会赋予1988年第24届奥运会举办权后，11月在没有竞争对手的情况下，又获得1986年第10届亚运会举办权。

自21世纪以来，韩国已举办过2002年釜山亚运会、2014年仁川亚运会，2002年韩日世界杯，以及更为切近的2018年平昌冬奥会。

紧接汉城亚运会，北京迎来了1990年亚运会，"亚洲雄风"响彻神州大地。2010年广州亚运会闭幕式上，亚运会进入"仁川"时间。

背影

大韩民国临时政府杭州旧址纪念馆

2018年平昌冬奥会，"北京8分钟"的惊艳呈现，拉开了2022年北京冬奥会的精彩序幕。而在2023年秋分时节将要开启的杭州第19届亚运会，韩国体育代表团将与其他亚奥理事会成员一起，齐聚美丽江南。

相近的地域，文化的源流，蓬勃的办赛景象，绵延，碰撞，浩荡向前。

汉城"跨越"

也许由于汉城在短短的两年内连续举办亚运会与奥运会，也许因为奥运会的影响力原本要远超亚运会，当问起汉城亚运会时，未亲历者似乎并没有特别深刻的记忆。"那时候我还在念书，"杭州亚运会宣传形象大使、中央电视台知名节目主持人沙桐老师回忆，"我记住更多的是釜山和仁川亚运会时的工作状况。"

但我们都记住了汉城奥运会的主题歌，那首旋律优美、大气磅礴的《心手相连》，时任国际奥委会主席萨马兰奇曾建议作为奥运会永久会歌。

青瓦台

火车站

黎明划破黑夜

用希望在你我心中燃起火焰

迈向崭新的一天

未来将是属于我们的世界

……

心与心相连

手和手相牵

带着骄傲一起飞向无垠的蓝天

……

当年用混杂的中英文跟谭咏麟录音带学唱的情景，犹在眼前，但一直清清楚楚记得的结束句"心手相连"，现在到网上查证时竟变成了"阿里郎"，英文版歌词也只有"Hand in hand"的不断反复。不得不说，那时的中译版已经相当超前。因为在酝酿杭州亚运会的主题口号时，就曾有过"携手向未来（Hand in Hand @ Future）的方案，但是组委会领导非常肯定地说，要比汉城奥运会更进一步，因此把"携手"改成了"心相融"（Heart to Heart），这才有了最终的"心心相融，爱达未来"（Heart to Heart, @ Future）这个发布版。

汉城亚运会，韩国以"水"为媒，用三颗平行交叠的水滴与亚奥理事会的太阳组合设计了会徽，既传达出韩国是个被海洋包围的国度，也用水的凝结传达出亚洲的紧密团结。那一年，韩国以东道主的姿态，以远超日本的优势名列奖牌榜第二，中国又一次以金牌总数第一雄踞亚洲体坛之首，中日韩三强格局进一步形成。中国体操运动员李宁以4枚金牌成为那届亚运会最多的金牌得主。

汉城亚运会为1988年奥运会积累了诸如交通和口译优化等方面的诸多经验，一些亚运遗产在奥运会时得到了二次开发和利用，奥运会和亚运会同用一个吉祥物就是这方面的典型例子。

在韩国，"老虎"是极其珍稀的存在，官方称"朝鲜虎"。在两场赛事中，一个名叫"虎多力"（Hodori）、萌态可掬的"太极虎"被选择为吉祥物，它同时承载了韩国人对于"勇猛"与"友善热情"的多重寄托。

汉城亚运会会徽、吉祥物

在赛事和更广泛的文化表达方面，韩国人一方面要彰显个性与辨识度，另一方面又常常情不自禁掉入对东方传统文化的深深眷恋，以致有时候分不清你我，表现出一种矛盾而复杂的心态。"太极"一词及其意象，既用于奥运会吉祥物的称谓，也在会徽设计中同时演变成了三原色的图案。只是不知道《易经》以来古人对"阴阳""八卦"的玄妙解读，韩国人是否感同身受。

"太极"，又称"太无"，彼时天地未开，囫囵一团。往后，太极生两仪，阴阳分，天地就出来了。天地生出的万物，也全都有阴有阳。阴阳合德，人安事宁。圈小一步跨出去，圈大宇宙乾坤都圈起来。

汉城奥运会会徽中的三个漩涡状条纹代表天、地、人的和谐，整合了"内向心"和"外离心"两种动态，分别表示五大洲选手走到一起，通过践行奥林匹克精神，走向相互了解和世界进步。奖牌延续了典型的希腊文化精神，正反面聚合了手持月桂花冠的胜利女神与衔着月桂树枝的和平鸽。

汉城奥运会会徽

汉城奥运会，东道主韩国以12枚金牌、10枚银牌和11枚铜牌名列奖牌榜第四，取得了国际推介和体育成绩的双丰收。

仁寺洞

清溪川

　　起步于20世纪60年代的韩国经济，70年代以来获得持续高速增长，到20世纪末达到高峰，由此创造了经济史上的"汉江奇迹"。汉城从亚运会到奥运会的跨越，正是在这样殷实的背景下展开。蚕室综合运动场（汉城奥运会主体育场）等一大批基础设施建成，交通拥堵得到极大解决。同时汉城奥运会犹如一场"成人礼"，让韩国的国家形象在全世界得以立体式展示，三星和现代汽车等大企业集团被成功推送到世界面前，韩国的国际地位空前提升。

釜山"名片"

　　由汤唯、朴海日主演的电影《分手的决心》中，有这样一段对话——

　　孔子说："仁者乐山，智者乐水。"我不是仁者，我喜欢海。

　　据说，这是导演朴赞郁和编剧郑瑞景为汤唯量身定制的台词。当汤唯饰演的女主角宋瑞莱对刑警海俊说出那段话时，我相信一切诚如编剧所为。

萦绕在男女主角与山峦间的迷雾与海浪，暖色衬衫与大海图案的背景墙，为真爱走向大海走向毁灭与救赎的宋瑞莱……

影片中，大海展开冲突与情节。

赛事中，水的意象被反复使用。

釜山是韩国六个广域市中的一个，也是韩国的主要港口。作为第二个举办亚运会的韩国城市，釜山用太极、海浪与相互啮合的对瓦（牝瓦和牡瓦），构筑了2002年亚运会会徽，还凭借灵动的线条与墨色、展翅高飞的海鸥设计出吉祥物"DURIA"，以此来接续汉城亚运会与奥运会关于"共同体""希望与超越"的多重文化表达。

釜山亚运会会徽、吉祥物

2002年9月29日的开幕式上，朝鲜女足运动员李贞姬和韩国手球运动员皇甫盛一一同高擎朝鲜半岛旗，引领两国的800名代表团成员手拉手步入运动场。这是亚运会历史上，44个亚奥理事会成员第一次全部参加。朝韩两国运动员一同入场，传为佳话。来自44个国家和地区的7500多名运动员，参加了38大类的400余项比赛，是历届亚运会规模最大的一次。

"共同的亚洲，走向世界的釜山"，这是亚洲的梦想，也是釜山的抱负。

汉城亚运会时还在念书的沙桐老师，彼时已成长为中央电视台体育频道的优秀主持人，对21年前的釜山转播经历，一经想起仍分明清晰。

"釜山亚运会期间，我们干得很轻松，那时中国体育处在一个飞速发展的阶段，尤其1990年咱们举办北京亚运会后，信心大增。记得我们在前方做了一档谈话节目，我们与马燕红、占旭刚、王涛等世界冠军和奥运冠军对谈，讲赛场上的见闻，釜山生活的一些趣事，一聊就是60分钟，整整一小时，作为节目的收尾，每天都很快乐。"

沙桐老师说的"快乐"，自然也离不开赛场上的果实，沉甸甸的收获同时给转播工作注入重量，让他们丝毫不敢放松。

"中国队的金牌银牌铜牌，是一会儿一个，一会儿一个，一会儿一个。"沙桐老师的表情幽默而真实，"亚运会不用看排名，中国肯定排第一，然后天天数金牌。就怕数错了少数了，因为在节目的播出过程中，当把字幕板全都做完之后，等发出去可能要半个小时之后，而就在那个时候，奖牌又有更新了，又多一枚了，所以既快乐，又有一点儿紧张，因为生怕数错了，因为要精准地向观众去传达。那时候的自媒体不像现在这么发达，很难做到实时更新。"

釜山亚运会是泳坛顶尖名将罗雪娟参加过的唯一一届亚运会。就在2001年，她已经获得日本福冈世锦赛的双料冠军，因此她是作为中国游泳的领军人物出征的，并在亚运会上获得个人和其他共3枚金牌。

"一共6天的比赛，3、4天就达到并超出了预期目标。结果非常漂亮，完全超出想象。"

让罗雪娟更为自豪的是，一批年轻小将崭露头角，在大赛中得到锻炼并经受了考验与挑战。第14届亚运会，中国代表团以骄人的成绩第六次蝉联"亚洲第一"，实现了锻炼队伍和提高金牌含金量的目标预期。"亚洲对于中国来说也许太小了"——韩国媒体发出了这样的感慨。

作为一项创举，釜山亚运会的颁奖典礼，一反过去先颁发金牌的传统，改为先铜后银，最后才是金牌的程序，以表示对金牌选手的尊重和赞扬。

除了亚运会，釜山还上演了更加频繁的颁奖典礼，那就是每年一届的釜山国际电影节。电影节创办于1996年，是韩国亦是亚洲最重要的电影节之一。除了推广新人新作，还致力于推动朝韩文化交流，全力将亚洲电影推广至全球。

值得一提的是一部名叫《釜山行》的科幻商业大片，电影讲述的并非釜山这座城市本身，而是发生在一列从首尔开往釜山的高速列车上的故事，是生死考验与灾难环境中的复杂人性。曾斩获包括"亚洲电影大奖""加拿大奇幻电影节"在内的三十多项提名与奖项。

釜山风光

与戛纳国际电影节一样，釜山国际电影节的设立首先是作为一个平台，一个把优秀电影人和作品吸引到一起并选出佼佼者的平台。釜山的真正抱负是走向世界，在文学领域也是如此。韩国"80后"女作家金爱烂，在她的作品还没有被成套译成中文前，我们就深深被她的文字吸引。相信她的作品，总有一天会被改编并拍摄成电影。而她，也正是韩国人预期的能获得世界性声誉的杰出作家。

仁者乐山，智者乐水。文化与体育，不同的城市名片，相同的熠熠生辉。

仁川"抱负"

仁川是韩国第三座承办亚运会的城市，位于首尔以西80公里。与釜山一样，仁川也是韩国的广域市与美丽港口，同时还有重要的国际机场。

我对仁川的关注，始于反复观看广州亚运会闭幕式上的"仁川8分钟"。他山之石可以攻玉，彼时我们因杭州亚运会雅加达接旗仪式工作需要，常找这一类资料学习借鉴。

"仁川亚运会，印象最深的是开闭幕式。"当沙桐老师接着釜山的记忆往下走，他的关注点似乎暂时从转播工作那个点跑开了一会。"没有太多的历史要去表达，就跳啊唱啊，各种组合出来，绚烂多彩。这也是韩国文化的一个特色吧！"

我们没有说"男团"或"女团"，一方面也许因为年纪，另一方面因为一下子叫不出具体名字。

水珠滴落，大鼓奏响，折扇舞动，跆拳道也搬上舞台，"仁川8分钟"的前半段热闹而饱和。随后是韩国青年歌手郑智薰及七人组，激情歌舞召唤观众"一起摇摆"。与节目的音乐变奏同步，8个分屏配合展示了会徽、太极符号以及"Rock"字样的背景。然后，在灯光短暂暗下的几秒，画风急转，一切都慢了下来，伴着飞舞的亚奥理事会大家庭成员旗帜，主唱的歌声像从另一个悠远的天空传来——

仁川风光

当你遭遇挫折希望破灭　当你没有朋友在身边　请不要忘记　我是你永远的朋友　如果我可以为你尽绵薄之力　如果我可以让你依靠　我会来到你身边和你一起　因为我是你的朋友

忧虑慢慢的会变成痛苦　痛苦慢慢的会变成孤独　当所有的努力都付诸流水　当一路上跌跌撞撞需要扶持时请想起我……

郑智薰领着身穿民族服饰的小朋友们，共同演绎主题歌《我和你一起》，与先前聚焦强调韩国文化的"阿里郎"元素不同，这首歌唱出了诚挚唱出了国际化。屏幕上吉祥物"风""舞""光"组合（白翎岛斑点海豹三兄妹）一个个飞过，会徽再度显影，最后赫然定格于"2014仁川"，向亚奥理事会大家庭成员发出诚挚邀约。

仁川亚运会会徽、吉祥物

沙桐老师没有具体讲述仁川亚运会开闭幕式的节目细节，让他记忆特别深刻的，仍是跟他工作最密切关联的那些部分。

"我不追星，你知道的张斌老师也一样。但不认识就无法做精准的介绍，所以我们拿到节目单后，就求助于国内网站的一些专门做流行音乐的编辑。请他们做一些资料提供，然后我们去筛选，做到既准确又点睛，有意识克制语言，让大家去听歌。"

"歌迷们有些什么反应？"

"很热情，也很较真。就像他们有一个组合名称按国际音标来说应该有一个'g'的音，但是歌迷有自己的叫法，我们也不知道这个情况，所以后台评论区也会有吐槽。调侃说'大叔，不这么念好不好'，但我们更愿意把它视作一个提醒，促使我们最大限度地去保持转播的准确性。"

从寂寂无名到"出道"再到走红，一般观众看到的，通常是"成团"者其后的光华与荣耀。这中间有漫长的"练习生"制度，严苛的训练与无情的淘汰机制。无数少男少女投入青春、泪水与汗水，最终脱颖而出的，到底极为少数。粉丝对于那样的偶像，难免会伴随偏爱、非理性有时甚至是无厘头，但爱和疯狂都同样真实。

对于观众的需求，优秀的央视主持人总是渴望自己做得更好。

不过张斌老师与沙桐老师的记忆重点有所不同。在张斌老师看来，仁川亚运会非常有特点，是韩国在一个历史周期中，国家、城市和地域一种较为蓬勃的景象展现。连同韩日世界杯与之后的平昌冬奥会，都表明韩国拥有非常强烈的办赛愿望。张斌老师还介绍：仁川当时把自己认定是亚洲发展的新中心。这让各地的媒体人，尤其来自中国的记者很错愕，因为对于仁川的这个自我定位，其实在当时大家体会并不深，今后恐怕也看不到。但是作为一个愿景，仁川真是这么去考虑的。

仁川风光

对于通过办亚运会让城市有突出的改变方面，仁川反倒没有特别高的预期，至少在宣传方面，保持着比较克制的基调。主要还是非常渴望被亚洲、也被世界有所了解，这跟它本身已是一个比较发达的城市有关。

仁川风光

电视转播方面，由于赛场设置的原因，一些比赛客观上关注度不高。但也有出乎意料的。张斌老师清楚地记得，某场在一个不断下雨、气温有点偏低的田径赛场所举行的比赛，在国内的收视率非常高。因为只要有中国的运动员参加比赛，咱们的老百姓就是喜欢看。喜欢看中国赢，看升国旗，听奏国歌。

怎么不是呢？仁川亚运会时，我也曾热切等在电视机前，看男子4×100米自由泳接力决赛。

发于"潮新闻"，2023-07-30。大公网转载。英文版发于杭州城市客户端Hangzhoufeel。

多哈"建构"

多哈天际线

　　最早关注卡塔尔，缘于2001年在首都多哈举办的"世界贸易组织第四届部长级会议"。当地时间11月10日18时39分，喜来登酒店萨尔瓦会议大厅内，随着世界贸易组织第四届部长级会议主席卡迈勒手中的击槌敲响，中国加入世界贸易组织的决定通过，中国正式成为世贸组织第143个成员国。

　　2016年G20杭州峰会时，置身于世界上最大的新闻中心（位于杭州国际博览中心内），我在"半岛电视台"的蓝色标识前颇踌躇探究了一番，才开始与工作间内的媒体人员招呼交流，琢磨着这个此前并不怎么了解的电视台，何以与英国广播公司（BBC）、美国有线电视新闻网（CNN）并称世界三大电视新闻频道。

与更为具象的卡塔尔相遇，则是2019年的北京世界园艺博览会。在一众国家馆中脱颖而出并得到永久保留，除了设计造型的新奇、投入的巨大，那个微缩版的卡塔尔究竟向来来往往的人们讲述了什么？

观摩2019年在多哈举办的田径世锦赛以及2022年国际足联世界杯，我们在走进真实的多哈时，感受到卡塔尔以体育作为国家战略与世界建构的联系，以及这种关联给卡塔尔带来的诸多变化。

卢塞尔体育场

"水"与"沙"的国度

"头顶一块布，世界我最富"，2022年世界杯时的一句网络流行语，形象勾勒渲染了卡塔尔的实力与概貌。

卡塔尔人确是穿着大抵相同的服饰。头巾、一抹色的长袍、皮质很好的拖鞋，是男女共通的标配服饰。不同的是男士的头巾上多了两圈头箍般的固定装饰，仿佛是担心那头巾一不小心会被风吹走；女子的拖鞋从平底换成了高跟，或者换成更为正规的鞋子。着一袭白色或黑色袍子的男女行走在日照长、气温高的夏日黄昏街道，恍惚中竟让人觉得像看着一个个二维码，同质化的只是表象，

卡塔尔服饰

每一个其实都具体生动。这时不禁想起廖一梅编剧、孟京辉导演的《恋爱的犀牛》中的台词："黄昏是我一天中视力最差的时候，一眼望去满街都是美女，高楼和街道也变幻了通常的形状。"但我还是喜欢看黄昏的多哈，看亮起的华灯与尚未褪去的夕阳，看迷蒙的城市轮廓线，看海风熏得棕榈摇晃路人醉，看笼罩着光晕与庄严气息的清真寺，看古老的集市中依然低头画画的女孩和她就要打烊的画廊，看驯鹰或手握刀具的男人凌厉的眼光。我还观察穿着黑色袍子走过青年中心，走过空旷广场的女人，看美丽如何包裹在神秘里，时隐时现。据说因为服饰的特点与遮蔽限制，卡塔尔的女人特别重视鞋、包、表与首饰，那些仅有的显露在视线与空气中的饰品，是她们审美的表达，身份的象征。只有在男女分而处之举行某种仪式的场合，她们才有可能互相打量那个不同于公共场合中的彼此与自我。

多金的卡塔尔，其财富主要来源于埋藏在沙漠中的石油和天然气，近年来天然气更成为其经济中的支柱产业与重中之重。年平均降水量不足80毫米的干旱之地渴望水，好在卡塔尔处于波斯湾西南岸的半岛，且拥有560多公里的海岸线。"水"与"沙"，既是卡塔尔的自然风貌，也是多哈的地缘环境。

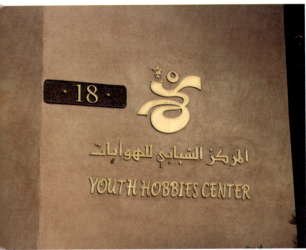

多哈街景

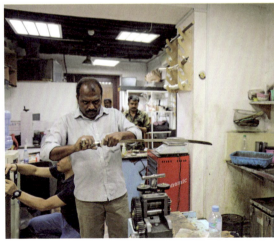

多哈集市

114

多哈的前身是一个名叫贝达的小渔村，位于卡塔尔半岛东岸中部的一个港湾。1863年，卡塔尔第一任国王萨尼对一位旅行家说："无论地位是高是低，我们都是一个主人的奴隶——珍珠。"可见捕鱼和采珍珠曾是历史上的多哈人赖以生存和获取财富的主要手段。这应该也是我们至今仍可以看到"贝壳与珍珠"雕塑屹立在多哈街头、19世纪的巴罗达珍珠地毯被珍藏在博物馆的原因，是多哈人感恩过往、记取历史的一种方式。

贝壳与珍珠

博物馆里的地毯

变化在20世纪20年代后发生，彼时日本成本低廉的人工养殖珍珠抢占了世界市场，卡塔尔的采珠业陷入衰败。与此同时，20世纪上半叶风靡中东的石油勘探拯救了困境中的卡塔尔。1939年英国帮助卡塔尔勘探出了巨大的油气资源储量，并钻出了第一口油井。当第一艘装满原油的油轮于1949年驶离卡塔尔港口，卡塔尔也从昔日的渔村逐渐转向西亚的能源经济强国。

"水"与"沙"，在2006年多哈第15届亚运会时，抽象成黄色的月牙状沙丘与奔涌的碧海，伴随着亚奥理事会的太阳标识，一个灵动和充满可能性的会徽跃然纸上。

与此对应，因热带沙漠气候限制了生物多样性的卡塔尔，选择了沙漠中的羚羊作为多哈亚运会的吉祥物。吉祥物"奥利"身着与会徽一致的黄蓝主色短运动套装，并衍生出高擎火炬、持球表演、挥臂奔跑、搭弓射箭等多种运动形态。"奥利"耐旱，体态矫健，一对剑一般的羊角直指天空，它充满激情与能量，象征着年轻国家十足的前进动力。

多哈亚运会会徽、吉祥物

多哈 16 年：从"亚运会"到"世界杯"

从2006年第15届亚运会到2022年第22届国际足联世界杯，多哈走过了16年的非凡历程。

关于第15届多哈亚运会，无论是否亲历，只要一经提起，人们似乎首先都会想起，哈里发国际体育场那场绝无仅有的开幕式圣火点燃仪式。百年一遇的连续降雨，策马加速的阿勒萨尼王子，百米高的点火台，骏马在坡道上打滑的惊

多哈亚运会开幕点火

险场面，那一刻，所有的观众都屏住了呼吸。最终，作为卡塔尔耐力赛马队队长的王子成功驾驭骏马冲顶，火炬点燃，高悬的巨轮与星盘转动，旋转出勇气与魄力、激越与震撼。

在一场马术比赛中，我曾目睹一匹未能成功跨越障碍的骏马将运动员从马上甩下，然后绕着场地狂奔，所幸那位运动员并没有伤得特别严重，短暂的倒地后她忍痛站起，向心爱的战马挥手，表示安抚，想让它安静下来，以便带它体面离场。不知道出于对失败的愧疚，还是有更多难以言喻的复杂感情，马无法平息和原谅自己，依旧兴奋狂暴，连跑数圈后竟直接跃出赛场的围墙。体育赛场不像文艺演出的舞台，没有对口型，没有提前录制，那一瞬发生了什么，就是什么。纵使训练有素，纵使身经百战，那一刻遭遇了什么别人其实无法知道，结果在那里，冰冷残酷，任谁都无法保证自己会是永远的王者。

多哈亚运会开历届亚运会先河的，还有赛会赋予媒体记者的空前礼遇。"早餐酒店解决，组委会提供每天一张的免费餐券。之后王后去视察，据说用她的'私房钱'又追加了一张餐券，后半程就等于全免了。"当时在媒体中心工作的记者朋友回忆，"不排除卡塔尔此举的背后，是为了能更好地宣传多哈亚运会，包括提前应对可能

出现的舆情。但卡塔尔对于媒体的善意，记者们还是收到了，那样的沟通是有效的。"

多哈亚运会中国代表团取得的165枚金牌中，有一位在世界田径史上闪闪发光的中国运动员，那就是男子110米栏冠军刘翔。正值雅典奥运会后的刘翔，意气风发，当时与他一起参加比赛的还有史冬鹏。2008年北京奥运会时，当我带着还在读小学一年级的女儿去鸟巢看刘翔比赛而未能如愿时，我庆幸我可以告诉女儿：刘翔叔叔严重受伤，他的脚很痛，暂时不能跑了。今晚让我们为史冬鹏加油，为更多的运动员加油。

时空切回到2019年9月29日凌晨的哈里发国际体育场，中国选手梁瑞摘得田径世锦赛女子50公里竞走的桂冠，为中国队赢得首金并向新中国70华诞献礼。10月2日凌晨，谢震业以20秒14获得田径世锦赛男子200米第7名，创造了中国田径当时在短跑项目国际大赛上的最好成绩。

2019年世界田径锦标赛 哈里发国际体育场

118

有人老去，也就有新人成长，这原本是新陈代谢和竞技体育的自然规律。我们要做的，只是学会爱、包容与致敬，爱他们登顶和巅峰时的耀眼华光，包容他们离场时的不甘、无力甚至绝望，因为唯有爱与包容，可以让他们在回忆过往的血汗付出时，让生命更坦然更倔强。

974 球场

官方球迷公园

国际广播中心

　　在以体育作为国家战略的征途中，卡塔尔不遗余力保持着长时间的勇猛突进。如果说1988年和2011年的亚洲杯赛为卡塔尔申办2022年国际足联世界杯做了铺垫，2022年卡塔尔世界杯的成功举办，则给国际足联和其他国家提供了借鉴与启示。回望北京世界园艺博览会卡塔尔国家馆的未来展区，当时只是匆匆走过包括卢赛尔标志性体育场在内的8个精致体育场模型展台，几年后才明白原来所有8个场馆都位于多哈市中心33.8公里半径范围内，且有7个是临时建造的。多哈"城市世界杯"的意义，在于它创造和提供的办赛模式与可能性，也许可以启示更多的国家与城市通过自己的努力与智慧，让人们享受到本土的世界杯大赛。

　　从亚运会到亚洲杯赛，从田径世锦赛到国际足联世界杯，多哈16年从不停歇，向亚洲和世界呈现了一次次精彩的赛事，不仅极大提升了本国的国际影响力，也点燃了整个中东和西亚地区对于国际大赛的渴望之火。

文化符号与对多样性的渴望

多哈继续赢得2030年亚运会承办权，就像一个被驱动和旋转着的陀螺，惯性已让它无法停下。与申办2022年世界杯时顾不上美国和近邻沙特的感受一样，再次申办亚运会的多哈依然顾不上竞争城市利雅得。

2030年多哈亚运会申办会徽由色彩丰富的四个半圆形图案错落叠加，呈现出一种静态的铺排气势。一眼看去无关运动而更像旅游广告和城市地标的随性组合。再看时却已不那么肯定，因为除了极具辨识度的"沙漠

2030 年多哈亚运会申办会徽

玫瑰"与伊斯兰艺术博物馆，不排除另外两个分别呈现现代与传统纹样图案的半圆，也可能跟运动主题或某个场馆存有关联。

这个没有在视觉上穷尽释义的会徽，也许正是卡塔尔留给亚洲与世界的想象及新邀约。

有"沙漠玫瑰"美誉的卡塔尔国家博物馆出自普利兹克奖得主让·努维尔之手，这位来自法国的建筑师以沙漠地区独有的酷似玫瑰的矿物结晶为灵感，用交错叠加的大型曲面圆盘完成了对博物馆的整体建构。同时通过馆内参观流线的设计，完成对卡塔尔历史、产业、空间尤其是世界地位的叙事展开。

"沙漠玫瑰"

"沙漠玫瑰"局部

伊斯兰艺术博物馆是华裔建筑大师贝聿铭的封山之作，低调朴素的石灰岩外墙、几何形状折射的变幻光影与蔚蓝的海水交相辉映，令人神往。但这个在卡塔尔航班座位屏幕反复出现的地标建筑，始终停留在无法抵达的人工岛屿。只有顶部矩形外墙两个弧状的采光口，像面具后神秘莫测的眼睛，不断提醒那里还有无穷的宝藏留待探索。

都说建筑是凝固的音乐，赛事的音乐却是另外的类型，它直接、燃情、充满正能量，呼唤此起彼伏或整齐划一的合唱，最好唱得满世界血脉偾张，当然还伴随尖叫、喧哗与呐喊。

你必须为理想而战
坚持荣耀赢得爱情圣杯
为生存奋斗下去
为它而战（是的！）
为它而斗（没错！）
你和我 Ale ale ale
Go go go! Ale ale ale

向前迈进，世界就在我们脚下

Go go go！Ale ale ale

1998年法国世界杯的主题歌《生命之杯》，是传唱度极高的经典。之后的歌，不知道到底是因为太多，还是说唱等的加入增加了传唱难度，抑或是作为观众的自己老了落伍了，总之是越来越记不住了。多哈派专机到韩国接上世界级男团成员参加开幕演唱，还让时尚活力女团加入推广，至少是站在年轻人的立场与角度，诚意满满地做了他们认为最贴近青年需求也算是最"潮"的事了。得益于滚动传播推送的视频，我也终于在等了很久的"时间之树"下，记住了一句"这是我们会做的事，这是我们对待事情的方式"。

在2022年世界杯会徽的设计上，卡塔尔更是做足了文章。弯曲交错的设计神似"无穷大"符号，又像阿拉伯数字"8"，远看还像一座白色的奖杯，并装饰有勃垦第红的阿拉伯特色图案。会徽以三维旋转的方式展示出来，象征了足球运动带来的无限可能，并表达了让世界杯源远流长的美好祝福。

2022 年世界杯会徽、吉祥物

卡塔尔没有让自己沉浸在世界杯的狂欢中太久，便又开始面向未来。

多哈2030年亚运会的意义，还在于它与卡塔尔的"2030国家愿景"相生相合。一直以来，卡塔尔力图摆脱单一依靠油气经济的局限，寻找更为多元的发展路径。一场场赛事，正是体育作为国家战

海滨大道

国际广播中心

由中国铁建国际承建的卢塞尔体育场

主媒体中心

略的具体实施，甚至埃米尔本人还亲自担任国际奥委会委员。作为一系列赛事和对外交往的红利，卡塔尔同时拉动了旅游、商业和教育的飞速发展。

2022年世界杯时，我昔日的同事去了多哈，亲见"中国制造"闪耀卡塔尔世界杯，自豪感油然而生。辗转于有"沙漠钻石"之称的卢塞尔体育场，以及贾努布等诸个球场，观摩见证了点球大战和冠亚军决赛，他们用老球迷的专业与新球迷的热血，写下了一篇篇世界杯报道的"号外"篇，硬生生把自己的写作水平提高到前所未有的高度。而我一边收看比赛，一边查阅此前在杭州召开的中阿广播电视合作论坛资料。在某些瞬间，我感到以往所有对多哈的零星认知，它所有的过去、今日与未来，突然像闪电般贯通了起来。

发于"潮新闻"，2023-08-09。大公网转载。

附 录
马丁·库珀与"移动"的人

"手机的诞生是为了实现一个梦想，即所有的个人通信将实现真正的可移动；手机号码应该代表一个人而不是一个地方。"

马丁·库珀及校友

这是生活中的一个真实场景——

一位老太太站在"浙江移动"（中国移动浙江公司）的某个门店前，抬头望向巨大的蓝色方块字，一脸困惑地问道：浙江，是要"移动"到哪里去吗？

不久前读完"手机之父"马丁·库珀《手机诞生记》的中译本，蓦地想起当时觉得荒诞无知的老太太，竟是如此这般地可爱与幽默起来了。因为，无论她是出于懵懂还是搞笑，她都无意间说出了发明家书中一个十分关键的高频词——"移动"！

马丁·库珀说："出于自然本质，人一生下来就是要移动的。"

而我与马丁·库珀的初见与相识，恰恰缘于一次"移动"。

那已是2004年初秋至2005年夏天期间，我在美国芝加哥伊利诺伊理工大学（IIT）读书时的事。

夏季的某个午后，当我走进一个大门半敞开的报告厅前，我并不知道那里正将开启一场重量级的"创业创新"论坛。随着报告厅中间的通道向前"移动"时，我才发现无论左边还是右边，都没有一个可以迅速安坐的空位。校长开始向讲台走去，已进到厅中间的我除了继续往前并尽快落座，其实无路可退。由于一直没有发现空位，就走啊走一直走到报告厅的第一排。

就是这段从报告厅入口直到讲台最前排的距离行进，让我结识了伊利诺伊理工大学最杰出的校友之一——马丁·库珀。

校长开始讲话，我"别无选择"地坐了下来，环顾左右，整个第一排就只坐了四个人，于是我十分唐突地成了不恰当的"第五个"。一位穿格子衬衫的先生朝我点了下头，同时微微一笑，他的优雅与微笑有效地缓解了我刚刚的紧绷与尴尬。于是我也朝他微笑，继而越过他再向一侧看去。我看到一个熟悉的形象，那是不久前与同学一起去拜访过的"全球500强"企业斑马技术公司的董事长与联合创始人艾德·卡普兰，由于此前已知他是IIT的校友，我意识到这是一场四位杰出校友的特邀分享会，随后瞥见的讲台边上的海报证实了我的判断。由于这冥冥中的误打误撞，我意外与他们紧邻而座。一时间我的心怦怦直跳，但很快就把那份不安与激动转换成表面的平静与专注听讲。

茶歇时，坐在身旁的"格子衬衫"先生已与我成为"熟人"，在他彬彬有礼的询问中，我告诉他我来自中国，到IIT是要学习公共管理方面的先进经验。他热情地与我交换了名片，那一纸小卡片与海报上的介绍相互印证，确认了这位"格子衬衫"先生就是IIT的终身受托人，摩托罗拉著名的电气工程师，世界上第一台移动电话的发明者马丁·库珀。他不仅名垂IIT校史，更永久留在人类科技发明与产业变革的历史长河上。

我心怀感激，请他给我一个做后续采访的机会，他就像刚才我在他邻座坐下时那样微笑着，他说他非常乐意与我分享"手机的故事"。我说由于这个领域有太多的专业术语，我需要再做一些功课才能让对话更加顺畅。他表示他愿意等待，并一定如约而至。

马丁·库珀演讲中

作者与"手机之父"马丁·库珀

数天以后，我在市中心一家宾馆的大堂里再次见到库珀。他依然穿着论坛那天的格子衬衫，或许是为了方便我记忆与辨认，也或许那原本就是他特别偏爱的一件衬衣，谁知道呢？

相机记录下的瞬间画面此刻正与《手机诞生记》摆放在一起，那时我还拥有敢穿无袖衣裙的上臂与肩颈，与库珀的合影也是我在数码年代还保留着的少数纸上相片之一。而送我这本书的朋友，正是因为看到这张相片，又碰巧在西西弗书店购得架上的最后一本，他感慨说尽管他在摩托罗拉中国公司财务部门工作了多年，却没像我一样幸运竟能与库珀面对面交谈。

"感谢您库珀先生，是您让我与大洋另一头的家人自如联系！"由于担心用英语交流科技话题难免有些吃力，我对自己的这个话题切入尚且感到满意。

库珀显然感觉到了我的真情实感。毕竟对于一个为了完成学业将与家人分开整整一年的国外留学生来说，手机的重要性不言而喻。虽然那时同学们用得更多的是MSN，我还是有不少时间一个人坐在深夜的走廊上用手机与家人朋友通话。

"Hi Vicky! 手机本来就是因为考虑人是移动的才研发出来的，我们不可能拎着一台座机走来走去，不管电话线有多长，与一个人要移动的距离比，它都太短太短了。现在你在这里，远离家人，就更能懂得我在说什么，对吧？"

我"嗯哼"了一下，表示我听懂了，从字面上说，至少这个开头，我的确听懂了，更何况我已经听过他的分享演讲。但是在多年以后我快速读完他的著作《手机诞生记》后，我明白我其实并没有全懂。

库珀在第一个回合的对话里，至少强调和隐含了以下几个方面的信息，即"移动的人""传统电话的限度"以及"无线电使手机成为可能"。我想他同时必然致敬了无线通信先驱、诺贝尔物理学奖获得者马可尼（意大利发明家），摩托罗拉公司的创始人保罗·加尔文，"创二代"鲍勃·加尔文，也许还有摩托罗拉激励创新不惧失败的文化，但我已记不起当时的细节。

"那么除了无线电，尊敬的库珀先生，还有什么使您成为世界上第一部手持式便携蜂窝电话的发明者？"

"不是我，是许多人，Vicky，我只是手机的构想者，当然也有人称我为预言家，是整个团队一起做成了这件事，"库珀的眼睛里闪着真诚的光芒，"至于成功，在很大的程度上依赖于不错的运气，敢于造梦以及坚持不懈。"

我并不相信库珀以似乎轻巧的方式说出的"运气"，但当他说到"运气"时，我们一起回忆了1912年那艘著名的邮轮"泰坦尼克号"，好莱坞大片刻画了一见钟情与至死不渝的爱情，但如果不是由于船上有马可尼的两名电报员发送了远距离国际莫尔斯电码救难信号（SOS），700多条最终得以存活的生命在邮轮向深渊沉没时就无法得到营救。

马可尼对无线电实用化的愿景意外地在一场毁灭性的海难事件中得到了检验，这让他看到无线通信在重塑人们之间联系和沟通方式方面的巨大潜力。库珀要做的，正是循着先驱开辟的这条线继续探索向前。

考察发明家库珀的身世，我们发现他原本就出生并成长于一个"移动"之家。库珀的父母都是乌克兰人，略去历经的种种曲折与动荡不说，曾先后移民加拿大与美国。库珀因为出生于美国顺利获得美国国籍，而他的父母和兄弟在这件事上就没有这么容易。他的父母以开杂货店为生，这与2022年获得诺贝尔文学奖的法国女作家安妮·埃尔诺相似。但是与安妮·埃尔诺经历被人们居高临下地称为"杂货店女孩"，她也以文学的方式犀利描述了阶层隔阂不同，库珀似乎没有这方面的敏感烦恼，他关注父母身上超强的销售与维护客户关系的能力，这种基因也成了植根于他心中的"企业家精神"。

进入伊利诺伊理工大学后，为了减轻父母的经济负担，库珀参加了美国海军并成为一名潜艇军官，这段独特的经历培养了他"不假思索立即行动"的能力。

在库珀看来，思考会让他变慢。因此，他无论在职业选择还是解决科技问题时，都果敢、神速而且肯定。

电传打字机公司研究工程师是库珀的第一份工作，但不满一年他就接受了摩托罗拉公司的邀请。摩托罗拉初创于1928年，总部大楼位于芝加哥的奥古斯塔大道，在公司发展的黄金阶段，库珀入了职。同时公司预见性地以1美元象征性地买下了库珀在职期间任何发明的专利权，这笔事后看来也许极不划算的交易，却让库珀心怀感恩，因为这让他从此有幸与一群才华横溢的专业人士相互碰撞与激发，不仅如此，还能从他们身上学习卓越的管理和强大的市场开拓能力。

几乎可以说，在摩托罗拉的全周期职业生涯，经常梦到未来、生活在未来的库珀都在"造梦"，或者为他心中的这个"梦"准备和斗争——那就是，基于人要移动和自由沟通的需要，库珀构想一个便携的无线通讯设备。有了它，人们可以在需要时与任何地方的任何人无障碍沟通。为了通讯方式的这种改变与更加美好世界的未来，库珀到底经历了什么？

"这条线并不是笔直的，"库珀说，"在很多时候，尤其受垄断行业的威胁时，它偏离了方向。"

历史上，贝尔系统［该系统由美国电报电话公司（以下简称AT&T）及一些关联机构、贝尔实验室和西部电气公司构成］曾长时间在政府监管下垄断电信业务。手机从诞生到普及与商用化，整整经历了10年时间持续地投入、研发、斗争、说服与争取。

也许我们多数人在做世界历史的考题时，都会清晰记住一些有名的实验室或公司在特定科技发明与制造领域的杰出贡献，倘若没有这场与库珀的跨文化对话，我不会真切理解当一种进步聚焦于紧紧捍卫因为这种进步带来的特殊利益时，会如何故步自封并竭尽全力阻挠新事物的诞生。

因此当马丁·库珀手持自己和团队研发的"砖头"（它是那么大，以至于20世纪70年代及之前出生的人记得它有个叫"大哥大"的俗称）DynaTAC——它是此后世上几百亿部手机的老祖宗——于1973年的4月3日从纽约的希尔顿酒店向南走并漫步在第六大道上时，他的第一个电话不是打给他的"准企业家"妈妈，不是打给他妻子，甚至也不是打给自己的办公室，而是打给竞争对手AT&T的乔尔博士。

"你好，是哪位？"

"嗨，乔尔，我是马丁·库珀。"

"嗨，马丁。"乔尔迟疑地说。

"乔尔，我是用手机在给你打电话。这可是一台真正的手机，一台个人的、便携式的、手持式的蜂窝电话。"

库珀说这是他能想出的最好的用词，而电话线那端是一阵沉默，库珀想乔尔或许会咬牙切齿。因为长久以来，在贝尔系统"眼"中，任何新事物都是有线电话系统的附加物，而库珀和摩托罗拉，则凭借无线系统和它所蕴含的自由打破了贝尔的驱动逻辑系统。

乔尔在AT&T的位置相当于库珀在摩托罗拉的位置，是负责蜂窝网通信项目的工程师，他虽然生气，却并没有觉得库珀给他的那通电话有多么了不起，至少在它将会革命性地影响未来人们的生存方式方面，他没有足够的预判。他极其生气，也许首先因为竞争对手仅仅用了3个月左右的时间就率先研制出了手机。尽管贝尔系统不希望以任何方式向公众透露他们有垄断的想法，在1972年，他们还是确定了对待手机的态度——如果必须有人来干这件事，那也应该是他们来干，因为他们原来就是电话公司，而且他们要有完全的控制权才肯干。而现在摩托罗拉和库珀却捷足先登，把一款"砖头"手机扔到了全世界的面前。

话题自然而然地转到了库珀的第三个关键词"坚持不懈"上，更准确地说，转到摩托罗拉与贝尔系统持续的合作与竞争上。

"这条竞争与合作之路始于新泽西，蜿蜒于芝加哥，止于首都华盛顿。"库珀说。

在当时的对话语境中，我一时还消化不了那么多的信息，但库珀的讲述已让我感到，他是如此清醒，以至于他对竞争与合作抱持一种完全实用主义的态度。库珀和摩托罗拉实际上采用了这样一种战略：既要在合作中分得一杯羹，又要暗下功夫突出重围出奇制胜。

这得以让我努力捕捉到一系列可以接续的情境——

1959年秋，新泽西州郊区，贝尔实验室一处全玻璃建筑内，库珀在对手强调"电话""监控"等有线电话术语的谈判中充分领受了其傲慢。

从新泽西返回芝加哥摩托罗拉总部，依然生着气的库珀说服决策层，无论喜欢与否，他们都必须参与车载无线电话（IMTS）项目。

几年后，贝尔实验室选择了摩托罗拉开发IMTS项目的无线部分，之后到固定无线基站业务，再到后来将IMTS扩展到新的450MHz频率（一种"超高频波段"，相对于"甚高频波段"。此后通过技术进步继续成倍突破）。

1960年，芝加哥警察局深陷信任危机，市长理查德·J. 戴利请来了一位名叫威尔逊的新警督。威尔逊需要一种既能在警车上、又能在步行巡逻时使用，且时刻与通信中心保持联系的便携式手持双向对讲机。摩托罗拉成功"被求助"。

因应芝加哥警察局这一客户需求，摩托罗拉创造了美国第一个可行的蜂窝网通讯系统。

一名皮带上挂着警棍、手铐、手电筒、枪、备用弹药等全副武装的警察，一面给库珀开罚单，一面说：瞧，我又多了这个你们发明的玩意（一种新的手持式收发两用机HT-220）。于是库珀开始构想更小更轻、便于携带的无线设备。

作者参观芝加哥警察局总部

摩托罗拉再次与AT&T不期而遇，围绕蜂窝通信技术的使用，两家具有不同历史、理念，在不同历史观和价值观指导下的公司，为通讯未来在首都华盛顿特区展开全面战争。

……

回到2004年秋至2005年夏芝加哥的某个夜晚，如果我和库珀的谈论依旧在进行，我们必然会谈及联邦通讯委员会（FCC），谈到政府监管。而在这之前，库珀会首先深入浅出地给我扫盲关于无线频谱的知识，它的公共财产属性，以及一种经由技术人员和工程师努力，容量可不断翻倍，因而永远不会被耗尽的资源。

"无线频谱是公共财产"，这是库珀的格言，也是他的信念。AT&T不希望如此，它一直致力于获得蜂窝频谱的垄断地位，不仅在有线电话系统，还要进入陆地移动业务和所有空对地通信领域。用库珀的话说，它想要拿走整个"蛋糕"。

FCC长时间对AT&T抱持一种极不合理的偏袒，但也不是一无是处。它早期已有防止AT&T一家独大的措施，虽然那些措施十分有限。在1973年5月由FCC举行的那场听证会上，摩托罗拉对推动技术进展的积极作用得到彰显。库珀雄辩地否证了AT&T对占有无线频谱的过度欲望，他得罪了世界上最大通信公司的董事长，却为手机与个人通信，以及FCC的公共政策（开放和共享无线频谱）赢得可能的未来。

与库珀的那场对话，部分地改变了我在IIT的课余时间安排。得益于移动电话构建的社交网络，我和同学有机会参加了时任芝加哥市市长理查德·迈克尔·戴利举办的"亚裔传统月"活动。我们拜访了芝加哥警察局，试图发现那个给摩托罗拉"出题目"（提用户需求）的老局长是否留下什么痕迹。在圣路易斯的地标建筑弧形拱门前，我们向设计了新泽西州贝尔实验室玻璃建筑的同一个设计师埃罗·沙里宁致敬。2005年7月上旬，我们再次拜访了斑马技术公司，并渴望与校友董事长艾德·卡普兰进行一场深入的交流。

"我们总是要走出去，才可能有机会。"

这是给我送《手机诞生记》的朋友，对"移动"的另一种理解。一个相信梦可成真、出生于清贫人家的孩子，从摩托罗拉干到另一家

作者与时任芝加哥市市长理查德·迈克尔·戴利

作者与时任斑马技术公司董事长艾德·卡普兰

作者朋友收集的摩托罗拉手机

全球顶级合资公司的首席财务官，"不断出发"便是他唯一的秘诀。

在芝加哥那个有限的夜晚，我和库珀实际上不可能交流得那么深刻，记忆与阅读早已交织在一起，相互纠缠又彼此帮衬。速读手机和网络不断进步的历程，故事的最后，摩托罗拉与库珀都迎来了童话般的美好结局，个人通信曾经的未来之梦变成了现实世界的神话。

这世界那么多人——那么多手机！

"人与人之间的相互联系与地点无关"，这是库珀继"人一生下来就是要移动的"之后的又一句经典话语。

写到这里，我多想给库珀拨一个电话，告诉他时隔多年，我依然真切地想念他。显然我已经丢失了他的名片，从摩托罗拉到后来的爱立信与诺基亚再到一代又一代的苹果与华为，不断更换的手机让我无法再找到那串珍贵的数字。在人类情感的永久维系中，技术同样显示了它苍白的一面，功能性的储存终究无法替代用心的记取。

时至今日，尤其是新冠疫情在全球流行的几年里，人类与手机的关系迎来了一场永久性的变革。我们可以几年不出国门，却不能一日一时无手机。学习教育、医疗卫生、支付与远程办公……手机已经成为我们生活甚至身体的一部分。

马丁·库珀留给作者的原始手稿

"便携式电话行业还处于初级阶段，我们才刚刚开始了解人机联系的重要价值，"马丁·库珀预言，"如果将手机和人工智能技术相结合，未来将有可能出现人机结合的混合体，即2.0版乃至3.0版的新人类……"

身为"手机之父"，马丁·库珀再次留给我们关于"未来"的思考。早已离开摩托罗拉创办自己公司的他，承继着他杂货店老板娘母亲的勇气与智慧，一如既往地向世界兜售他的"点子"与"梦想"。

"我们只需不断学习，不断前行，这是我们唯一的生活方式。"

——马丁·库珀

"The cell phone was created to fulfill a dream that all personal communication would be truly mobile.

A phone number should identify a person not a place."

发于"天目新闻"，2022-12-18。英文版发于杭州城市客户端Hangzhoufeel。

代后记
从骨骼到精神的行走

　　见证《赛事之城》从构思到成书，深感写作之不易。一方面，亚运临近，正如每一个书写者都有自己的赤诚表达，再瑰丽的设想也需在一字一句中落到纸面；另一方面，任时间如何追赶，铺陈仍得讲求严谨，文字仍得有其气韵。于是在数月逼近极限的写作之后，呈现在读者面前的这本书，也许依然从容不够，却也生猛鲜活。

　　应当如何写"赛事"？浏览社交媒体，不难查到围绕亚运百科与故事的系列报道，体育记者们或许早已爬梳了赛会的前世今生。这本书做了同样的事，但也尝试着走得更远。譬如，美学的实践经验，是否能为珍藏在博物馆一角的会徽、吉祥物和宣传片注入新生？又譬如，对世界的观看积累，是否令台前幕后的点点滴滴拥有了"现场感"？

　　而至于应当如何写"城市"，似乎是一个更难的问题。古今中外，许多优秀的游记、影视作品、地质学书写甚至社会科学研究给出了自己的答案。面对丰富的文化剧目、智识与见闻的熔炉，这本书谦逊而"贪婪"。马尼拉的胶片，封存了女性移工的欢笑与血泪，借由社会学者蓝佩嘉对性别、阶层与国界的思索，逐渐显影。雅加达的不眠夜，以一辆摩托车拉开序幕，几十年前，年轻的政治学家安德森怀抱胆怯与热情，同样骑着摩托走街串巷。阿巴斯与王家卫大概是人们了解某座山村、某条公路的窗口，《广岛之恋》与《中亚行纪》或许都触及了人们对社会剧变和内心核爆的隐忧。穿行于洛桑街头，虚虚实实的相遇，是令人想起《剑桥的陌生人》里那在洛桑车站下车的奈斯毕特，还是约翰·伯格那句使人迷醉的

"我们从骨骼到骨骼，从大陆到大陆地旅行着"？

正如唯有多样的文本才能够吸纳如此多样的资源，我想，这本书同样欢迎多样的解读。某种程度上，它可以是新闻报道、工作手记、影评、书评，也可以是俏皮的实验性写作、对其他作品严肃的引介。希望这些诚恳的文字能够满足或进一步激发读者的好奇。循着书中的线索，我们能够抵达的地方，也许远远超出我们的预期。

陈嘉禾

2023年夏至于巴黎政治学院

致　谢

　　书稿放下时，朋友手书至。

　　"写作如雁过长空，影沉寒水。雁无遗踪之意，水无留影之心。"

　　雁过长空，瞬即无痕，但天空给了雁飞翔的无限空间，天空也有了雁飞过时的优美弧线。

　　影沉寒水，恍惚如梦，互为镜像的彼此，如镜花水月，重新认出与发现另一个自己。

　　作者与作品，做书的人与读书的人，便是这样无情又有意的关系。了无牵挂，互相成全。

　　感谢浙江教育出版社，特别感谢周俊社长和编辑与审校的老师们。

　　感谢所有支持、参与和帮助本书的相关单位，感谢专家老师、同学朋友、同事家人与读者。

作者于2023年初秋

《拼搏》（常青作品）

CITIES OF SPORTING EVENTS

ZHOU SHU

PROOFREADER

Jeans ZHOU Jian
Director of Media & Broadcast Department, Olympic Council of Asia

CHEN Jiahe
Bachelor of Arts, Beijing Foreign Studies University, Master Student of Sociology at Paris Institute of Political Studies

TRANSLATOR

CAO Xiaochuan
Master of Translation and Interpreting, Middlebury Institute of International Studies at Monterey

WEN Hui
Master of Quality Management, Hong Kong Polytechnic University

LIU Jing
Master of Translation and Interpreting, Beijing Foreign Studies University

WANG Xiaoxuan
Master of Science, National University of Singapore

ZHENG Kaiyuan
Master of Translation and Interpreting, South-Central University for Nationalities

CHEN Yijun
Master of Public Adminstration, Zhejiang Normal University

JIANG Miao
Master of Translation and Interpreting, Renmin University of China

The Road to Championship（by CHANG Qing）

Contents

Meet the Genesis in New Delhi

It was in the spring. A turbaned man stepped onto the bank of the Qiantang River in the dusk light, pondering as he looked out at the stadiums lit up in a surreal mix of blue and purple.

Hangzhou Olympic Sports Center

I was, at the moment, heading to a nearby hotel's concierge for a book that a Hong Kong friend left me before departure. It was a collector's edition of Chetan Bhagat's *The Three Mistakes of My Life.*

There were two gentlemen in the tea lounge who looked just like twin brothers. They were conversing about things they were doing at the moment and an approaching event they both looked forward to.

Here's exactly where a parallel session of the Conference on Dialogue of Asian Civilizations (CDAC) was held years ago. Parallel as it was, the scale was unparalleled. It could be the effect of seeing Chetan's signature. I found myself involuntarily picturing the scene of "Meet in Hangzhou for the Asian Games 2022", an exhibition that put on display the "three treasures" handed over to us at the closing ceremony of the 18th Asian Games, i.e., the torch and flag of the first Asian Games and the OCA flag. The treasures came from New Delhi, the capital of India, and the host city of the first and the 9th Asian Games. Among those present for the event, there was Timothy Fok, Senior Vice President of the OCA (East Asia) and President of the Sports Federation & Olympic Committee of Hong Kong. I recalled seeing him spending a lot of time standing before the torch and flags. His eyes were glinting with emotions.

First Asian Games flag, First Asian Games torch and OCA flag

Then I picked out the headwrap. He had returned from outside and seemed to have noticed the book in my hand while I was looking at his attire and wondering if he might be from New Delhi. The subsequent plot should involve us exchanging glances and smiles and going on our ways like strangers do.

The Games (and Its Managers) in the Past

A walled part of New Delhi in the city's north is the so-called "Old Delhi". A quip says that "New Delhi is too new to have a history, while Old Delhi is too old to know its history". New Delhi came as an extension of Old Delhi, and standing between them is the iconic landmark of the city "India Gate" (or "Delhi Gate"). The Gate was once taken as a line that divided the present from the past, dreams from realities and the rich from the poor. However, with the passage of time, the line is getting increasingly blurred.

New Delhi marks the commencement of the Olympic Movement in Asia. The city hosted the first Asian Games and witnessed developments and changes in the Asian Games Federation (now known as OCA). It's been filled with the "first" moments and thrills coming afterwards.

Asia's earliest regional multi-sport event, initiated by the Philippines, China, and Japan in the early 20th century, was the Oriental Olympics Games or Far East Championship Games (FECG). It was held 10 times from 1913 to 1934. Japan's insistence on Manchukuo's participation in FECG in 1934 led to China's protest and withdrawal, which resulted in the ultimate dissolution of the Far Eastern Athletic Association and FECG itself. As the first international competition the continent had ever known, the Games demonstrated the best athletic performance in Asia back then and was therefore deemed the forerunner of the Asian Games.

The Asian Games Federation was founded after the end of World War II when delegates of Asian sports organizations signed the Charter in New Delhi on February 13, 1949. New Delhi was thus given the opportunity to host the first Asian Games in 1950, and the organizing committee was formed in no time. It was postponed to 1951, though, due to a range of factors including the trauma of the war, lack of funding and the unavailability of sports facilities and equipment. The Games eventually welcomed 500 athletes from 11 countries and regions who competed across 6 sports and 57 events, 6 of which were also on the Olympics sports list. Athletes from India, Myanmar and Iran in particular, gained entry to all the sporting events.

The emblem of the first Asian Games (New Delhi) in 1951

The emblem of the Olympic Council of Asia

The Asian Games Federation was renamed the Olympic Council of Asia (OCA) on November 16, 1982, with its headquarters in Kuwait. As the organization that oversees the Olympic Movement in Asia, OCA is Asia's representative in contact with the International Olympic Committee (IOC) and other continental sports organizations.

Inside the OCA headquarters

"If you were to write about New Delhi, you would have to highlight the part concerning the history of the Olympic Movement." Later, when I read *The Three Mistakes of My Life* in the lounge where I ran into the "twin brothers", they advised me as such. "A person who can tell history is wiser than a person who simply desires the future." The philosophy of a senior flashed in my head.

"But I need to remind you that New Delhi has not only the 'beginning' but the 'afterwards'. " The turbaned man joined our conversation. By then we had confirmed that he was indeed an Indian from South Asia.

The emblem of the 9th Asian
Games (New Delhi) in 1982

"Appu" — Mascot of the 9th Asian Games
(New Delhi) in 1982

We knew what he was referring to. He wanted us to remember that, in addition to the first Asian Games, New Delhi also hosted the 9th Asian Games in 1982. And, of course, we won't forget that it was at that Games China overtook Japan for the first time on the medal count with 61 golds in the pocket, became the foremost sporting nation in Asia.

Dangal and the Rise of Female Athletes

Dangal is a sports-themed Indian film directed by Nitesh Tiwari, based on true events. The film portrays the inspiring story of former wrestling champion Singh, who managed to train his two daughters (eldest daughter Geeta Phogat and second daughter Babita Kumari) to become national women's wrestling champions, and Geeta the world champion, challenges the common stereotypes in Indian society. The film was released on December 23, 2016, and was honored as the winner of the 62nd Filmfare Awards. On May 5, 2017, it was released in China and earned approximately 1.3 billion in box office revenue and positive word of mouth.

Streetscape of New Delhi

When the two young girls were obliged to accept their father's arrangement to become female wrestlers and they were distressed and felt the need to push back because they couldn't understand the arrangement, let alone approve it, until a girl who married early changed their mind:

"I wish God had given me such a father who thinks about me. Otherwise, a girl's fate is to cook, clean and do all the household chores. And once she comes of age, marry her off, to relieve the burden of the family, hand her over to a man whom she has never met. Then she bears children and raises them. That's all she's good for. At least your father considers you. He is fighting against the whole world. He is silently tolerating their taunts. Why? So that the two of you can have a future."

Words from the girl of a similar age served as a wake-up call. The daughters began to follow their father's instruction, forged ahead no matter what, and eventually secured the title of women's wrestling championship.

There was no lack of twists and turns. But let's just fast-forward to the day before the Commonwealth Games final. The father was doing the pep talk:

"If you win the gold medal, you will become a role model, a very good one, and the children will remember you for the rest of their lives. If you win tomorrow, you will no longer be alone, and many girls will join you in the fight against those who discriminate against women, who make women perform chores and marry at a young age. Tomorrow's match is crucial because your real opponent is not Angelina Watson (an Australian female wrestler), but rather everyone who looks down on women."

At the end of the story, the Indian competitor defeated her Australian peer in the women's 55kg wrestling at the 2010 Commonwealth Games, winning the championship and qualifying for the Olympic Games—an unprecedented achievement in the history of Indian Olympic Movement.

The film is a work of reality being recreated. Perhaps only Indian women know the true situation they are in in terms of competitive sports and other facets of social and political life.

"Would you mind, sir, if I ask how the status and role of Indian female athletes have changed since the first Asian Games?"

"In fact, female athletes were there at the first Asian Games."

We soon discovered that the turbaned man was none other than Mr. Bhupinder Singh Bajwa, Chef de Mission of India NOC delegation to the 2022 Hangzhou Asian Games.

He was not offended by my question. Instead, he smiled and thanked me for my interest in Indian films and Indian female athletes.

"I am betting on our female athletes winning more medals than their male counterparts at the upcoming 19th Asian Games." With wit and fact-based prediction, he answered the tricky question I challenged him, driven perhaps by my perspective as a woman.

The "Afterwards" that Appear to Be Unrelated to New Delhi

"Aside from women's wrestling, what else do you know about India's sporting prowess?" The "older brother" inquired.

I pointed to the young man wearing a red T-shirt and holding a cricket bat high in his right hand on the left side of the cover of *The Three Mistakes of My Life* and blurted out "cricket". I had just spotted a line written by my friend right next to the author's autograph, "If you read this book, you will understand how much Indians love cricket". It could have been his wicked way of demanding my lasting appreciation for his generosity even after I finished writing about New Delhi. Anyway, thanks to his remarks, I was able to answer the older brother's query.

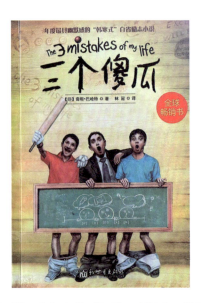

Chetan Bhagat's bestseller *The Three Mistakes of My Life*

"A book that appeals particularly to young people." stated the younger brother. He looked young, so I guess his statement should be convincing enough.

"Three young people, each with their own aspirations, run a cricket shop together. They try to protect a boy named Ali who is incredibly talented in cricket, but the protection costs them too much. For some, the price is their life."

He took the book, flipped through it only a few times, and then showed me page 184.

"If I join this team, which side will I play for?"Ali asked.

"Australia."Mr. Cutler replied.

"But I'm an Indian."Ali stated.

"However, you can be both an Indian and an Australian. Our society's culture is highly diverse."Mr. Greener spoke up.

"No."Ali said.

"What?"

"I'm an Indian. I play for India. Not for other countries."

Born in New Delhi in April 1974, Chetan Bhagat earned a Bachelor of Science degree and a Master of Business Administration degree before working as an investment banker in Hong Kong for 11 years. Later, he became a writer, reshaping the Indian English novel single-handedly and presenting to the world the social image of modern Indian youth passionately.

My instinct tells me there is more to the book than just cricket. I'm inclined to believe that the author chose cricket on purpose for its universal popularity and its ability to evoke emotional resonance.

When I think about it, I used to spend almost a week with a New Delhi family before my encounter with this turbaned gentleman in front of me. Not in New Delhi, but in a homestay in Chicago while I was studying abroad. A girl from Nanjing and I were placed in an Indian-American home, which was quite frustrating for us not least because the couple spoke English with an Indian accent, but because there were no other girls in the family. So, we had to move into the rooms that once belonged to the two boys the family had. I remember I was quite taken aback when I saw them taking food with their bare hands.

It was later proved that every homestay experience inspires in some way. The father was a talented doctor, and the mother was a housewife. She drove us to the mall early in the morning on Thanksgiving for what was supposed to be the biggest discount of the year. They sent us to another American home in the neighborhood at lunchtime because they didn't make turkeys themselves. As we parted ways, the mother proudly displayed a photograph of her son and daughter-in-law at the presidential reception.

The fact that the "second-generation entrepreneur" of the family were

Hangzhou Olympic Sports Centre Stadium (By ZHAI Mofan)

all tech-savvy IT people impressed me more than the photo. Many of the Indian students from our school also majored in IT.

"In New Delhi, we have lotus-shaped buildings as well, and your stadium reminds me of my hometown. The facilities built for the Hangzhou Asian Games are excellent, even better than many of the Olympic venues throughout the world. I can say Hangzhou is more than qualified for hosting the Olympics. Of course, India will bid for the Asian Games for a third time, and I believe this will be the case."Mr. Bajwa said, interrupting my train of thought.

"In your opinion, Mr. Bajwa, will technological innovation, particularly in the IT industry, have a revolutionary impact on competitive sports, particularly large-scale sporting events?"

The question is faced by both India and the world at large, especially at a time when ChatGPT piques public interest and Elon Musk kisses his robots. The sky had grown considerably darker during our conversation. We smiled at each other for the one last time, shook hands, bid farewell, and left the question unresolved. The lights of the "big lotus" and "small lotus" remained bright, and the Hangzhou Century Center towered silently over the vast city. Life was as wonderful as it could be.

Back to Ashgabat

It's been quite a long while before I understood that, if not for sports, it wouldn't be easy to enter Turkmenistan, a Central Asia country, and stay in its capital, Ashgabat, for a period of time – because of its relatively strict requirements for visa application and the duration of stay, with even more restrictions as well.

I said all this because it was in Ashgabat that Hangzhou won the bid to host the 19th Asian Games. It was on September 16, 2015, a distant date yet still being clearly remembered. As the president announced that "Hangzhou, China, has the right to host the 19th Asian Games in 2022" at the 34th OCA Congress, everything had been well in place.

So let's move close to Ashgabat, the enigmatic, yet still tangible city, with the recall of such a milestone event.

Nature, Culture and History

To describe exceptional Turkmenistan and the city of Ashgabat with only a couple of words, if possible, we might choose "fire", "water" and "stone".

Turkmenistan, a member state of Central Asia, is also one of the world's youngest nations. The suffix "stan" from Persian refers to "place" or "land", hence the meaning of Turkmenistan "a land for Turkmen".

"Fire" means "The Gate of Hell" in the desert.

The country itself is an infinite desert (covering over 80% of its territory), and the "Gate of Hell"is actually a burning natural gas pit in the Karakum Desert. In 1971, Soviet geologists prospecting for natural resources in the Karakum Desert (also named the "Black Desert", a most unsafe part of the Silk Road) — 260 kilometers north of Ashgabat — discovered gas fields there. The drilling caused the ground to collapse, leaving a massive hole 60 meters wide and 20 meters deep. To prevent methane leakage from hurting nearby villages, scientists ignited the gas—all the flames melted together to produce an oval-shaped, orange vast blaze.

"The Gate of Hell"

But the pit fire estimated to last for only a few weeks has remained alive for over 50 years. The flames have contracted, yet they are still burning. Even the country's supreme decree failed to "stop" or "brake" the uninterrupted flow of gas and flames from underground.

Though the President once ordered a full evacuation from the frightening "hell", the pit has, to people's surprise, become a wonder that looks particularly "beautiful" from afar. It is nowadays a tour destination in Turkmenistan.

Turkmenistan is one of the driest places on earth, yet Ashgabat actually means the "City of Love" in Arabic. The city is "water-thick", and densely furnished with fountains of all sizes and shapes. They are the sources of life for an oasis, gurgling, flowing, and self-cycling. People of Ashgabat believe that their city is second to none in the world when it comes to the number of fountains.

Ashgabat set another world record in 2013 — it is the city with the most marble buildings per square kilometer in the world.

The capital is now packed with apartment buildings bearing snow-white facets, let alone the Presidential Palace, state and local authorities, and mosques that are all luxury white marble structures. For visitors, the marbled Ashgabat is completely a world of dazzling whiteness — without any blots.

Legend has it that the Turkmen people were so thirsty for marble that they almost emptied the Carrara Mountain Quarries. To make Ashgabat an exuberant Carrara-marbled fortress, its prominent buildings are usually the masterpieces of some very gifted architects from France and Turkey.

Just in between the East and the West, parts of Central Asia saw a boom thanks to the Silk Road bridging the two continents. Meanwhile, the location also invited troops from alien nations, like Persians, Greeks, Mongols, Arabs, and Turks.

"Turkmenistan is sandwiched between the East and the West, totally exposed to them. The country defends itself with nothing but the harsh deserts", said Norwegian journalist, author and social anthropologist Erika Fatland in her travelogue *Sovietistan*. This may partially explain why Turkmenistan later worked so hard to become a neutral state.

Russians, during the age of Tsars, controlled Central Asia for economic interests. The ancient tribal society (loose in organization) was later reshaped to embrace socialism. After the demise of the Soviet Union, Turkmenistan, as an independent state, secured its path toward the future. The "Belt and Road" is one of the significant tracks. Among the

Fountains

A glance of the "marbled city"

five Central Asian countries, Turkmenistan is undoubtedly a powerhouse in both economy and sports. In 1995, Turkmenistan was recognized as a neutral state by the United Nations, and later became the only permanent neutral state in Asia.

Turkmenistan is unusually rich in oil and gas, particularly the world's fourth-largest proved reserves of natural gas. In Turkmenistan, water, electricity and oil are free or extremely low in price. Turkmens admire and love their Presidents – Ashgabat is loaded with statues and portraits of them, always smiling to visitors.

AIMAG and the Akhal-Teke Horse

When I visited Turkmenistan with the Hangzhou Asian Games Organizing Committee (HAGOC) delegation in 2017, the 5th Asian Indoor & Martial Arts Games (AIMAG) was happening in Ashgabat.

AIMAG is the largest indoor multi-sport event in Asia. Asian Indoors Games was held every two years, merged with the Asian Martial Arts Games, it is now held every four years.

AIMAG welcomes diverse sporting events (for example, e-sports in AIMAG Ashgabat 2017 for the first time), its rich and trendy sports choices never fail to attract young Asians. The 2017 session proved that Turkmenistan is capable of hosting world-class events, and Turkmenistan became the first country in Central Asia to host the Olympic Council of Asia (OCA) Games. In a more far-reaching sense, sports diplomacy helps Turkmenistan join the world Olympic family.

AIMAG took place at the new 156-hectare Olympic Complex (at the intersection of four main roads) in Ashgabat. President Berdymukhamedov composed and sang the theme song in person.

The Olympic Complex

Infinite space awaits you and me. A colorful world is the condition for success. No matter how high the mountain is, we will cross it. In moments of liberation, we create a dream and release the power. Young hearts want to fly into dreams. Facing the sky and the ocean, let's see our hope coming true. Crossing the horizon, let's embrace a brand-new day.

I don't speak the local language, but the translated lyrics I found seem sporty and easy to spread.

Like the previous AIMAG hosts, Turkmenistan did not miss the chance to add its traditional sports, such as wrestling and equestrian.

The Akhal-Teke horse, a national treasure, naturally appeared on the AIMAG 2017's emblem. At the bottom right of the horse, the OCA sun shines on the name of the host country and city, while on the left there is a green crescent and the name of the Games. A few simple, sleek lines are enough to draw a handsome horse, and the yellow ribbons flying around the neck make it even more graceful. The modernist-style emblem echoes and contrasts strongly with the mascot, the Alabai shepherd dog, which is the loyal guardian of caravans along the ancient Silk Road and also a treasure of the country.

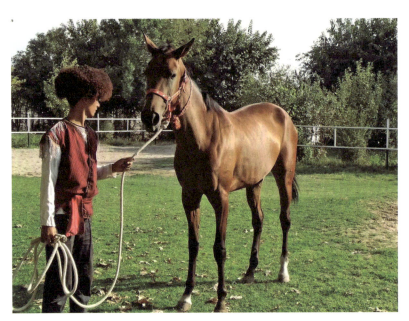

The Akhal-Teke horse

The mascot of the 5th Asian Indoor & Martial Arts Games

At the 1960 Rome Olympics, an Akhal-Teke horse won a gold medal in dressage. It was many, many years before Turkmenistan secured its first Olympic medal in weightlifting, which is also the country's strength, in Tokyo 2020.

Needless to say, horses are extremely precious to locals. If a horse makes a mistake, it may even be easier to forgive than a man. Although horses were once forbidden to be raised privately or even slaughtered, the Turkmen people, with amazing perseverance and unremitting efforts, proved the unique value of horses. Today, horses live a good life, have many chances to write a splendid chapter in history, and play a critical role in diplomacy and national development. Many towns have built a brand-new race course, and the country has a horse racing authority. At Akhal-Teke Horse Festivals and Horse Days, high-level international academic conferences, exhibitions, marathons, and many more, are held or staged. Turkmen people never eat horse meat, and they treat Akhal-Teke horses almost with religious respect.

Ashgabat's Internet and Hometown's Moon

In addition to learning from organizational experiences in the AIMAG, the more important task of our delegation was to participate in the 36th OCA's General Assembly and the 70th Executive Board Meeting, and report on the preparations of the Hangzhou Asian Games.

The 36th OCA's General Assembly

The background of the General Assembly was yellow and green, and the name of the meeting was white. Green is the color of the flag of Turkmenistan, a much-beloved color by locals for

The 70th OCA Executive Board Meeting

generations. I didn't have time to delve into the symmetrical traditional patterns in the background, but considering the country's well-developed carpet industry, I guess visual symmetry matters in this place.

In Turkmenistan, we met a delegation from Aichi-Nagoya, the host of the Asian Games after Hangzhou. We were surprised to learn that Japan had twice as much time to prepare as us. We shook hands and talked, but I was thinking about Haruki Murakami, the Japanese best-selling author who is also passionate about running. "Japanese people plan early," I told myself in many encounters with them in later years.

The Sports Committee had a side meeting during the General Assembly, joined by OCA Vice President Song Luzeng, the members of the Sports Committee, and other experts. Compared with the General Assembly, it focused on the competition at the Asian Games. The sports proposed by HAGOC were discussed, debated, and guided. In any case, this meeting held in the hometown of Akhal-Teke horse had an impact on whether equestrian should be included in Hangzhou's schedule, for its venue, quarantine, logistics, and other requirements are quite unique.

After crossing most of the tasks off the list, we had a brief tour and came across a "weird" building. Its uncanny resemblance to the hotel "Burj Al Arab" in Dubai had confused me for a while. Later, the driver dropped us off at a place close to the ruins of an ancient city for about 15 minutes. We were no closer to the "The Gate of Hell" or Kizkalesi, the "Girl's Fortress" that Erika Fatland encountered. It is conceivable that people in the desert began living together behind defensive walls very early, but it is impossible to know what is buried inside the walls of distant ruins and beneath the soil.

I tried to send photos to my daughter who was at a particularly curious age. After several failed attempts, I remembered that before we left Hangzhou, we had set up a group on Alipay as an alternative channel of communication. The last few days had been so busy that I forgot I hadn't used WeChat for a few days. The Internet in my hotel was not stable as well. But compared to the old days when there was no access to the Internet at all, Ashgabat had already made a solid step forward.

The ruins of an unknown city

My memory flashed back to September 2015, when the Chinese Olympic Committee, Hangzhou Municipal Government, and OCA signed the Host City Contract in Ashgabat. In just two years, the terms on the paper had been transformed into a "fishbone diagram" and implemented. At the same time, in my 5,000-km-away hometown, the Archaeological Ruins of Liangzhu City were applying for the UNESCO World Heritage, and the digital economy there was still flourishing at an incredible speed.

Tens of kilometers north of Mary, the economic center and second-largest city of Turkmenistan, is the Bronze Age site of Gonur Depe. Archaeologists told us that as early as 4,000 years ago, there was a well-organized large city with complex irrigation systems and even sewage facilities. The similarities and wonders of history seem to explain

Ashgabat's ubiquitous water scenes. I could not help tracing and imaging the major civilizations during the Bronze Age, as well as the more ancient and pioneering oriental wisdom.

"We'll have a delegation of more than 100 athletes and officials for the Hangzhou Asian Games." Maksat Gokov, representative of the Turkmenistan Olympic Committee and head of the Ministry of Sports, said.

The past tells us in unfinished words, and we are destined to be the "future".

Designing Tokyo

Tokyo was one of the last cities I visited before the COVID-19 spread around the world.

I didn't know much about Tokyo, so for a long time, my impression of Tokyo was replaced by my impression of Japan.

My perception of Japanese sports was once limited to the Japanese women's volleyball team nicknamed the "Witches of the Orient". The unique smile of Kojika Jyun, and the ball that jumped into the air with a clear shout of "Clear Sky Thunderbolt" and flipped several times before it was spiked, were probably our generation's collective memory of volleyball.

Of course, I learned more about Tokyo and things related to Tokyo with time. Examples included *The Chrysanthemum and the Sword* (first published in 1946), ACG (the anime craze that took shape worldwide in the 1990s), *Doomsday: The Sinking of Japan* (released in 2006), Katsumi Masaru (design critic and central figure in the design team of the 1964 Tokyo Olympics), Tadao Ando, Yohji Yamamoto, Issey Miyake and Yayoi Kusama...

It was a long time later when the 19th Asian Games Hangzhou 2022 was being organized that I really got to know Tokyo and met a real Tokyo.

Streetscape of Tokyo

The "Most Expensive" Olympic Emblem Ever

My journey of approaching Tokyo began with researching the publicity and public engagement of 2020 Tokyo Olympics. More specifically, it began with a focus on its visual system, particularly the emblem, a key visual symbol.

The first version of the 2020 Tokyo Olympic emblem, released on July 24, 2015, resembled the letter "T", and the Paralympic emblem was a vertical equal sign. This pair of emblems were quite similar to the logo of Théâtre de Liège in Belgium, so when they were first released, they caused quite a stir in the design community and the global media, and were even accused of plagiarism. This was certainly a big deal for Japan, which is famous for its design worldwide.

Perhaps because of this episode, in March 2019 when I went to Tokyo with the delegation of the Hangzhou Asian Games Organizing Committee, and saw the new version of the emblems and mascots at the entrance of the Tokyo Organizing Committee building, I was overwhelmed with emotion and could not move my feet.

The design community will remember a designer named Yusaku Kamekura at the 1964 Tokyo Olympics, who later became known as the father of modern Japanese graphic design. In that year, the rays of the Olympics shone for the first time in Asia. Yusaku Kamekura designed the first Olympic emblem in Asian history by boldly placing the Japanese flag above the Olympic rings.

In the golden age of Japanese graphic design (1950s–1970s), Japanese graphic designers, centered on the Japan Advertising Artists Club (JAAC), already began to design the logo, posters, medals, diplomas, event schedules, venue maps, tickets, commemorative coins and stamps for the 1964 Tokyo Olympics in a holistic and systematic way. It was a design system that coordinated the central elements with the whole. This approach ushered in a new era of systematic design in the history of the modern Olympics.

As we can imagine, a country and a city with such a profound design tradition could not accept a clearly flawed logo. Therefore, on September 1, 2015, the Tokyo Organizing Committee announced that the already released Tokyo 2020 emblems would be scrapped.

The new emblems were designed by Asao Tokolo. He was born in Tokyo in 1969, graduated from the Department of Design of Tokyo Zokei University, and received a master's degree from the AA School, UK. He founded the Tokolo Studio and is a part-time lecturer at Musashino Art University.

Ichimatsu Moyo (a check pattern popular in the Edo period) which originated in the Edo period in Japan and became popular later, was an important inspiration for the new emblems. The emblems took an abstract form to reinforce the sense of "connecting rings" in a forceful shape. The three different rectangles represented different countries, cultures and ways of thinking. The Olympic and Paralympic emblems were connected by the same shape, meaning that Tokyo 2020 would be a diverse platform that connects the world. Since the events took place in summer, Asao Tokolo selected a blue color that presented a sense of freshness and purity. The designer strove to bring together the profound history and culture of the East and the elements of Western culture, to achieve the multiple aesthetic effects of harmony, simplicity, and silence.

The emblems I saw at the Tokyo Organizing Committee building reminded me of the Sapporo 1972 emblem I saw at the China Design Museum in the China Academy of Art (CAA) before I arrived in Tokyo. It was in a

Tokyo 2020 emblems

group exhibition of works by famous contemporary Japanese designers. The exhibition was curated by Professor Yuan Youmin, the designer of the logo for the 11th G20 Summit, the emblem and sports icons for the 19th Asian Games, and director of the China Design Museum in CAA. Kazumasa Nagai, designer of the Sapporo 1972 emblem, continued to use the design concept of the Tokyo 1964 emblem designer Yusaku Kamekura. He put snowflakes, a symbol of winter, between the rising sun and the Olympic rings, as a sketch of the ancient Japanese family crest pattern. Under the Olympic rings, he added the words "Sapporo'72".

I have to point out that Japan has always been extremely enthusiastic about bidding to host international sporting events. This is why Japan has successfully hosted two Summer Olympic Games, two Winter Olympic Games and two Asian Games, and has successfully bid for and is now preparing for the 20th Asian Games that will be held in Aichi-Nagoya.

The design of the visual system is an essential and critical part of major sports events. I have been part of the organization and international communication of the main visual signs for the 19th Hangzhou Asian Games and Asian Para Games, Hangzhou International Day and Hangzhou International Sister City Mayors Conference. Therefore, I totally understand that even for the best designers, it is extremely difficult to create works in a two-dimensional world that strikes a chord with people at first glance. Even highly skilled designers may create works similar to others without any intention of plagiarism.

Plagiarism checkers have evolved with the times and become very important, and the increasingly advanced Internet technology has made it possible to compare a large number of graphics. Trying to find the perfect emblems, the Tokyo Organizing Committee was meticulous in the selection. They spent a lot of money on research to check if there were any other works out there that were clearly similar to the collected works. When Asao Tokolo's work was selected, the Committee spent another 10 days investigting and publicizing it before it was officially chosen as the emblem for the 2020 Tokyo Olympics. Therefore, we may boldly infer that in the history of the Olympic movement in Japan, the Tokyo 2020 emblems are undoubtedly very "expensive". In addition to the possibly unprecedented cost, this expensiveness also reflects the desire and respect for truly original designs, as well as the courage to face reality and correct mistakes.

Olympic Mascots Chosen by Children

Fumio Ogura, head of the International Department of the Tokyo Organizing Committee, introduced to us the preparations for the Olympics. After listening to him, I was once again drawn to the mascots standing at the entrance of the meeting room. I looked back at them and had a silent conversation with them.

Inside the TOCOG Headquarters

The first mascot in the history of the Olympic Summer Games was named "Waldi". It was a short-legged, long-bodied dachshund, created for the 1972 Munich Olympics. The 1964 Tokyo Games did not actually have a mascot. In spite of this, some enthusiastic netizens later made up a virtual "cherry blossom doll" for it. They probably thought that the mascot of Tokyo 1964 could only be the cherry blossom, which is very popular among Japanese people, as opposed to the image of the rising sun.

It was at the 18th Winter Olympic Games held in Nagano, Japan in 1998 that the flower became an independent image for the main visual identity of Japan's major events. It was not a "baby flower" as imagined by netizens, but a flower designed by Masanori Shinozuka as the emblem. The emblem consisted of a dynamic image of athletes and a snowflake pattern. The whole resembled a mountain flower, and was thus named Snowflower. The mascots of Nagano 1998 were four owlets designed by Landor Associates. It was the first time in the history of the Olympics that four animals were used as mascots.

The four mascots were named Sukki, Nokki, Lekki and Tsukki, representing the four different components of forest life: fire, air, earth and water. The few letters of the four names reform the word "snowlets", which is the common name of the four owls. "Snow" refers to the winter season, "lets" refers to "let's", and "Owlets" means little owls.

The mascot of the Nagano Winter Paralympic Games is a rabbit named "Parabit", which is composed of the prefix of "Paralympic"and the English spelling of "rabbit". The image of this mascot is said to have originated from a painting by British painter Watts.

As is the general rule in the preparation of major international sporting events, the release of the mascot usually follows that of the emblem, as the emblem must be shown in the mascot. In the history of the Olympic Movement in Asia, the Olympic Council of Asia (OCA) has required that Asian Games mascots must present the emblem in a prominent position. What was striking about the Tokyo 2020 mascots was that the main structure and essential elements of the emblems were subtly and intrinsically integrated into the mascots.

The Tokyo Organizing Committee released the Olympic mascot on February 28, 2018. Later, on July 22, it announced the mascot's name Miraitowa on its official website. "Miraitowa" was a combination of the Japanese words "mirai" (future) and "towa" (eternal). This name was chosen to promote a future full of eternal hope in the hearts of people all over the world.

Miraitowa came in blue and white with cat-like ears, big anime-style black eyes, and an athletic frame. Its forehead bore the emblem of the 2020 Tokyo Games, and the pattern on its face dated back to the helmet worn by ancient Japanese warriors. Miraitowa was lively, loved sports and was amazingly athletic. It was upright, selfless and honest, and was a character living in the digital world. It could use the Internet to move freely between the digital and real worlds. Its special skill was instantaneous movement, which allowed it to move wherever it wanted to go. The mascot showed respect for tradition and pursued innovation in line with cutting-edge information.

Correspondingly, the mascot of the 2020 Tokyo Paralympic Games is called "Someity", which comes from a combination of the Japanese word "Someiyoshino" (a cherry blossom variety) and the English phrase "so mighty" (omnipotent). Someity has a cherry blossom tactile sensor, presenting red (rose) and white colors. It has strong psychological and physical strength, representing Paralympic athletes who overcome difficulties and redefine possibilities.

The mascots were designed by Ryo Taniguchi, a freelance designer based in Fukuoka Prefecture. He creates original characters and designs illustrations, and also makes sofubi toys. The designer's traditional and futuristic style echoes the Tokyo 2020 philosophy of "everyone at their best", "diversity and harmony", and "future-oriented succession".

It is obvious that Miraitowa and Someity show contrasting colors, matching shapes and expressions. In addition, they are also good friends.

2020 Tokyo Olympic and Paralympic Mascots

This pair of futuristic robots have the traditional Japanese Ichimatsu Moyo. They were chosen by Japanese elementary school students with high votes.

This way of selecting mascots is undoubtedly the most creative and interesting thing about Tokyo 2020.

An Olympics without Spectators

In the history of the Olympic movement, the IOC does not change its set plans for major events easily, unless there is force majeure.

Tokyo 2020 was certainly an exception.

Back on September 7, 2013, at the 125th IOC session, IOC President Jacques Rogge announced Tokyo as the host city for the 2020 Summer Olympic Games.

Due to the outbreak of the COVID-19 pandemic, the IOC agreed to postpone the Tokyo Games for one year.

The subsequent waves of COVID-19 spreading around the world led to speculation that the Tokyo Olympics would eventually be canceled. On

Streetscape of Tokyo

March 30, 2020, IOC President Bach announced that the Tokyo Olympics would be held from July 23 to August 8, 2021, the Tokyo Paralympics would be held from August 24 to September 5, 2021, and they would still use the name "Tokyo 2020 Olympic and Paralympic Games". It wasn't until then that the dust settled.

During this period, we also learned in the media that the Tokyo Olympics would not be suspended even without spectators. In other words, nothing could stop the IOC, especially the Tokyo Organizing Committee, to make the Games happen.

The significance of the Olympic Games for the host country and the host city has never been limited to the sport itself.

Take the 1964 Tokyo Olympics as an example. The first line of Japan's Shinkansen, the Tokaido Shinkansen connecting Tokyo and Osaka, opened on October 1, 1964, before the opening of the Games. This marked the beginning of Japan's high-speed railway era. At the same time, to watch the Olympics in a country where the Internet was not yet around, more and more people started to buy color TVs. The proportion of household color TVs increased dramatically, which led to the rise of color TV business in some brands such as Panasonic and TOSHIBA. Japanese landmarks such as the Yoyogi National Stadium designed by Kenzo Tange and the Tokyo Tower designed by Tachu Naito, as well as some other urban structures, were built and formed a distinctive architectural style. Undoubtedly, the 1964 Tokyo Olympics not only drove the rise of Japan's economy after World War II, but also reintroduced Japan to the world. In 2013, when Tokyo achieved the successful bid for the 2020 Olympics, the Games were estimated to bring in an economic value of about 3 trillion yen. Therefore, from the very beginning, this Olympics carried people's dream and hope of reviving Japan's economy. There was a new designer for Japan's new National Stadium, the main venue for the 2020 Tokyo Olympics. The famous Japanese architect Kengo Kuma, also the designer of the Folk Art Museum of CAA, designed this "stadium of trees". We can see how the designer made efforts to respond to both economic and ecological challenges with natural materials, and we can also glimpse the possible

A view in Shinkansen station

differences between Tokyo 2020 and Tokyo 1964.

In fact, the spillover effect of Tokyo 2020 was felt throughout the entire process of preparing for it. For instance, Tokyo carefully "designed" international communication.

After the promotion video for the 2020 Olympics bid, another promotion video "Tokyo Tokyo" was released and became a hit. The video uses split-screen shots to show the contrast between traditional and modern Tokyo: tatami and

Screenshot of the promotion video "Tokyo Tokyo"

Simmons, paper umbrellas and modern umbrellas, kendo and e-sports, traditional kimono and modern kimono, ukiyo-e and Hatsune Miku (sound library), handwritten calligraphy and mechanical ink splashing... All of this vividly shows how Tokyo has changed drastically. In fact, this split-screen technique did not originate in Japan. It may have been created by filmmaker Andy Warhol, an American pop art master and father of pop culture. As Andy Warhol expected when he first designed this filming technique, a split screen is more attractive to viewers, and more information is delivered for the same length of time, so double effects are achieved.

The greatest design is often hidden in the opening ceremony. Nevertheless, perhaps due to cultural differences, the impact of the pandemic, the quietness of not having speculators, or for some other unexplained reasons, most viewers are more impressed with Tokyo's eight-minute show in the handover ceremony during Rio 2016's closing ceremony.

In the eight minutes, Hello Kitty, Captain Tsubasa, Mario, Doraemon and other characters shone on stage, taking the stadium into an ACG world, evoking both nostalgia and imagination. In the end, then Japanese Prime Minister popped up on stage dressed as Mario, bringing the connection between ACG and the reality to a climax.

As the Tokyo Organizing Committee once said: the purpose of the show was to present Japan and Tokyo, and ACG is one of the powerful tools that Japan has. This is a global consensus.

I haven't thought about the economic value behind the anime images in Tokyo's eight-minute show, and I'm not sure if anime technology has succeeded again in becoming the focus of Tokyo 2020. That's because I am much more intrigued by Japan's fashion industry, with Issey Miyake's folds that conquered the world, Yohji Yamamoto's restrained yet shiny black, and Yayoi Kusama's distinctive polka dots and pumpkins. What I do know is that Tokyo 2020 has been through ups and downs, but in the end they were held, in an unprecedented way. In the most difficult time of the Games, the IOC gave Tokyo a rare "exemption" from responsibility— " No government or health department can guarantee absolute control of the pandemic. Everyone is likely to get infected. This is a risk we all have to take." Therefore, the IOC informed athletes that they had to sign a waiver to exempt the Tokyo Organizing Committee from COVID-19 responsibility.

Just one year apart, some athletes known as "evergreens" were no longer young, some ambitions to win gold encountered setbacks, many beautiful hopes of going to Tokyo and watching the Games together shattered like scattered cherry blossoms ...

The city of design, the distant Tokyo.

Man proposes, God disposes.

Tehran's Cinematic Art

"When you go to Tehran, which book will you carry with you?"

"Jin Yong's *Heaven Sword and Dragon Saber*."

My answer was half-serious, half-joking. In addition to world history, the ancient empire and its kings that I had memorized since I was a child, Xiaozhao in the book was probably the first Persian I had ever known. And she is a beautiful leader with great martial arts skills.

"You were still young when Tehran hosted the 7th Asian Games."

That was in 1974. And I was indeed young. All I recognized were probably words and pictures of ping-pong on cards.

"Go watch the film *Children of Heaven*. There's a match in the film, about a boy competing with his own heart and against his own limits."

When it comes to Tehran, I usually look at its unique location along the Silk Road, both by sea and by land. Getting to know the city through films is another perspective.

There's an excellent group of filmmakers in Tehran. Unlike Hollywood movies, Tehran movies are not heavily invested. They use warmth, truth and power to touch the audience's heart, thus winning one award after another in the international film industry.

"They depict women, portray children, reveal the pain of men, and tell the meaning of life and death."

What's more, a famous Tehran-born director named Abbas Kiarostami used to visit Hangzhou several times for the preparation of a film named *Love in Hangzhou*.

Run, *Children of Heaven*

There is a unique running race, where the hero does not want to come first or second. All he wants is third place, because the prize for it is a pair of sneakers. That's the prize he has promised his little sister. Therefore, when he runs far ahead, he turns back and slows down to let a kid run before him, and then let another go before him. Suddenly, he is tripped by a boy behind and has a fall. As the finishing line is getting near, he regains his footing and desperately runs forward...

As I stared at the boy who stood on the winner's podium but was filled with tears of despair, my tears dropped on the screen and I felt as down as he was. At that moment, I understood why the film was nominated for the 72nd Academy Awards for the Best Foreign Language Film, and why hundreds of thousands of people gave this low-budget movie an impressive score of 9.2/10 on Douban, a Chinese film-rating app.

In 1974 when Tehran hosted the 7th Asian Games, Iran was already prosperous and developed, which shocked people from many countries.

Born in Tehran in 1959, Director Majid Majidi directed *Children of Heaven* in 1997. He sets the film in a poor family who can't afford rent, where the brother and sister have to take turns wearing the same pair of old sneakers and dash to school. Majidi said that the movie was a combination of the need for beauty and poetic expression, his

A still from *Children of Heaven*   Poster of *Children of Heaven*

The emblem of the 7th Asian Games   Main stadium of the 7th Asian Games

understanding of that social class and that kind of life, and some of his own childhood experiences.

Children of Heaven is not a typical sports movie. It focuses on character building and a poetic display of human nature. The older brother Ali and his sister Zahra are sensible, righteous and responsible, keeping all the hardships and grievances to themselves.

The scene set in *Children of Heaven* is cramp: the alley between home and school is almost the home base of the young siblings' childhood. They go to school at different times, hastily change their shoes in hidden corners, and run desperately nonstop. Life is so hard. When they make considerable efforts to look for Zahra's lost red shoes, only to

A still from *Children of Heaven*

find them on the feet of a blind girl, they give up and return home with profound disappointment.

The shoes are all they dream about in their hopeless daily life. A children's running race climaxes the story and opens up a different world. Before the race, a teacher tells young players that sportsmanship is more important than ranking. At the end of the film, Ali dips his blistered feet into a pool of water, and a school of red fish swims around them. Meanwhile, Ali's father hurries home with new shoes for his children.

A running boy also appears in the film *Where Is the Friend's Home?* directed by the master director Abbas Kiarostami. In this film, the hero Babek Ahmed Poor runs to find his deskmate to return his notebook, so that his friend won't be punished or even expelled the next day for failing to finish his homework again.

Ali is running, Babek Ahmed Poor is running, and lots of other boys are running. Small shoes turn into big shoes, and then into professional running shoes. The camera moves up from the shoes to the faces of the children who grow up running and become famous athletes. They won't forget that Iranian athlete Baghbanbashi, who won gold in the men's 5,000m and silver in the men's 3,000m steeplechase at the first Asian Games, lighted the flame at the 1974 Asian Games in Tehran.

Although sports films are rare in Iran, directors are enthusiastic about this topic and relevant elements. During the 2008 Beijing Olympics, the director of *Children of Heaven* directed the promotional video *Colors Fly* which presented Beijing through the eyes of children. Football, Iran's dominant sport, usually appears in Iranian films in various ways.

Offside, which tells a sad story about female football fans, won a Silver Bear at the 2006 Berlin International Film Festival. In 2019, after all, 500 Iranian women were allowed to attend football games. Football, which rarely appears in but runs through Abbas' *Life and Nothing More,* is almost a heroic dream in the Iranian people's difficult and tiring life.

"Do you know what time the game is on?"

"Seven to nine. But we already know who will win."

...

"The earthquake has caused such serious damage. Everyone is in grief. You still want to watch the game?"

...

"The World Cup comes every four years. Life still goes on. Earthquakes happen every forty years..."

In the film, dialogues about football also occur among kids and between father and son.

As director Majid Majidi hopes, the world shown in his films should be peaceful, tranquil and beautiful.

The Azadi Stadium in Iran

"Footballers play better at home, even though rules are the same everywhere. My best work is probably what I make at home." Abbas used this metaphor to express the same deep affection for his homeland as the younger director Majid Majidi.

Tehran Actress Who Won The Best Actress at Cannes

Fans cannot decide who wins the Palme d'Or, despite their passion.

While South Korean director Park Chan-wook won the Cannes Film Festival's best director award for *Decision to Leave*, Iranian actress Zar Amir-Ebrahimi won the Best Actress award for her leading role in *Holy Spider*.

It was on the evening of May 28, 2022 Cannes time, at the 75th Cannes Film Festival.

While feeling sorry for Tang Wei, fans gave *Holy Spider* a different kind of attention. Zar Amir-Ebrahimi, the leading actress, and Ali Abbasi, the film's director, were both born in Tehran in 1981. In popular terms, they are two millennials in Tehran.

Poster of *Holy Spider*

"When you say you love me, your love ends. When your love ends, mine begins." Audiences who've seen *Decision to Leave* will not forget the classic scene where Song Ruilai (played by Tang Wei) utters these heartbreakingly beautiful words before she makes up her mind to end her life in the sea.

Excellent production and special effects, plot twists of the suspense film, as well as the overall aesthetics and tragic nature... All this got Tang Wei several Best Actress awards shortly after Cannes, including the Chunsa Film Art Award, Busan Film Award, Blue Dragon Award, Baeksang Art Award, and Asian Film Award. This, in a way, comforted fans who were upset about Tang Wei missing the Cannes Award.

Unlike *Decision to Leave* and even unlike many other serial-killing films, the focus of *Holy Spider* is not on the hunt for the killer, and the identity of the killer is revealed not at the end of the film but halfway through. Despite this, the female reporter as the heroine, while facilitating the investigation of the serial killing, still encounters numerous obstacles from the public and beyond.

Paradoxically and thought-provokingly, judges almost always have to compare completely different films and choose the best one out of them—because that's the rule.

"I've come a long way to get here tonight..."
"But I'm standing here with the award..."

Zar Amir-Ebrahimi's acceptance speech was as much about the actress herself as it was about the extraordinary journey of shooting the film. On the one hand, the actress made a difficult journey from fleeing her homeland to finding her way back into acting in a foreign country. On the other hand, the film was ultimately shot in Jordan rather than in Iran, and even after it won the award, it still encountered some resistance.

In fact, one gets depressed and down when watching *Holy Spider*. Adapted from a real case more than 20 years ago, the film cannot avoid violence and bloodshed. In the certain background, tone and atmosphere set by the film, there exists a hidden yet growing tension between "deep-rooted traditions and modern spirit". The heroine's dauntless bravery and genuine fear, her tenacity, and her final limited triumph, are the film's one and only beam of light.

Perhaps the director's courage is touching in the first place, when he presents the topic of the crime thriller, the predicament of women living at the bottom, the heroine's perseverance and how she manages to get the criminal arrested.

The story takes place not in Tehran but in Mashhad, Iran's second-largest city. Possibly, the director has chosen Iran's holy city to tell the story based on the background and culture of the real event that the film is adapted from. In addition, both the director and the leading actress had been away from Tehran for years before the film won the award. Zar Amir-Ebrahimi is an Iranian actress whose exile years ago was more of rebirth than escape. Ali Abbasi, a Danish director and screenwriter, moved to another country for further education or other reasons. Since they have long been "living elsewhere", as Milan Kundera puts it, will audiences question or even contest the film's Iranianism?

In festivals and exhibitions with global influence, there are works that initially lack sufficient attention in their own countries, or are heavily criticized, but are easily awarded internationally. It cannot be ruled out that in some cases, discourse hegemony and value export can directly or indirectly influence the result, but for awards with relatively high authority and recognition, audiences will respect professional judgments, and content creators will value the honor bestowed by the jury.

"I am here, but my heart is with my fellow Iranian men and women..."

When Zar Amir-Ebrahimi made a speech as the Best Actress at Cannes, many viewers would at least believe in her bravery and sincerity just from the perspective of cinematic art.

Abbas and His Unfinished *Love in Hangzhou*

When trying to enter the unknown world of Tehran, I had the honor to know Abbas. This talented Tehran director started but never finished *Love in Hangzhou,* which gave me more surprise and pity.

Following the map of Abbas' films, we come to *Taste of Cherry.* A middle-aged man named Badii plans to swallow sleeping pills and lie down in a ditch by the roadside in the suburbs of Tehran. He is looking for someone to help him kill himself, someone who will bury him the next morning. The theme of suicide is reminiscent of the Swedish film *A Man Called Ove* and the Brazilian writer Paulo Coelho's novel *Veronika Decides to Die.* Usually, the main characters of such works do not die in the end, because in the process of attempting suicide, many "accidents" will happen. In the end, they either can't die, or don't want to die.

Death is by nature a very personal thing. Death could arrive through unexpected accidents or careful plans (death caused by disease is not discussed here). Death is silent. It does not say hello or goodbye. When people die, they go with the wind.

The structure of *Taste of Cherry* is taken from a Persian poem about a butterfly, which flies around a candle flame, and gets closer and closer to it until it's burned by flame. Badii drives around until he falls into the grave he has dug for himself. The film is inspired by the legend of a man chased by a lion: the man who jumps off a cliff is caught by plant roots on the mountainside, while two rats are gnawing on the roots. In such a dangerous situation, the man sees a strawberry growing on the mountainside. He reaches out cautiously, picks it and eats it.

As a successful psychological drama, *Taste of Cherry* won the Palme d'Or for best film in competition at the 50th Cannes Film Festival. Perhaps the significance of this film lies more in the enlightenment Abbas gave to subsequent works on similar themes.

In contrast to "death", another film directed by Abbas that won him worldwide fame is called *Life and Nothing More*. It tells the story of a film director who drives back to a region in Iran where he filmed *Where Is the Friend's Home?* a few years ago. The place has recently been struck by an earthquake, and the director wants to find the two children who played leading roles in his film to make sure they are safe.

Similar to Wong Kar-wai's *My Blueberry Nights*, *Life and Nothing More* is a distinct road movie. Abbas let the actor drive his own Land Rover, pulling in at times to ask passersby how they understand life after the disaster.

The film was set three days after the earthquake, but the actual filming took place months later. The earthquake caused different tragedies. Large areas of houses were damaged or collapsed, countless families' loved ones were killed, and devastation and desolation were everywhere. Still, life went on. Those who planned to get married got married anyway without waiting for all kinds of time-consuming prayers or mourning. Antennas were erected on the hillside. After all, the World Cup is held once every four years. The world will outlast the life of any individual, and "we" are transient. Survivors are supposed to rebuild homes and provide for families. Everything else is secondary.

"When I asked the survivors to clutter up the few possessions they had retained, many refused, and some even borrowed new clothes to wear for the film. Their survival instincts were strong, as was their desire to maintain self-esteem in such a hostile environment. "

"The idea of a journey, of moving from one point to the next, is important in Iranian culture," Abbas believed, "the road expresses people's search for necessities, for the ever-restless soul, and for things that don't end."

Abbas, who had planned to visit Hangzhou for the fifth time, passed away on July 4, 2016, Paris time. *Love in Hangzhou,* which he had been contemplating and preparing for a long time, thus remained in a profound "unfinished state".

From *Taste of Cherry* and *Life and Nothing More*, which correspond to the themes of death and life, through the other two films of Abbas' Koker Trilogy (*Where Is the Friend's Home?* and *Through the Olive*

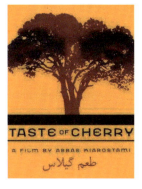

Poster of *Taste of Cherry*   Poster of *Life and Nothing More*

191

Trees), to Abbas' *Certified Copy and Like Someone in Love* shot in Europe and Japan respectively... When Abbas handed us his unfinished works as he did in the workshop, how should we continue under the long-established themes?

During Abbas' four trips to Hangzhou, he went to a bookstore in December 2014 to buy books about China. I believe that among those books, there was at least one about poetry of the East, because poetry was always a source of inspiration for his films. "When in Rome, do as the Romans do." Would he read the poems of Su Dongpo, a renowned Song Dynasty poet, who served as "mayor" of Hangzhou? Well, not necessarily, but his *Love in Hangzhou* must be poetic.

In June 2014, during Abbas' first trip to Hangzhou, he wore sunglasses and held a camera to capture things around all the time, as if saying once again to himself and to his Chinese friends in front of him, "Why can't a director just start with images?" "Silent thoughts, feelings and expressions are not only possible, but also should be encouraged." Having fully appreciated the beauty of "Paradise on Earth", would Abbas use more images to express themselves in *Love in Hangzhou?*

In May 2015, Abbas came to Hangzhou for the third time. This time, he brought with him a Tehran actress, Afsaneh Pakroo. He took her to the Xiangshan Central Campus of the China Academy of Art, Phoenix International Creative Park, Yuangu Creative Park and LOFT49 Creative Industrial Park. Afsaneh Pakroo spoke a little Chinese, which she had learned for two months. Did the director want her to ask strangers in Chinese? In fact, the scene "asking a stranger for directions" appeared many times in Abbas' previous films. Would it continue to be the director's poetic and philosophical way of exploring and knowing Hangzhou?

Abbas' last trip to Hangzhou was in September 2015. After several close encounters with Hangzhou, he decided to choose Faxi Temple in Upper Tianzhu and Xiaohe Street as shooting locations. On October 10,

The portraiture of Abbas (By ZHAI Mofan)　　　　The portraiture of Afsaneh (By REN Zhizhong)

Abbas met with the press in Beijing's 798 Art Zone, where he revealed that the film would be about a female Iranian student's experiences in Hangzhou.

Imagining Abbas' film *Love in Hangzhou* is an extraordinarily peculiar experience, for it is only after countless viewing experiences of his films that this imagination can be based and pointed to. Abbas said he liked half-finished films, because he requested his audience to make more effort than they usually do when watching a film. At some moments, I wanted the Tehran girl who was walking from Faxi Temple to Xiaohe Street to play some video games at the Asian Games' e-sports venue, because Abbas' film is in essence a never-ending game. As he hid away to never see us, he was creating a journey where more responsibilities are given to actors and audiences and the director can eventually be forgotten.

After Abbas, the mutual choice between Iranian directors and Hangzhou continues.

Gao Shiming (2nd from right), headmaster of the China Academy of Art engaged Majid Majidi (2nd from left) as a visiting professor

Hiroshima's Narrative

"Even if it becomes a ruin, or even collapses to just a little part of the building, as long as it's still filled with narrative power, it is architecture."

The famous Japanese architect Tadao Ando's definition of architecture and understanding of the architectural spirit may, at a certain moment, remind us of the Atomic Bomb Dome (a permanently preserved memorial located in the center of Hiroshima, the ruins of the original Hiroshima Prefectural Industrial Promotion Hall), the city in ruins, and a reborn Hiroshima.

Atomic Bomb Dome

The laureate of the Nobel Prize in literature Kenzaburo Oe's *Hiroshima Notes* and female French writer Marguerite Duras' screenplay *Hiroshima mon amour* seem to be the concrete carriers and different versions of this narrative power.

"What did you see in Hiroshima?"

I had never been to Hiroshima, so I asked everyone who might have been there: what did you see in Hiroshima?

Surprisingly, many people, like me, had not been to Hiroshima. They'd been to Tokyo, to Kyoto, Osaka, Nara, but never to Hiroshima.

Later, I finally found three people who had a real connection or brief encounter with Hiroshima: a painter, a sportsman and an overseas Chinese student. They said they didn't know much about Hiroshima which I wanted to explore, but they had indeed been there.

Hiroshima · Love

"I went to Hiroshima, at first, to refresh myself," said the painter, "but then something else happened."

After the outbreaking of the Russia-Ukraine conflict, the painter drew one picture a day according to the information he could get. He painted 400 pictures, and the conflict was still ongoing. He felt lost, not knowing whether he should continue or not.

When the painter went to Hiroshima many years ago, he had already completed a massive drawing on the history of Nanjing. The subject of war, the tragic atmosphere, innocent civilians and brutal executioners weighed on him for a long time. Meanwhile, because of long-term hard work, when the piece was finished, he was left with severe "post-painting syndrome". At one point he vowed that he would never paint such pictures anymore. He wanted to draw the beauty of the world, and he ended up in Hiroshima.

"A paradoxical place. On the one hand, militarism has its own to blame there. On the other hand, the city and its people have suffered an unprecedented calamity and destructive catastrophe."

Therefore, in Hiroshima, the painter could not paint beautiful women. Wherever he went, he couldn't avoid the wreckage, ruins, disaster and pain of the past.

"Hiroshima is once again covered with flowers. There are cornflowers,

Inside Hiroshima Peace Memorial Park

irises, morning glories and three-colored bindweed everywhere. They are reignited from the ashes with remarkable vigor hitherto unseen in flowers."

These are lines from Marguerite Duras's play. In her book, Duras noted that these sentences were copied almost word by word from John Hersey's excellent report on Hiroshima.

At first, the painter just wanted to paint oleander, the city flower of Hiroshima, to paint the flowers quoted by Duras that were as tough as oleander. When the flowers first grew from the crevices in the ruins, they undoubtedly became a source of comfort for people in Hiroshima (at the

The red pine reborn in the ruins

197

time, there was a widespread curse that "for 75 years, no grass, no people could grow here"). However, the later development predictably exceeded the painter's expectations.

"In Hiroshima, you can't control yourself."

So the painter went crazy, painting works he had sworn he would never paint again. He was so crazy that wherever he went, he carried his portable case (propped up as an improvised easel) and sketchbook, his hands, eyes and brain in a state of rapid rotation. Until one day, he was admitted to a hospital in Hiroshima.

The painter went through a period of trance and blankness. When the doctor told him he had to have a heart stent, he couldn't believe it was something happening to him. He thought about how young and strong he had been, and how his portraits from different periods of his life were vivid records of growing up from childhood to adolescence, and then from youth to adulthood. Like most oil painters who eventually consider thematic painting as the highest level of painting, the review and artistic reproduction of history became his youthful memories and glory days.

The doctor handed the painter a document and told him that a relative of his needed to sign it. The painter shook his head and said that if the document must be signed, he would have to do it himself. He came alone to Hiroshima without detailed plans. Even if he had any plan, he would still be alone, facing the ruins of his love that had collapsed. However, the doctor said that according to the rules, a family member must sign.

"I'll sign it!"

This voice came from a nurse beside the doctor. The painter and the doctor looked at her at the same time as if she were a dream.

"I've seen your paintings about Hiroshima. They're so beautiful." The nurse said.

The painter noticed that it was the face of an Asian woman. He couldn't tell which country she came from, but her eyes were as sure as her voice. At that moment, time and space seemed to stand still.

Later, the painter drew that scene and named it "Hiroshima · Love". Afterwards, the nurse became his wife. Then later, they had a son.

Personal Experience

"It is impossible to talk about Hiroshima. All we can do is talk about the impossibility of talking about Hiroshima."

These are also words from Marguerite Duras.

After all these years, *Hiroshima mon amour* is still what it should be, a classic that lives on. Hiroshima, the "city of no man", is no longer full of desolation.

"It is not only possible, but also relevant to talk about Hiroshima. Sports make it more possible." A veteran in the sports circle said.

He happened to have been to Hiroshima and seen the 1994 Hiroshima Asian Games.

As the question "What did you see in Hiroshima" led to more rounds of dialogues, Duras finally made it possible to tell the story of "impossible" love in the shadow of war, by combining the heroine's immediate experiences with her past.

After visiting Hiroshima twice in 1963 and 1964 respectively, Kenzaburo Oe, who wanted to use Hiroshima and the real Hiroshima people as a file to test the hardness of his heart, recorded the images of

Hiroshima mon amour by Marguerite Duras

Hiroshima Notes by Kenzaburo Oe

tragedy and majesty that were about to be declared dead one by one. He put forward the serious proposition of how humanity should prevent tragedies from happening again.

In artistic reflection and literary criticism, in a more general sense and way of expression, peace has been the theme of the Hiroshima narrative.

This theme was also reflected in the 1994 Hiroshima Asian Games.

In 1984, at the 3rd General Assembly of the Olympic Council of Asia (OCA) held in South Korea, the OCA conferred Hiroshima the right to host the 12th Asian Games. Hiroshima managed to get the rare opportunity to host the Asian Games for the first time outside a capital city.

Bearing the OCA's vision of "Integrating Asians", Hiroshima, slowly recovering from the shadow of war, did not forget the cultural expression of the games.

The emblem of the Hiroshima Asian Games is a distinctive representation of the city's spirit. The upper part of the emblem is the sun rays, which symbolize the OCA. The main part of it is the letter "H" formed by two white doves, which symbolizes the host city of Hiroshima.

The image of doves also appeared in the mascots of the 1994 Asian Games, as the male dove Poppo and female dove Coccu. It was the first time in the history of the Asian Games that mascots were shown as a pair of cartoon figures. As the ambassador of the 1994 Asian Games, the white dove conveyed the desire for world peace and the anti-war spirit.

The emblem and mascots of the 1994 Asian Games

"Apart from these abstract yet concrete symbols, what else did you see in Hiroshima?"

He was silent. He did not say that Iraq was disqualified that year, or that five Central Asian nations took part in the Asian Games for the first time that year. He did not say any of this.

He said nothing because China Central Television sent a 54-member press corps to the 1994 Asian Games. That was the year CCTV set up its first studio abroad to broadcast directly to China. This feat in China's television history made it possible to pass on the vivid memories of the 1994 Asian Games.

"What do you think of the match between Deng Yaping and Koyama Chire?" I changed the subject.

"In Hiroshima, Deng Yaping began another kind of 'completion'." This time, he was not silent.

What Deng Yaping needed to defeat was nothing more than herself. She defeated herself, so later in the 1996 Atlanta Olympic Games, she won the gold medals in women's singles and women's doubles. Therefore, she is still the brightest table tennis star in the world.

"Do you know who carried the Olympic torch on its last leg in the 1964 Olympics? " Now it was his turn to test me.

"A young man born in Hiroshima on the day the atomic bomb was dropped?" He didn't seem to have me stumped.

"It was a body that was striking in its own strength. With a smile of relief from any uneasiness, he dashed on the huge track." Kenzaburo Oe wrote.

"In Hiroshima, I saw the human potential unleashed by sport, and the healing power of that potential and strength."

Before leaving Hiroshima, he visited the Hiroshima Peace Memorial Park again. When he boarded the plane, he had two more books with him, *Hiroshima Notes* by Kenzaburo Oe in Japanese, and *Summer Flowers* by

Tamiki Hara, another Japanese author.

"Hiroshima-Style" People

If it wasn't for Yuxiao, a Chinese student who studied in Japan, the only Hiroshima person I knew would have been Issey Miyake.

On August 5, 2022, the renowned Japanese fashion designer Issey Miyake died of cancer at the age of 84. His fans grieved the demise of the great master.

Miyake was born in Hiroshima in 1938. When the atomic bomb was dropped on the city, he was about 7 years old. His mother and most of his relatives were injured and died, and he himself suffered from ill health. After moving to Tokyo, he was admitted to Tama Art University at the age of 21. He went to study in Paris and then in New York, and learned from Hubert de Givenchy, a renowned haute couture designer and a lifelong friend of Oscar-winning actress Audrey Hepburn.

Miyake, a war survivor, once confided, "I've tried to hide this memory deep inside. I chose fashion design partly because it symbolizes creativity and rebirth."

Miyake conquered the world with his unique folds. He broke the western pursuit of extremely tight dresses, and designed clothes that made it easy for women to move around. The black turtleneck he designed for the former Apple CEO Steve Jobs and the ideas behind it were loved by Jobs, which has become a much-told tale.

In the process of learning about Hiroshima, I came to know a term called "atomic bomb aftereffects". The aftereffects actually include at least two aspects, the immediate destruction and injury, and the psychological trauma caused by this, which combine into a new and possibly more serious condition.

From what he achieved, Miyake might not be associated with the term, or the signal of liberation conveyed in his design was originally a powerful counterbalance and cure for this disease. I don't know if he was, in this sense, what Oe called a "Hiroshima-style" person. However, when he went out into the wider world, "Hiroshima"was already one of the things that defined him.

"In Hiroshima, there is a tour guide named Shintaro." Yuxiao Said.

Yuxiao studied at the Ritsumeikan Asia Pacific University in the Kyushu region. He'd been to Hiroshima twice. The first time he went there around New Year's Day during his 20th birthday, and the second time he stayed there for nearly a month. He traveled with his good friend Nanaka to see what life was like in Hiroshima long after the atomic bomb was dropped.

"We call him Shinchan. Shintaro is the name given to him by his grandfather. It means 'believed to be able to walk out of the shadow of war'."

Yuxiao celebrated his 20th birthday briefly in an average-sized izakaya in Hiroshima. While cooking Hiroshima-yaki, the restaurant owner learned from others that it was Yuxiao's birthday, so he cooked with greater efforts. That night, in addition to Hiroshima-yaki, Yuxiao also ate baumkuchen originated in Hiroshima.

Yuxiao couldn't explain why he chose Hiroshima for his birthday. Perhaps subconsciously, he thought Hiroshima was a city suitable for contemplating life.

Yuxiao met Shinchan on his second trip to Hiroshima while riding around the Peace Memorial Park. On that day, Shinchan was showing several tourists around. When he discovered Yuxiao was a Chinese student, he tried to communicate with him in Chinese.

It was when Shinchan took the visitors to the alley at the side entrance of the Japanese Red Cross Society that Yuxiao learned that in addition to the world-famous Atomic Bomb Dome, a dilapidated wall had also been restored there.

In *Hiroshima Notes*, Oe wrote about a group of "Hiroshima-style" people, represented by Dr. Fumio Shigeto, who arrived at the Japanese Red Cross Society just a week before the bombing. These were "unyielding people" with human "dignity". They would not give up under any circumstances and were always working hard.

Wherever the visitors saw a site, Shinchan would explain its origin and how horrible it was when the bomb dropped. These stories might be told in similar ways by all tour guides, but Yuxiao could not forget what Shinchan's parents and grandparents went through.

Here goes the story of Shinchan's grandmother. On the day the atomic bomb was dropped, Shinchan's pregnant grandmother sent water to the injured and bandaged their wounds without caring for herself. The

Remains of Japanese Red Cross Society in Hiroshima

plight of the injured made her deeply frightened, and too much work gradually wore her out. She passed out and was then saved by others. Later, she gave birth to Shinchan's father and died a few months later.

The second story is about Shinchan's grandfather. Thrown from a tram but not seriously injured, he saw a child trapped under a beam. He worked with several others to move the beam, but failed. After they dispersed in disappointment, Shinchan's grandfather continued to try for a long time, but had to give up eventually. The child screamed hysterically: "Help me! Help me!" But he felt powerless. He covered his ears and ran away. After that, every day he would utter the words "I failed to save that child, after all... "

Shinchan said his father often taught him, "You should make a whole lot of friends in the world, because when everyone becomes your friend, peace will come." That was why Shinchan chose to be a tour guide in Hiroshima.

Yuxiao found himself at the end of the ride, in front of the Great Fountain. It's said that Hiroshima hosts a fountain that spouts the most water to the greatest height in Japan to commemorate victims who died of thirst in the bombing.

There are streetcars around the park. It is said that although the streetcars were halted on the day of the bombing, they resumed operation the next day after roadblocks were cleared. Even though practically no one took them, they kept running, free of charge. There

The Great Fountain in Hiroshima Peace Memorial Park

A tram in Hiroshima

was one train that ran on the tracks at that time and has not been retired to this day – No. 651. It happened to be resting at the headquarters of Hiroshima Electric Railway Co., Ltd., so Shinchan took the chance and let visitors take photos with it.

The number, schedules and routes of Hiroshima's trams are dazzling, and the roads are exceptionally wide.

"If you have time, you may also visit the Hiroshima City Naka Incineration Plant. It's a waste processing factory, but Yoshio Taniguchi's design made it look like an art museum."

Looking at Shinchan, who was smiling broadly, Yuxiao seemed to suddenly realize that Shinchan wanted to show them more than just the heavy tragedies of the past. Walking past the ruins in the rebuilt city, this Hiroshima guide, who wanted to make more friends in the world, intentionally made himself feel less pain. In this way, the visitors could see the vibrancy of the "City of Peace".

"Brains" of Lausanne

It was not until the train from Paris arrived in Lausanne, a city in southwest Switzerland, that the girl realized her European SIM card had no cellular mobile network services in this neutral country. She came in a hurry, and could afford only a half day. Though the travel plan was simple and clear enough, she suddenly felt at sea without a data map.

"Don't guess the way – just ask for directions!" The girl recalled what her parents said when she was still a child and looked around. People paced back and forth, but she fixed her eyes on a pole with four road signs.

The signs showed a museum just on her way, and it wouldn't take much time to get there. She decided to find the museum first, and then secure the final route.

Road signs   In search of the IOC headquarters

The girl's red pullover, with cryptic Chinese characters on the front, was a staff award she received as a volunteer at Han Meilin Art Museum. Before she went to France, Han, the eminent artist, took out his Pierre de Coubertin medal and allowed her to wear it around her neck for a few minutes. The book *Olympic Memoirs* by Coubertin, the founder of the modern Olympics, was in the girl's backpack, and now she was going to the headquarters of the International Olympic Committee and the Olympic Museum.

A Great Vision for the Future

The IOC was headquartered in Lausanne on April 10, 1915.

For a considerable period of time after the establishment of the IOC, Coubertin's residence in Paris was also the IOC headquarters. To find a haven away from World War I, the headquarters were relocated in 1915 and then called the "Modern Olympian World Management Center and Archives Center". Between 1915 and 1922, the IOC Secretariat was located directly at Coubertin's residence in Lausanne. With the IOC's proclamation of Lausanne as the "Olympic City" and "Olympic Capital",

The IOC headquarters

the IOC headquarters and the Olympic Park eventually forged the magnificence of today.

The IOC's first and only president before Coubertin was Demetrius Vikelas, who actively supported Greece's hosting of the Athens Olympic Games (the first modern Olympic Games). The "rotation" rule was that "the IOC president should be a citizen of the Olympic host country". Vikelas was therefore elected the first president and devoted all his life to the Olympic movement.

Since the girl's knowledge and memory of the Olympics basically started with the time she went to the "Bird's Nest" and "Water Cube" to watch the 2008 Beijing Olympics when she was eight years old. She did not know much about the four IOC presidents after Coubertin. Even for Juan Antonio Samaranch, who was often on the lips of her parents' generation, she just knew that "he spoke highly of Deng Yaping" and

Coubertin's *Olympic Memoirs*

"he was very supportive of China's bid to host the Olympics". Jacques Rogge and current IOC president Thomas Bach have close ties to her hometown of Hangzhou, but she only hears about them on the news or from the talks of her parents.

Coubertin is different—He is a French citizen and she is studying in France, but it's more than that. The first emotional bond that connected her to Coubertin was not so much Paris as Greece.

The girl had a spontaneous trip (her first) to Olympia, Greece. The heroic Pheidippides, who collapsed after running more than 40 kilometers to send the victory news to his compatriots, the ancient Olympic site, the glories and ruins—all Greek philosophy, history, art, and literature summoned her there.

When the Olympic Games were revived in 1894, Coubertin made a lonely pilgrimage to Olympia. After 33 years of hard work, he went there again on April 16, 1927. At 10 a.m. on the 17th, the history of the modern Olympic movement ushered in an important moment: the inauguration of the Olympic revival monument was held in Olympia, and the letter *To the Young Athletes of All Nations* was announced on radio:

... We have resumed a 2,500-year-old activity in the hope that you will become disciples of the faith in sports designed by your ancestors. In a modern world full of great possibilities and threatened by dangerous depravity, Olympism can be a school that cultivates both noble spirits and good sentiments, as well as physical endurance and strength, provided that you constantly raise your notions of sporting honor and non-utilitarianism to heights commensurate with your physical strength. The future is in you.

As Coubertin himself said, when he conceived the Olympic Games from a fully international perspective and gave them a global framework, he not only took the only practical means that could make them perpetual (including making "independence" the most basic weapon of the IOC and maintaining autonomy in elections), but also supported the culture of ancient Greece in the best way that served its true interests. For he did not represent the historic Games and cultural spirit as "things of the past" worthy of respect and reflection but strove to present them as "things of the future" commensurate with our faith and loyalty.

This "future" orientation of the modern Olympic movement, through the joint efforts of the core figures and members of the IOC, has ensured the sustainable development of the Olympic Games around the world. There will be a total of 33 modern Olympic Games, including Paris 2024.

Home in a Remote Country

It was Sunday, and the girl could only take photos outside the IOC headquarters. Some were buildings and scenery, and some were cyclists passing by. People are manic to cycling and running in Lausanne—sport is part of the city and of their lives.

She spent most of time in the Olympic Park, especially at the Olympic Museum. Visitors were encouraged to try sports and have fun. She attempted to cup the shot, her face flushing scarlet, and saw the stark contrast with the world record marked on site. Failing as an athlete, she continued the tour at the Olympic Museum as a photographer.

Sculpture in the Olympic Park   View from the outside of the IOC headquarters

Like the IOC headquarters, the Olympic Museum was designed by IOC members Pedro Ramírez Vázquez (Mexican) and Jean-Pierre Cahen (Swiss). It was completed on June 23, 1993, with an opening ceremony attended by IOC honorary President for Life Samaranch (He was the recipient of the 2018 China Reform Friendship Medal, by the way). The museum is by far the most comprehensive, famous, and vibrant sports

Olympic Museum

museum in the world. The Olympic flame is always burning on the square in front of the museum.

Usually, the girl sees her visit as "a magnificent journey towards the other", but in Lausanne, in such a special scene, she could not help looking for cultural symbols of her home country among the many sculptures and displays.

She first discovered the names of the two torchbearers of the 2022 Beijing Winter Olympics, Zhao Jiawen and Dinigeer Yilamujiang, on the stone steps and then photographed the torches of the 2008 Beijing Summer Olympics and the 2022

Steps engraved with the name of the torchbearer

Beijing Winter Olympics. She was also thrilled to spot Fuwa, Bing Dwen Dwen, and Shuey Rhon Rhon when visiting the zone that displayed the mascots of all the Summer and Winter Olympics.

The SMART Beijing 2022 (By WU Dayong, WANG Ziyan)

She recalled reading Han Meilin's stories and sketches about Fuwa at his Art Museum and buying Bing Dwen Dwen more than once (what an adorable smile! It's related to Pan Pan, the panda mascot at the 1990 Beijing Asian Games).

Mascots display in the museum

Seeing the plaque "Recognizing the Contribution of All Beijing People", she took pride that her college life was well spent in the capital city.

During 2008 Beijing Olympics, Belgian Jacques Rogge was the 8th IOC president. He was also the founder of the Youth Olympic Games. Ever since he took the presidency, he has supported Beijing's bid for the Olympics. When an American journalist asked him why Beijing, he replied cleverly, "The IOC wants the world's most populous country to host the Olympics." In his closing speech, Rogge praised the Beijing

Olympics as truly "unparalleled".

In 2017, the then IOC honorary president visited Hangzhou to give guidance on Zhejiang's sports undertakings and preparations for the Hangzhou Asian Games. Rogge also put forward a series of important reform ideas, such as anti-corruption, anti-doping, and event streamlining.

After Rogge, Bach was elected the 9th IOC president on September 16, 2013, becoming the first Olympic champion to take this position. He was a German fencer who won gold for the men's foil team at the 1976 Montreal Olympics and several world championships. At the Youth Olympic Games held in Nanjing, his selfies with athletes went viral, capturing the young generation's hearts.

The IOC's support for Beijing's hosting of the 2022 Winter Olympics with Bach as its soul has enabled Beijing to write history through extraordinary efforts, realize its commitment to bring 300 million people to participate in ice and snow sports, and become the first city to host both the Summer and Winter Olympics.

The plaque engraved with the words "2008, All Beijing People" and "2022, All Beijing People" recognizes the contribution of the Beijing people during the Summer and Winter Olympics

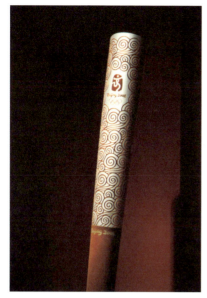

Torch of the 2008 Beijing Summer Olympics   Torch of the 2022 Beijing Winter Olympics

Despite the ravages of COVID-19, the IOC and Beijing delivered fantastic games. "The Beijing Winter Olympics showed that it is possible to organize a successful Olympic Games even under very difficult circumstances. It can transmit hope and confidence to all humanity." Bach praised the event as "extraordinary" and "unparalleled". At the closing ceremony, Bach said "Thank you, China" in Chinese. In a congratulatory video speech on the first anniversary, he again gave Beijing credit for "opening a new era of global ice and snow sports".

On his third visit to Hangzhou on May 9, 2023, the president showed again his belief that Hangzhou Asian Games would be very successful!

Cultural Exchange and Translation

When the girl was about to leave, she came to the marble column in front of the museum, walked past two pillars engraved with the times and cities of the previous Summer Olympics and Winter Olympics, and

Olympic Museum

then looked at the names of the IOC presidents on the other pillar. "They are the 'steersmen' of the modern Olympic movement!" The girl thought. She then noticed that by the burning flame on the square stood a lady with short hair and a familiar face. It was Eva Lüdi Kong.

Eva came from her home in Biel, the German-speaking part of Switzerland. The girl learned about her achievements in the translation of famous books and cultural exchanges from a book club and wrote an email to her. It was a surprise that Eva showed up.

Like the masterpiece *Journey to the West*, which she translated, Eva's life has been somewhat legendary. She began studying Chinese at the age of 14 and then lived in Hangzhou for 25 years, receiving a bachelor degree in printmaking at the China Academy of Art and a master degree in Chinese at Zhejiang University. Later, in addition to lecturing and researching, she spent more than a decade translating *Journey to the West*. It was the first cover-to-cover

The German version of "*Journey to the West*"

216

A sculpture behind the Olympic Museum

A burning flame on the square in front of the Olympic Museum

German version, published by the well-known German publisher Reclam, reprinted many times, and won the translation prize at the 13th Leipzig Book Fair.

"How was your visit?"

"Epic!"

The dialogue between Eva and the girl started spontaneously in Chinese. The context was organically generated and flowing. As the sky grew darker, the burning flame illuminated the museum's white marble parapet as well as a wise, middle-aged face and a pair of young, radiant eyes.

The girl said that she needed to practice French so that she comd interpret Annie Ernaux's Nobel Prize-winning *The Years* to Chinese readers and become a qualified volunteer for the 2024 Paris Olympics. Eva said that practice takes time. In *Journey to the West*, Tang Sanzang and other characters had ordeals. So do normal people. Just do the right thing and believe in yourself.

Eva's presentation of the richness and diversity of *Journey to the West* won praise from the Leipzig Book Fair — "She not only translated one language into another but also built a bridge between the cliffs of different ways of thinking in different eras, which is the true meaning of world literature, a kind of literature from the world and for the world."

Since the revival of the Olympic Games, literary and artistic creations inspired by sports have become increasingly integrated into the quadrennial event, although twists and turns were seen in the earlier days. Architecture, sculpture, music, painting, and literature, as well as new technologies represented by artificial intelligence, make the occasion richer, younger, and more splendid.

All the creatures of this earth seek the highest good, what grows out of it will eventually realize virtue. If you want to understand which force determines the cycle of existence...

The girl recited a passage at the beginning of Eva's epic translation of *Journey to the West*. It uncannily fit their encounter. In fact, Eva always feels that, although she translated the book, the book also interpreted and fulfilled her.

"Feel free to send me emails. I may not check it frequently, but it's the way to reach me." Eva expressed her wish to keep in touch.

"May I experience more people, things, and events and grow myself into a bridge, a river, a memorial book, and a melting pot."

The girl hugged Eva and left Lausanne behind.

Sleepless in Jakarta

Somehow, Jakarta is the only foreign city that I have visited frequently in a short period of time. All my trips were for a pure and grand event.

As I traveled for business other than for leisure, my memories of the capital of Indonesia are mostly about the scent of the palm trees and tropical shrubs, the mist of water on the lenses, and the vehicles that perpetually congest the roads. The meeting place with the director of the closing ceremony of the 18th Jakarta-Palembang Asian Games, the rehearsal venue for the flag handover to Hangzhou, and the office building of the Indonesian Asian Games Organizing Committee formed a sector of all our activities.

Jakarta displayed at the opening ceremony of the 18th Asian Games

The sector absorbed the energy from conversations and communications and witnessed the moments when morning suns bid farewell to starry nights.

On that passionate night at Gelora Bung Karno Stadium, we were thrilled to be part of the large crowd, like a drop of water in the vast ocean.

The Opening and Closing Ceremony:
A Gorgeous Show Outside the "Coconut Shell"

Whether you were there or not, the president's way of entering was unexpected.

The opening video of the opening ceremony of the 18th Asian Games

The screen lit up. The spectators saw President Joko Widodo, who was planning to take a car from the presidential palace to downtown, switch to a motorcycle due to traffic jams. He went through the streets and alleys and let kids go first when passing a school. Then the video stopped, and the president appeared on a motorcycle. When the lights once again focused on his seat, he stood up and greeted the spectators. The stadium soon filled with laughter and applause.

The president did not seem to mind showing off his motorcycle stunt. It's impossible to come up with a better way to show the horrible traffic jam than this creative video. His ridicule of the "Most Congested City" was apparently well-received.

If you have been to Jakarta, you will understand what I mean. It is said that 10 million residents own some 9 million motorcycles and 3 million cars. If you consider the vehicles from other cities, at least there are 13 million motor vehicles! I was almost devastated when I got stuck in traffic at rush hour. Sitting by the street, I had an epiphany. It seemed that there was no traffic police, few cars changed lanes, and nobody was complaining. People were patient, and finally they would move a little.

Benedict Anderson, an expert on Southeast Asia, talked about riding a Vespa for field work in Jakarta in the 1960s in his book *A Life Beyond Boundaries*. The little motorcycle quickly navigated him around the neighborhoods of the small former colonial city in no time. More than half a century later, motorcycles still seem to be the magic tool for locals.

"Coconut shell" is an idiom that likens someone to a frog that lives under a coconut shell and believes the shell to be its entire world. For Anderson, a life beyond the coconut shell is his perspective of Southeast Asia and his academic research and intellectual journey. Therefore, when I use the "coconut shell" metaphor to describe the grand opening and closing ceremony of the Jakarta Asian Games in September 2018, the first thing that pops up in my mind is an "open" stage.

The event's theme song, *Meraih Bintang* (*Reach for the Stars*), was undoubtedly extraordinary. Asia saw its sweeping popularity.

When young Indonesian singer Via Vallen took the stage in a white suit embellished with flowers and a peacock, the atmosphere of the stadium was immediately ignited.

A gorgeous show outside the "coconut shell"

Everything that I have dreamed of
All the gold that I have longed for
Every goal that I've inclined to
This is the moment of truth

The stage behind Via Vallen presented the huge metal emblem of the 18th Asian Games, and she faced the area where Indonesian athletes gathered after the entrance ceremony and sang passionately to the spectators. The lyrics were a mix of English and Indonesian. The spectators and athletes were immediately evoked when the melody started.

Now the game is tight, get my focus right
One thing in mind, I'm a winner
I can't quit now
I reach for the stars

When the singer was arousing people's enthusiasm, the lyrics were the simplest. Everyone joined spontaneously, even if it was the first time for him or her to hear the song.

Yo yo ayo... yo ayo
Yo yo ayo... yo ayo
Yo yo ayo... yo ayo
Yo yo ayo... yo ayo

...

Don't let anyone shake your resolve
No matter how challenging, don't underestimate yourself
Grab the victory star

Athletes waved small flags, everyone couldn't help singing, including the president, who just showed off his motorcycle tricks and now waved arms from the left to right happily. The close-up of the president on the screen once again strengthened the atmosphere. It reminded me of the Queen's performances of *Bohemian Rhapsody* and *We Are the Champions* at London's Wembley Stadium decades ago, despite the differences.

There was a string of highlights of the opening and closing ceremony: the "Javanese show", as well as the cultural symbols of the

Sundanese, Madurese, and Malay, showing the splendid vitality of the "country of a thousand islands". The mingle of flying waterfalls and burning volcanoes at a certain viewpoint vividly portrayed the slogan of the 18th Asian Games: Energy of Asia!

"Javanese show"

"Images of Paradise" and Hangzhou's Eight-Minute Show

It is customary for the host city of the next Asian Games to stage a performance and receive the flag. After the spectacular eight-minute show to promote the Beijing Winter Olympics in Pyeongchang earlier in 2018, Hangzhou's stunning same-length presentation in Jakarta became the headline of almost all the media that night and the next day. Was it exactly eight minutes? Well, it's not important.

Expression is the art of time. People crave precision, but restrictions sometimes stimulate a stronger desire for expression. Not all the promotion videos of previous flag-receiving cities were watched globally in real time. But Hangzhou was confident it would be done. The extra three minutes brought infinite space and possibilities to the story-telling of paradise on earth.

"That's the window," we thought, "images of paradise."

We first had to find a way to narrate it so that it wasn't just a simple collection of photos and videos. So we thought about screenplays and films, trying to present incredible results with post-production techniques on a low budget.

Then we came up with an idea. A girl who wore jade, carrying a bow, and arrows from the ancient Liangzhu Period traveled thousands of years to today's Hangzhou, where the pleasant modern society and state-of-the-art facilities made her curious. In the end, she ran into the main stadium of the Hangzhou Asian Games, meeting another girl who looked exactly like herself. The girls disappeared, and then the "Big Lotus" and the emblem of the 19th Asian Games appeared and froze.

The promotional video, like an ink-wash painting, brings out the oriental spirit. Each frame of the image was beautiful, authentic, and powerful.

"Streamline it. Don't try to convey everything. Don't carry burdens as you move forward." A wise man instructed the team on video preparation.

"To reach an international audience, let the music and pictures speak for themselves. Keep the characters subtle." A leader of China's State General Administration of Sports also gave insightful guidance when the video was finalized in Jakarta.

Promotional video of Hangzhou

The performance, which began planning earlier than the promotional video, was in the good hands of Chen Weiya and other veterans in the opening and closing ceremonies of the 2008 Beijing Olympics and the 2010 Guangzhou Asian Games. In addition to the signature songs and dances of the southern Yangtze River Delta, the smart screens that moved horizontally and vertically were the brainchild of Chen Yan, the chief

Bridge (By CHANG Qing)

Lotus (By CHANG Qing)

artist of the Beijing Olympics. Another big surprise was Yi Yangqianxi, who appeared in a large international sports event for the first time.

In order to create a song that was appropriate for the flag handover ceremony and suitable for a young singer, composer Meng Ke studied the theme song of the 18th Asian Games thoroughly. In his opinion, the reason why the theme song was loved by Asian youth was because of its catchy rhythm and fashionable melody. It felt like reggae, combined the rhythms of Brazilian music and Indian music well, and sounded like Western pop

Smart screens at Hangzhou's eight-minute show (Designer: CHEN Yan)

Yi Yangqianxi singing *Longing* (lyricist: ZHU Hai, composer: MENG Ke)

music but with a strong Asian style, especially the chorus. Since Zhu Hai already wrote the lyrics, Meng Ke integrated the techniques and timbre of electronic music on the basis of the symphony, highlighting the eclectic coexistence of tradition and modernity and thus conveying the aspiration to move from a beautiful today to a vibrant tomorrow.

The girl rising from the high platform slowly poured a jug of water from the clay pot of Liangzhu, turning Jakarta's stadium into Hangzhou's West Lake. Jakarta and all of Asia cheered simultaneously. At the end of the performance, Hangzhou invited Asia and the world to participate in the 19th Asian Games. After the solemn national anthem of the People's Republic of China was played, the flag was handed over, and the torch of the first Asian Games, the flag of the first Asian Games, and the flag of the Olympic Council of Asia were taken to Hangzhou.

Hangzhou's eight-minute show

Chinese athletes at the closing ceremony

A Community of Imagination and Reality

As early as 1962, Jakarta hosted the 4th Asian Games. Vietnam was due to host the 18th Asian Games in Hanoi in November 2019 but backed out in 2014. In September 2014, the Olympic Council of Asia General Assembly approved Indonesia's bid to host the 18th Asian Games. Therefore, Jakarta-Palembang had quite a short time window, which naturally affected the opening and closing ceremonies that involved many matters.

Since the host usually makes strict restrictions on the venue of performances for the next host, the director team of the latter had to manage to make it work regardless of the facilities.

In the countdown days to the flag handover ceremony, the performance team was still only able to rehearse at a place far from the main stadium. Prior to that, although the two director teams met regularly, they were both vague, fearing that their creatives would be disclosed. So both sides were guessing what the other side was doing while doing their best for their own side.

Once the promotional video and the eight-minute show were presented, loud and long applauses in the Gelora Bung Karno Stadium proved a fact: it was ours party!

The sleepless night in Jakarta is a distant memory. Time flies, stars move, everything updates, Hangzhou will usher in another glorious Asian Games. I miss Jakarta badly: the sports posters, the mascots (Bird of Paradise, One-Horned Javan Rhino, and Bawean Deer) that dotted three special districts (Jakarta, Jogyakarta, and Nanggroe Aceh Darussalam), and the rupees that I was too busy to spend. I also miss the occupied night without hugs or farewells, the starry sky high above the main stadium, and the lonely long-haul flight.

The mascots of the 18th Asian Games

Is Jakarta still so congested and people so patient?

Weng Xuanxiao, an Indonesian girl studying in Henan, China, wished that high-speed trains could be available in Indonesia as well. The "Global Maritime Fulcrum" and "The Belt and Road Initiative" made her dream come true. In February 2017, she became an interpreter for the No.1 tunnel of the Jakarta-Bandung High-Speed Railway, a cooperation between China and Indonesia. In April 2023, 90% of the civil construction was done, all 13 tunnels were dug, and the track was laid.

I hear the theme song of the 18th Asian Games again:

Hold my hands and join in this grand event
Legends will continue to be recorded...

Messages from Bangkok

While doing art design for the latest issue of *Asian Sports* (June 2023, Issue 61), I met Mrs. Khunying Patama Leeswadtrakul. It has been a long while since we last met.

Patama chairs IOC Culture and Olympic Heritage Commission and the OCA Cultural Committee. On February 25, 2023, she attended the Olympic Day activity held by the Thai Olympic Committee in Chiang Rai, a small city in northern Thailand. Holding a starting gun and wearing sportswear, her eyes were playful, as a happy child. On March 8, The Bangkok Post announced her as the "Woman of the Year" in recognition of her business excellence and contribution to expanding Thailand's international reach. A different picture, the same smile. She is always elegant and vivacious.

Patama on the "Olympic Day"

Memory
All alone in the moonlight
I can smile at the old days

Ever since Patama performed *Memory*, the most well-known song from the Broadway musical *Cats*, in Bangkok on March 2019, I have seen her infinite possibilities. At this very moment, my memory flashed back to Bangkok in the spring of 2019 and even further to the longer history of Thailand's Olympic movement.

Bangkok in the Spring

Perhaps the first thing that comes to mind when people think of Bangkok is Thai massage, elephants, and the royal family that is constantly in the headlines. But once you set foot in the city, even if it is for a short stay, you will feel its unique vibe.

Streetscape of Bangkok

The commercial center is modern. The corridors between the malls remind me of the Wulin CBD in Hangzhou. It's not uncommon to find large malls at BTS (Skytrain) stations. Shopping is encouraged anytime, anywhere.

Bangkok is also full of human interests. Food stalls at night are bustling. People indulge themselves in seafood or liquors and chat loudly with friends or even strangers, toasting the short night away.

Temples are also convergences of spiritual pursuits and earthly prayers. Although people are told that the sensory world is an illusion, they still wish for such as "prosperous business" "career promotion" "high score in examination" "good luck" , etc.

Thailand, back in history known as "Siam", is the only country in Southeast Asia that has not been colonized. It began to open up to the outside world and carry out social reforms at the end of the 19th century, changed its autocratic monarchy to a constitutional monarchy in June 1932, and was officially named "Thailand" in 1949. Bangkok is the only provincial-level municipality among the 77 "provinces" in Thailand's five regions. Bangkok is sitting on the east bank of the Chao Phraya River and bordering the Gulf of

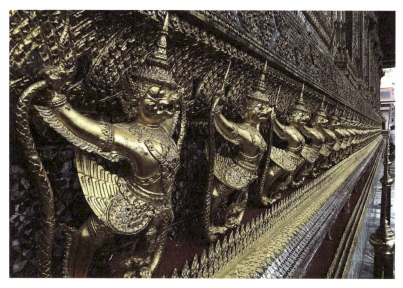

A corner of the Grand Palace

Siam to the south, the military, royal family, big business and a large middle class (ethnic Chinese make up a large proportion) gathering here.

When the 38th OCA General Assembly was held in Bangkok, the Hangzhou Asian Games Organizing Committee made a presentation on the preparations for the Games. Venue construction, competition events, news propaganda, public participation, and market development all became hot topics.

Outside the meeting room, the tropical monsoon blows and palm trees sway in the unique atmosphere of this big Southeast Asian city.

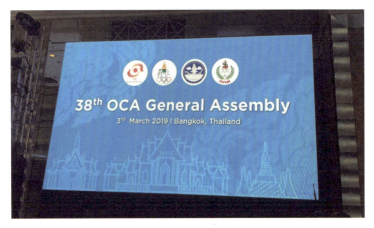

The 38th OCA General Assembly

Bangkok's green plants

I went to Rajamangala National Stadium to watch a major sports event. I wore short sleeves on that spring day and felt how strong the sun was.

At the Suphachalasai Stadium, the continuous planning and holding of public activities such as "Olympic Day" kept the old structure exuding a charm of spring.

Rajamangala National Stadium

Suphachalasai Stadium

The One and the Only

Bangkok is still at the top of the Asian Games cities list.

From 1966 to 1998, Bangkok hosted four Games — the first three were staged when the Asian Games were still in their infancy.

In 1966, Bangkok, which first bid to host the Asian Games (the 5th Asian Games), did not have any competitors. The infrastructure built by the government underpinned a successful event. After that, Bangkok hosted the 6th Asian Games in 1970 and the 8th Asian Games in 1978, since South Korea and Pakistan backed out due to financial difficulties. In 1998, Bangkok, which had accumulated rich experience hosting the Games, won the right to host the 13th Asian Games.

In the history of the Asian Games, Jakarta was also asked to host when another country quit in the preparation stage. Bangkok's contribution is evident: it dared to take on the challenge, and avoided the disruption that the Asian Games might have experienced in their early days. By the way, the simplest and most straightforward proof of Bangkok's success in every Asian Games is the presence of the King of Thailand at all four sessions.

Usually, if a country has won the right to host the Asian Games multiple times, it will consider placing the event in different cities to drive infrastructure construction and economic development. For example, South Korea used Seoul, Busan, and Incheon respectively as the hosts. Indonesia added Palembang as a co-host for Jakarta when it hosted for the second time (the 18th Asian Games). Bangkok is an exception, perhaps because in the early days, the organizer had neither time nor conditions to think as much, or perhaps the OCA and the Thai government had a fondness for Bangkok.

Completed in 1935, the Suphachalasai Stadium (also known as the National Stadium) was the main venue for the first three Asian Games. By the time of the 13th Asian Games in 1998, Rajamangala National Stadium was built and ready to serve.

Bangkok also made a significant contribution to the aesthetics of the Asian Games. Taking the design of the main visual identity as an example, the emblems of the 5th and 6th sessions marked the venue, the number of sessions, OCA's sun, and the slogan "Ever Onward". The emblem of the 8th session added some more Thai elements. Two patterns that resemble arms and Thailand's national bird, the Siamese fireback, embrace the sun, showing the spirit of Thai culture while highlighting the vitality of the Asian Games. The emblem of the 13th Asian Games used the spire of the stupa, a symbol of Thai Buddhist culture, to form an "A" shape representing Asia. Together with the sun above, it expressed the vision of "Asia as a Family".

The emblem of   The emblem of   The emblem of
the 5th Asian Games   the 6th Asian Games   the 8th Asian Games

The mascot was an elephant, one of the signatures of Thailand. Interestingly, its name, Chai-yo, happens to be a local exclamation for joy, happiness, and victory. The slogans of the four sessions, from "light" to "sportsmanship" and "friendship without borders", convey Thailand's good wishes for the ever-evolving Asian Games.

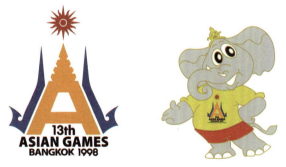

The emblem and mascot of the 13th Asian Games

The 13th Asian Games inevitably suffered from the financial crisis that swept Asia in 1997. Thanks to the blessings of the optimistic Chai-yo and, of course, the benefits brought by the Asian Games, the Thai economy began to recover in 1999. In July 2003, it paid off the loan provided by the International Monetary Fund during the crisis in advance.

I Was Beautiful Then

I was beautiful then
I remember
The time I knew what happiness was
Let the memory live again...

On that spring night in 2019, Patama's singing was mesmerizing. Despite lowering the pitch, she successfully sang this difficult song with the best emotions and skills. Equally excellent was the Royal Band. While Patama was performing, two young female singers were singing and dancing on the makeshift stage, switching between Thai and English lyrics.

With the exception of Patama's costume (probably because she is an advocate of Thai silk), the whole scene was quite Western.

Thai culture was once Americanized, but with the rise of national power, Thailand has emphasized its own identity while being international. When ethnic Chinese Queen Suthida attended the British King Charles' coronation, she was wearing Thai costumes (with modern fashion elements). Sometimes she wears Chinese cheongsam.

Bangkok is where diversified cultures meet.

The film *Tropical Malady*, directed by Apichatpong Weerasethakul, a well-known Thai independent director, screenwriter, and producer, is a great example of such a cultural collision. Apichatpong's *Uncle Boonmee Who Can Recall His Past Lives* won the Palme d'Or at the 63rd Cannes International

Film Festival. *Tropical Malady* was shot even before Ang Lee's *Brokeback Mountain*. The director used the metaphors of "turning a man into a tiger" and "jungle tiger" to narrate soulmates and a destined separation in a subtle and mythical way. Since it was about same-sex love, it was only screened in three theaters in Bangkok for a week. The film's enormous international fame contrasted sharply with the low viewership in Bangkok, and even the reactions in rural and small towns and Bangkok were completely different.

The royal family theoretically represents the "orthodoxy" of Thai culture. Rumors and news about the royal family tend to trend on social media, and some can be rather bizarre. Yet Princess Sirindhorn has always been liked and respected. She is proficient in many languages, loves oriental culture, and has visited China 50 times to promote cultural exchanges between the two countries.

Princess Sirindhorn is an old friend of the famous artist Han Meilin and his wife, Zhou Jianping. During her visit to China in April 2018, the Han Meilin Art Museum in Beijing was one of her stops. Touched by Mr. Han's brilliant artworks and the profound cultural traditions, she gladly wrote the four characters "Rooted in Fertile Soil" in the studio, and then Mr. Han completed her calligraphy with Chinese seals. She also sent one of her Chinese books to Mrs. Zhou. In January 2020, she visited Mr. Han's exhibition in Thailand and took a group photo with his team. It was the beginning of the COVID-19, and the head of the Tourism Authority of Thailand gave Mr. Han more than 300 masks before he flew back to China. Those gifts were more precious than gold.

In April 2018, Princess Sirindhorn went to the Three-Su Memorial Hall and Three-Su Ancestral Hall in Meishan, Sichuan Province, and wrote "The Su Family has Talents" in Chinese to pay homage to Su Shi, the great writer of the Song Dynasty. Su Shi was the "mayor" of Hangzhou, and the princess visited Zhejiang several times. What a lovely coincidence.

I didn't look up the exact age of Princess Sirindhorn, but Han Meilin, in his 80s, joked that he is a "young man born in the 1980s". In the film *Youth*, there is a line saying, "A generation's youthful days have completely gone. Although they talk and laugh as before, it is not difficult to see the changes that the years have brought to everyone." How insightful yet sad.

And they, and the singing lady, and many people like them, may have experienced all the vicissitudes, but they are still glowing.

When the dawn comes
Tonight will be a memory too
And a new day will begin

The 42nd OCA General Assembly

On July 8, 2023, at the 42nd OCA General Assembly in Bangkok, the Hangzhou Asian Games Organizing Committee made a report that Harbin has won the bid to host the 9th Asian Winter Games in 2025, and the OCA Outstanding Contribution Awards were conferred.

Manila in Camera

Manila is far away, like the youthful years of movie stars in Wong Kar-wai's *Days of Being Wild.* Manila is close, like a coconut just picked and exported.

Manila is simple yet colorful. The black-and-white video shot by Japan's NHK at the 2nd Asian Games in 1954 and the gold medal for Men's Water Polo displayed in the National Museum of Singapore tell vivid stories since the launch of the Far Eastern Championship Games in Manila, a "coconut city".

Streetscape of Manila

Seaside

The cockfighting traditions, the modern advertisements, the ancient monuments, and the romantic coast—what a hectic place.

Some flock to Manila, and some can't wait to leave. In *Days of Being Wild,* Yuddy was trying to find out his real mother, and Tide was a ship crew member, and their stories continued in the Philippines. Filipino women, on the other hand, are living drastically different lives across the world.

Exterior Scenes in
Days of Being Wild and Manila Scenarios

From November 28 to December 5, 1989, film director Wong Kar-wai, who always wore sunglasses and often treated actors toughly, spent 8 crazy days in Manila with Hong Kong superstars such as Leslie Cheung, Andy Lau, and the production team of *Days of Being Wild.*

Yuddy is the main role. He had a famous line "I've heard that there's a kind of bird without legs that can only fly and fly and sleep in the wind

244

Aerial view of Manila

when it is tired." When loved by both the docile So Lai Chun and the less dignified dancer Mimi, he remained unmoved. Because the spell of fate has long foreshadowed that "The bird only lands once in its life. That's when he dies".

Scenes in the movie resonate well with dreamlike Manila.

"The air in Manila is sluggish than in Hong Kong, making people tired easily."

But this was only the feeling of the production team when it arrived. Shooting in Manila was different. The crowd was so attracted by the cast and crew that it turned into a carnival.

It is said that in the Philippines, theatergoing was once the cheapest pastime, so Filipinos developed the habit of watching movies, and there were many theaters. As time goes on, consumer goods and real estate advertisements presented by nice-looking men and women have become a new sight on the streets of Manila. New entertainment, such as KTV and bars, is the natural extension of the watching and acting tradition. Barbands are not only important cultural exports but also the way of life for some breadwinners.

In the movie, Yuddy, the illegitimate son of a Filipino noblewoman, was raised by his adoptive mother, who was a dancer. The adoptive mother did not tell him who her biological mother was until much later because she was afraid of losing him, so he was a spiritual orphan. It was not easy to find his biological mother. When he finally arrived at Villa Escudero, she refused to meet him due to her high social status.

In a large coconut forest, Yuddy walked on a path that seemed to have no end, leaving his helpless but resolute back only. "I just want to see her face. Since she didn't give me a chance, I won't give her a chance." After the monologue, the director showed the audience a panoramic view in slow motion, indicating that Yuddy's self-redemption was not successful and he was completely lost.

The Philippines is the "Land of Coconuts", and Manila is home to numerous tropical coconut palms. Coconut is the fruit of survival, nourishing the body and repairing wounds. In the movie, Yuddy's heart was bleeding, his wounds were mercilessly torn, and his hope for more than 20 years was just an empty dream. Wong Kar-wai set Yuddy's "broken dreams" and "dead heart" in "a state of hope", but after all, Yuddy was a legless bird—he could not make it.

Trees and fruits

Tide, who worked as a ship crew in the Philippines, came across the heartbroken Yuddy next to a 19th-century building. The director did not show a full picture of the ancient building. Instead, he presented horse-drawn carriages, stairs, and shaky close-ups of western wrought iron windows.

In Manila, there are quite a few such historic buildings, especially churches, reflecting the Philippines' long history of colonization by Spain and the United States.

And that encounter allowed Tide to witness how the fate of Yuddy took a sharp turn. Because of a fake passport, Yuddy fought and stabbed someone with a knife. Former policeman Tide helped him and took him to board a train. The injured Tide blamed Yuddy for being reckless. Yuddy was so indifferent that the two argued, and Tide left angrily. When he returned, Yuddy had already been shot dead.

Yuddy's sad and pale face, Tide's helpless pain, and the dense rainforest and large coconut groves all moved hazily. Knowing that the audience would not accept what happened to Yuddy, the director treated this orphan's death with a dash of hope: he was finally free and perhaps would be reborn. Everyone could be Yuddy, everyone could be a legless bird.

The plots of *Days of Being Wild* and Wong Kar-wai's unique aesthetic style make it impossible for the movie to fully tap what Manila has to offer. Tutuban Train Station, built in 1832, was quite abandoned when the movie was shot. But with the completion of the first phase of the Clark section of the Philippine National Railways in 2022, it restored its vitality. More convenient transportation makes it possible for people to enjoy the unique customs of the Philippines, such as the Water Buffalo Festival, Nipa hut, and Luzon tobacco leaves, on a high-speed train. The nationwide cockfighting fever has also been upgraded to an international derby. The most aggressive cock from a foreign country could become a superstar in Manila.

Timeline

Before going through the major events in sports development in the Philippines, there is a time that needs to be mentioned that is not only epoch-making in world navigation but also related to the destiny of the Philippines.

In March, 1521, Magellan led a Spanish expedition (Moluccas) to the Philippine Islands, becoming the first to extend the seafaring record from the Americas to Asia. Magellan spent some time in Cebu (now the second-largest city in the Philippines), a trading hub in the southern part of the archipelago. The crew traded glass beads and mirrors in exchange for gold, while he himself socialized with King Humabon of Cebu and spared no effort to spread Catholicism. He was assassinated on April 27 while attacking Mactan Island, ending his ambitious adventure and conquest.

Spain then gradually invaded the Philippines and began its rule, which lasted for more than 300 years. The Philippines declared independence and became a republic in 1898, but was soon occupied by the United States and Japan until it regained independence on July 4, 1946.

The first Far Eastern Championship Games, staged in Manila in 1913, was a regional international competition initiated by the Philippines, China and Japan. As the predecessor of the Asian Games, it was the world's first continent-wide international competition, held 10 sessions from 1913 to 1934. In those 10 games, Chinese men won the championship in football 9 times.

From May 1 to 9, 1954, the 2nd Asian Games was held at the Rizal Memorial Sports Complex (RMSC) in Manila. About 1,000 athletes from 18 countries competed in 8 sports and 76 events.

RMSC, located on the site of the Manila Carnival Grounds, is also known as the Philippine National Stadium and is named in honor of the national hero Jose Rizal. Built in 1927 and inaugurated in 1934 at the Far

East Championship Games, it can accommodate 30,000 people.

Like other stadiums, it has been opened to the public, hosted concerts, etc. At one point, it was almost sold and rebuilt, but it was preserved due to fierce opposition and declared a National Historic Landmark. It was renovated to get ready for the Southeast Asian Games, and then used for local and international sporting events. During the COVID-19, it was converted into a quarantine facility to house patients with mild symptoms from the Philippine General Hospital.

Visual design was still in its infancy at the 1954 Manila Asian Games, so the emblem followed the style of the first Asian Games in New Delhi, and the mascot was not yet on the agenda. However, this session had its stamps and postcards. The blue, 5 centavos, is for discus. The green, 18 centavos, is for swimming. The pink, 30 centavos, is for boxing. These 3 stamps stay on the upper right of the postcard. The left side of the postcard is filled with high and dense flags, a diver, and buildings. In the lower center of the postcard stands a male athlete holding the torch high in his right hand.

The emblem, stamps, and postcard of the 1954 Manila Asian Games

The gold medal from the 1954 Manila Asian Games can be seen at the National Museum of Singapore. It was also Singapore's only gold medal at that session, won by the men's water polo team.

The Philippines, as the host, jumped from 4th in the medal table in the previous Asian Games to 2nd in 1954. Filipino athlete Haydee Coloso Espino, who was just 16 years old, rose to fame after beating 2 Japanese to win the 100-meter freestyle. That was a good start. Later, she won many medals in international competitions and became known as "Asia's Swim Queen".

The gold medal of the 1954 Manila Asian Games

Among the athletes who had attracted much attention at the Manila Asian Games was Nambu Atsuko from Japan, a winner of the 100-meter women's race. She was dubbed the "Sweetheart of the Games" for her "humble" interactions with the local fans.

NHK captured the Hong Kong team's entrance into the stadium in the opening video. Wong Kar-wai stated during the filming of *In the Mood for Love* and *2046*, both the *Days of Being Wild* sequels, that the music in the movies was greatly influenced by Spanish or Latin American music because most musicians in Hong Kong at the time were from the Philippines.

Jose Rizal opened an eye hospital in Hong Kong's Central before moving back to the Philippines. To this day, the commemorative plaque erected at Rizal House can be seen.

The business card used by Dr. Rizal in Hong Kong

A commemorative plaque at the former residence of Dr. Rizal

At the 2020 Tokyo Olympics (the 32nd Summer Olympics held in 2021), female athlete Diaz won the final of the weightlifting 55kg category, securing the first gold medal for the Philippines and ending the country's 97-year "gold medal drought".

City Women and Country Men

"You need a vacation — a really good vacation — to enter a new world. You once had such a dream, and we can quickly make it come true."

This was an ad in a Manila magazine, trying to use rose-colored romance to recruit Filipino women to work in Japan.

Women from Manila or elsewhere in the Philippines, married or single, constantly leave their country and then send their hard-earned money home. Coping with unemployment, making more money, getting out of trouble, seeking development, and perhaps fantasies of living abroad make it possible and necessary for them to fly away. Fluent in English, many college-educated, they work in different or roughly the same jobs in different countries. They are often referred to collectively as "Filipino maids", though sociologists prefer the term "female migrant workers".

Probably Filipino women have set foot in as many cities as possible in the world. Their contribution to the country's economy has made them uncrowned "heroes".

In his play, *A Doll's House,* the Norwegian playwright Ibsen effectively revealed the conflicts between patriarchal society and women's liberation, and the play ended with the awakening and angry departure of the heroine Nora. If Ibsen's focus was to inspire women to fight for freedom and equality, then Lu Xun put forward a more serious question, "what happens after Nora walks out?"

A dock where life stories unfold

How are "heroes" made? How far can they go across national borders and gender barriers?

Most of the families who have hired Filipino maids have a positive comment on their professionalism and ethics, and they pay a salary that is relatively higher than that of local nannies or other foreign nannies.

The bargaining finesse with employers on matters such as salary and holidays is inseparable from the organized services of Filipino maids. The realization of such rights, in turn, fosters a culture of "reunification".

Taking off their work clothes, applying lipstick, moving from the employer's home to the public area, meeting with friends for a short time, eating hometown food, consuming moderately when happy, and letting go of themselves — such good times would be the "medals" awarded to themselves by Filipino maids, which are the bright colors of their life on the edge of the city.

They run away, they get rich, and then they Went home. Ibsen and Lu Xun seem to have only predicted half right.

These breadwinners have changed their roles. They are able to support their parents, sponsor their siblings' education, or use their own money to hire servants for their families so that they can continue to live and work in other cities for a longer period of time. Some foreign maids became foreign brides.

Growth varies widely

Assuming that there is an ideal family model, it is difficult to say whether this is a success. Everyone has a long story to tell. Anyway, they move forward and make something happen.

The Laughter of My Father is a novel written by Filipino writer Carlos Bulosan based on his personal experience in the countryside. Set in a disaster-ridden village in Luzon, the author wrote about the 9 members of the family from a first-person perspective. Dad is a master cock fighter and a male chauvinist. Mom is a professional mourner who punches her husband when she is angry. The eldest brother, returning from the battlefield, has become a gloomy alcoholic.

The Laughter of My Father

The second brother steals things at home; the third brother is a nerd. The fourth brother wants to get married and has children at the age of 12... And the protagonist himself drinks spirits at the age of 5. "Our family is a little weird, but thankfully we still have each other. Every day, the whole family laughs," Carlos further concluded, "laughter is the only treasure of our family."

The novel is witty, occasionally sarcastic, and it was rated by The New Yorker as a hilarious "Filipino Story". Although it is a story of the author's hometown, it portrays the general life of Filipino farmers.

The dream of going abroad in search of a better life is deeply rooted in the cultural and historical context of the Philippines. In the novel, as the protagonist grew up, he was passively "blind dated" while being quietly arranged by his dad to go abroad. "We only live once." Dad said. So, dad wants his son to "go and see what everyone else in the world is doing".

In the Philippines, patriarchy restricts women's participation in the local labor market while retaining their place in the global labor market. Women have even more access to overseas jobs than their husbands.

Is this a paradoxical reality or the soil of dreams?

Dream of the sea

A Tale of Three Cities

1981 was an extraordinary year for Seoul, the capital of South Korea. After being granted the right to host the 24th Olympics in 1988 by the International Olympic Committee (IOC) in September, the hosting of the 10th Asian Games in 1986 was awarded to the city in November without competitors.

After 21 century, South Korea has hosted the 2002 Busan Asian Games, the 2014 Incheon Asian Games, the 2002 Korea-Japan FIFA World Cup, and more recently, the 2018 Pyeongchang Winter Olympics.

Rear view of a South Korean woman

Memorial of the historic site of the South Korean provisional government in Hangzhou

Immediately following the Seoul Asian Games, Beijing hosted the 11th Asian Games in 1990, and China was resonating with the theme song *Asian Mighty Winds*. At the closing ceremony of the 16th Asian Games in Guangzhou in 2010, Incheon was ready to host the next session.

At the 2018 Pyeongchang Winter Olympics, the stunning Beijing eight-minute show was a prelude to the 2022 Beijing Winter Olympics. At the 19th Hangzhou Asian Games, which will be inaugurated at the autumn equinox in 2023, the South Korean sports delegation will gather Hangzhou together with other members of the Olympic Council of Asia (OCA).

The two neighbors, with shared cultures, are writing splendid chapters in the history of sports.

Seoul: The Leap

Perhaps because Seoul has hosted the Asian Games and the Olympics back-to-back in just two years, or perhaps because the influence of the Olympics was far greater than that of the Asian Games, when asked about the Seoul Asian Games, those who have not experienced them do not seem to have a particularly deep memory. "I was still in school at the time," Sha Tong, the ambassador of the Hangzhou Asian Games and a well-known CCTV presenter, recalled, "I remember more about my work during the Busan and Incheon Asian Games."

Blue House

Seoul Station

We all remember the theme song of the Seoul Olympics, the melodic and majestic *Hand in Hand*, which Samaranch, then IOC President, suggested as the permanent anthem of the Olympics.

See the fire in the sky
We feel the beating of our hearts together
This is our time to rise above
We know the chance is here to live forever
For all time

...

Hand in hand we stand
All across the land
We can make this world a better place in which to live

...

The song was translated into Chinese and sung by Alan Tam, a Chinese pop singer. I still remember listening to his tape again and again. The ending sentence was "heart and hand connected", while it was "Arirang" in Korean and "Hand in hand" in Chinese. What a beautiful translation. When brainstorming the slogan for the Hangzhou Asian Games, "Hand in Hand, @Future" was proposed. The leaders of the organizing committee decided to go beyond the Seoul Olympics, so it was changed to "Heart to Heart, @Future".

At the Seoul Asian Games, water was the key element of the emblem. Three overlapping water droplets and the OCA's sun indicated not only the fact that South Korea was sea-enveloped but also the close unity of Asia. That year, South Korea ranked second in the medal table with an advantage far ahead of Japan, and China once again topped Asian sports with the most gold medals. It consolidated the "top-three" pattern of China, Japan, and South Korea. Chinese gymnast Li Ning, who won four golds, was the athlete with the most gold medals in that Asian Games.

Many lessons and experiences learned at the 1986 Seoul Asian Games proved useful at the 1988 Seoul Olympics, such as traffic and interpretation. Some of the legacies of the Asian Games was redeveloped and utilized at the Olympics as well. The same mascot for these two events was a typical example.

In South Korea, the tiger is extremely precious and is officially called "the Korean tiger". In the two events, a cute tai-chi tiger named "Hodori" was chosen as the mascot, which was brave, friendly, and peppy.

The emblem and mascot of the Seoul Asian Games

In terms of events and broader cultural expressions, Koreans wanted to show their individuality on one hand. But on the other hand, they were deeply attached to the traditional Chinese culture — so much, so that with an ambivalent and complex mindset, sometimes they can't even tell which parts are purely Korean. "Tai-chi" and its imagery were both used as the name of the Olympic mascot and had morphed into the three primary colors in the emblem. The Chinese first proposed "yin", "yang", and the "eight diagrams"(ba-gua) in *The Book of Changes*, yet I am wondering how Koreans would now interpret them.

Tai-chi, or "Grand Unity", describes the time when heaven and earth were still one. Then it split into "yin" and "yang", thus heaven and earth were separated. All things in heaven and earth, either of "yin" or "yang", exist in concord to make this world so harmonious. You can take just one step out of a small circle, yet the whole universe can be wrapped up in a big one.

The three swirling stripes in the emblem of the Seoul Olympics represented the harmony of heaven, earth, and people. The inward unity and outward movement indicated that athletes from five continents came together for mutual understanding and progress through practicing the Olympic spirit. The medals look still Greek-like – with a goddess of victory holding a

The emblem of the Seoul Olympics

winner's crown in her hand on the front side, and a dove, the symbol of peace, holding a laurel branch in its mouth on the back.

At the Seoul Olympics, the host country ranked fourth with 12 gold, 10 silver, and 11 bronze medals, harvesting a promoted international image and a record high in sports as well.

The Korean economy, which started recovering in the 1960s, has witnessed sustained and rapid growth since the 1970s and peaked at the end of the 20th century, thus creating the "Miracle of the Han River" in economic history. From the Asian Games to the Olympics, Seoul

Insa-dong, Seoul

Cheonggyecheon River, Seoul

saw such a leap against such a solid background. A large number of infrastructures, such as the Jamsil Sports Complex (the main stadium of the Seoul Olympics), were built, and traffic congestion was solved. In addition, the Seoul Olympics were like a coming-of-age ceremony, showcasing the country's strength, promoting large corporations such as Samsung and Hyundai, and elevating South Korea's international status to an unprecedented level.

Busan: The Signature

In the movie *Decision to Leave,* starring Tang Wei and Park Hae-il, there is a dialogue:

Confucius said, "The benevolent enjoy the mountain, the wise enjoy the water." I'm not benevolent, I love the sea.

It is said that this was a line tailored for Tang Wei by director Park Chan-wook and screenwriters. I guess it's true, when I heard the heroine Song Seorae said that to Jang Hae-joon, a detective.

The mountain fog and sea waves around the hero and heroine, the warm-colored shirts, the sea-scene decorated walls, the heroine who committed suicide in the sea to destroy and redeem herself...

In the movie, conflicts and plots unfold at sea.

In sports, the image of water is used repeatedly.

Busan is one of South Korea's six metropolitan cities and a major port. As the second South Korean city to host the Asian Games, Busan put tai-chi, waves, and matching tiles in the emblem of the 14th Asian Games in 2002. Its mascot, "DURIA", a flying seagull painted with cute lines and ink, was coherent with the spirit of "community" "hope and transcendence" in the Seoul Asian Games and the Olympics.

The emblem and mascot of the Busan Asian Games

At the opening ceremony on September 29, 2002, North Korean female footballer Ri Chong-hui and South Korean handball player Hwangbo Sung-il held the flag of the Korean Peninsula and led 800 members of the delegations of the two countries into the stadium. This was the first time in the history of the Asian Games that all 44 OCA members participated. The North and South Korean athletes entering the venue together were praised far and wide. More than 7500 athletes from 44 countries and regions participated in over 400 competitions in 38 categories, it was the largest of any Asian Games.

The slogan "One Asia, Global Busan" revealed the dream of Asia and the ambition of Busan.

263

Sha Tong, who was a student at the time of the Seoul Asian Games, had become an excellent presenter of the CCTV Sports Channel during the Busan Asian Games. After 21 years, he still has vivid memories.

"We had an easy time during the Busan Asian Games. Chinese sports were in a stage of rapid development, especially after we hosted the 1990 Beijing Asian Games. We launched a show in which we talked with world champions and Olympic champions such as Ma Yanhong, Zhan Xugang, Wang Tao, etc. We talked about things at the sports venue and funny anecdotes in Busan for 60 minutes every day. It was the end of the reporting. Every day we were extremely happy."

The "happiness" that Sha Tong said was naturally inseparable from the exciting results of the competition, which made exhilarated journalists very careful all the time.

"The medals showered." Sha Tong's expression was humorous and genuine, "We did not have to look at the medal tally, China was definitely No.1. But we needed to count the gold medals to avoid mistakes. Because it took time to prepare the subtitles and captions, like 30 minutes before we went live. When the audience saw it, we might already have new medals! We were both happy and nervous. We wanted to announce accurate information. Self-media was not as developed as it is today, so it was difficult to update in real-time."

It was also the only Asian Games for Luo Xuejuan, the great swimmer. She secured two gold medals at the FINA World Championships in Fukuoka, Japan, in the previous year. So, she was a leader in Chinese swimming team and won three gold medals as an individual and as a member of the relay at Busan.

"There were six days of competition, and in three or four days we met and exceeded the goals. The result was very beautiful and completely beyond expectation."

What made Luo even more proud was that young players had

emerged and withstood tests and challenges in the competition. At the 14th Asian Games, the Chinese delegation won "first place in Asia" for the sixth consecutive time with an impressive result, achieving the goal of testing the team and bringing home more gold medals. "Asia may be too small for China." The South Korean press pointed out.

To show respect and praise for gold medalists, the award ceremony of the Busan Asian Games took the initiative to award bronze first, then silver, and finally gold, which was opposite from previous procedures.

In addition to the Asian Games, Busan is a witness to frequent award ceremonies at the annual Busan Film Festival. Founded in 1996, the event is one of the most important film festivals in South Korea and Asia. Besides advocating new works and new professionals, it is also committed to promoting cultural exchanges between North and South Korea, and making every effort to present Asian films to the world.

It is worth mentioning a sci-fi blockbuster, *Train to Busan*. The movie is not about Busan itself but about a high-speed train to the city from Seoul. Portraying complicated human nature in the face of horrible

A view of Busan

disaster and death, it has won more than 30 nominations and awards at the Asian Film Awards, the Fantasia International Film Festival, etc.

Like the Cannes Film Festival, the Busan Film Festival was established first and foremost as a platform to attract outstanding filmmakers and their works and select the best ones. Busan's true ambition is to go global, and the same is true in the field of literature. Ae-ran Kim, a Korean female writer born in the 1980s, had a huge fan base even before her complete works were translated into Chinese. I believe that her works will one day be adapted and made into films. She is also an outstanding writer whom Koreans expect to gain world fame.

The benevolent enjoy the mountain, and the wise enjoy the water. Culture and sports are both signatures of Busan that shine brightly.

Incheon: The Aspiration

Incheon, South Korea's third city to host the Asian Games, is 80 kilometers west of Seoul. Like Busan, Incheon is a metropolitan city with a beautiful port as well as an important international airport.

Our attention to Incheon began with repeatedly watching the "Incheon eight-minute show" at the closing ceremony of the Guangzhou Asian Games. At that time, we constantly learned from such materials to prepare ourselves for the flag-receiving ceremony at the Jakarta Asian Games.

"The opening and closing ceremonies were the most memorable parts of the Incheon Asian Games." As Sha Tong continued to recall, his focus seemed to temporarily divert from reporting from Busan. "There was not much history to express. People were dancing and singing. Lots of colorful groups. That was a typical Korean culture."

We didn't say "boys group" or "girls group", on one hand, maybe because of age, and on the other hand, because we couldn't remember the exact names.

A view of Incheon

Water dropped, drums played, fans swayed, taekwondo performed...
The first half of the eight-minute show was lively and full. This was followed
by a seven-man group led by Korean super idol Jung Ji Hoon (Rain), who
sang and danced so passionately that the spectators moved their bodies
spontaneously. The eight screens showed the emblem, the tai-chi symbol, and
the word "rock" along with the rhythm. Then, the lights were dimmed for a
few seconds, and everything slowed down, OCA member flags were flying,
and Rain's voice came surreally from the deep sky:

*When you are frustrated and your hopes are dashed, when you don't
have friends around, I am your friend forever, don't forget. I can do my
best for you, you can count on me, I will come to you and be with you,
because I am your friend.*

*When worry slowly turns into pain, when pain slowly turns into
loneliness, when all efforts are wasted, when you stumble along the way
and need support, think of me.*

Rain led the children in national costumes to perform the theme song *I'm with You*. Compared with the traditional "Arirang" things in the previous Games, it was more of a song for the globe. The mascots, "Wind", "Dance" and "Light" (three seals from Baengnyeong Island), were flying, the emblem was displayed again, and the last image, "Incheon 2014", issued a sincere invitation to the OCA members.

The emblem and mascots of the Incheon Asian Games

Yet Sha Tong did not specifically describe the details of the opening and closing ceremonies of the Incheon Asian Games. The most impressive part for him was still closely related to his work.

"I don't idolize celebrities, and neither does Zhang Bin (famous CCTV presenter). But if you don't know it, you can't make an accurate introduction. So, the moment we received the program plan, we turned to editors of Chinese pop music websites and asked them to provide some information. Then we prepared some proper and short narratives to encourage people to listen to the music."

"What was the reaction of the fans?"

"Passionate but also nit-picking. For example, there was an idol group whose name has a letter 'g'. I pronounced the 'g' according to the International Phonetic Alphabet, but fans complained to us, 'Hey, uncle, your pronunciation was wrong!' It was a nice urge for us to do a better job as reporters."

From being unknown to debuting in the entertainment world to becoming popular, it's a long journey before a group gets brilliant and glorious. The public doesn't see those long, long days as trainees, the tough training, or the ruthless elimination mechanism. Countless boys and girls invested in youth, tears, and sweat, and only a very few could make it. Fans of such idols are inevitably obsessed, irrational, and sometimes even ridiculous. But love and madness are equally real.

Committed to serving the audience, excellent CCTV presenters always aspire to seek perfection.

Zhang Bin's memory was different from Sha Tong's, though. In Zhang Bin's view, the Incheon Asian Games were one-of-a-kind and were a relatively prosperous scene for a country, city, and region in a historical cycle. Together with the previous Korea-Japan FIFA World Cup and the subsequent Pyeongchang Winter Olympics, it showed that South Korea had a very strong desire to host the competition. Moreover, Incheon identified itself as the new center of Asian development. This made global journalists, especially the ones from China, very stunned because this self-positioning was not obvious at the time and would probably not be feasible in many years to come. But it cannot be denied that it was Incheon's vision.

Incheon did not have particularly high expectations for the massive changes made in the city by hosting the Asian Games, at least in terms of publicity, it maintained a restrained tone. The point was that the city was

A view in Incheon

A view of Incheon

eager to be known by Asia and the world, which was related to the fact that it was already developed well.

In terms of television broadcasting, some matches had not attracted much attention due to the schedule. But there were exceptions. Zhang Bin clearly remembered a competition held in a track and field venue with constant rain and low temperatures registered very high ratings in China. Because as long as there are Chinese athletes, Chinese people want to watch it. People want to watch China win, watch the national flag be raised, and listen to the national anthem.

How is it not? At the Incheon Asian Games, I also waited eagerly in front of the TV to watch the men's 4×100m freestyle relay.

Doha's Construction and Connection

Doha skyline

Qatar first caught my attention was the 4th WTO Ministerial Conference held in 2001. At 6:39 pm, on November 10, in the Salwa Banquet Hall of the Sheraton Hotel, Youssef Hussain Kamal, the conference chairman, banged the gavel to announce that the WTO has ratified China's accession and thus China has officially become its 143rd member.

At the G20 Summit in 2016, when the Hangzhou International Expo Center was a mecca for global journalists, I stopped at Al Jazeera, and hesitated for a while before saying hello to their staff. It struck me that it is one of the world's three major TV news channels, along with BBC and CNN.

An even more concrete encounter with Qatar was at the 2019 International Horticultural Exhibition in Beijing. Compared with other national pavilions, Qatar's heavily-invested buildings were eye-catching, hence preserved forever, so that a miniature version of Qatar could showcase its enchanting stores to visitors.

At the 2019 World Athletics Championships and the 2022 FIFA World Cup, we saw with our eyes how Qatar has leveraged sports as a national strategy to connect with the world and benefited from it.

Lusail Stadium

A Land of Water and Sand

"With a keffiyeh on my head, I am the richest in the world", a witty description of Qatar's economic strength, went viral during the 2022 World Cup.

Qatar does do wear much the same clothing. Headscarves, single-colored robes, and slippers with good leather are standard for both men and women. The difference is that men's headscarves are secured by two rings ogal, as if worrying about a sudden wind blow, and some women prefer high

Qatari clothing

heels or formal shoes. People in white or black robes walking on the streets of a hot summer dusk look similar, like a throng of QR codes on legs, but they are actually not. It reminds me of a line in *Rhinoceros in Love*, a drama directed by Meng Jinghui and written by Liao Yimei: "My eyesight is at its worst at dusk. All the women seem beautiful, and the tall buildings and streets look different." Doha at dusk never ceases to fascinate me: lights are on, the sunset has not yet gone, the skyline is blurred, the sea breeze sways palms, mosques are crowned with halo and majesty, a girl is drawing in the old bazaar, a falconer is holding a knife in his hand... Local women's charm is wrapped in black abayas, so their taste and status are well reflected in shoes, bags, watches, and jewelry. It is only when men and women are separated for some kind of ritual that they may look at each other and themselves differently from the public.

Qatar's wealth comes mainly from oil and gas buried in the deserts, and in recent years, natural gas has become a pillar industry and a top priority in its economy. Arid lands with an average annual precipitation of less than 80 millimeters are eager for water, but fortunately, Qatar is

Streetscape in Doha

Bazaars in Doha

located on a peninsula on the southwestern shore of the Persian Gulf and has more than 560 kilometers of coastline. Water and sand are not only the natural features of Qatar but also the geographical environment of Doha.

Doha was formerly a small fishing village called Al Bidda, located in a harbor in the middle of the eastern coast of the Qatar Peninsula. In 1863, the first ruler of Qatar, Thani, said to a traveler, "Whether our status is high or low, we are the slaves of a master: pearls". Fishing and pearl diving were the means of survival and wealth throughout its history. This is probably why the sculpture "Shell and Pearl" is on a street and the 19th-century Baroda pearl carpet is treasured in the museum. They are a salute to the past.

"Shell and Pearl"

Carpets in the museum

Things changed after the 1920s, when low-cost cultured pearls from Japan seized the world market and Qatar's pearl diving industry went into decline. Meanwhile, oil exploration, which swept the Middle East in the first half of the 20th century, saved Qatar from its troubles. In 1939, the British helped Qatar explore huge reserves of oil and gas and drill its first oil well. As the first tanker laden with crude oil sailed in 1949, Qatar gradually transformed itself from a fishing village into an energy and economic powerhouse in West Asia.

At the 15th Doha Asian Games in 2006, water and sand were abstracted into yellow crescent-shaped dunes and the rushing blue sea of the Arabian Gulf, accompanied by the sun logo of the Olympic Council of Asia. The emblem perfectly illustrated the vitality and possibilities of the event.

Though the country's biodiversity was not that great due to its tropical desert climate, the desert antelope served very well as the mascot for the Doha Asian Games. Orry, wearing a short sports suit in the same yellow and blue colors as the emblem, was carrying a torch, playing balls, running fast, or shooting an arrow. It was drought-tolerant, well-shaped, and had a pair of sword-like horns pointing straight to the sky. Its passion and energy symbolized the strong momentum of the young country.

The emblem and mascot of the Doha Asian Games

16 Years in Doha: From the Asian Games to the World Cup

From the 15th Asian Games in 2006 to the 22nd FIFA World Cup in 2022, Doha has gone through an extraordinary journey of 16 years.

Whether people watched it in person at the 15th Doha Asian Games or on TV, the one-of-a-kind flame-lighting ceremony at the Khalifa International Stadium is absolutely unforgettable. The unusual rain in the last couple of days, the galloping Prince Al-Thani, the more than 100-meter-

Flame lighting at the opening ceremony of the Doha Asian Games

tall platform, the heart-stopping moment when the horse slipped on the ramp, the gasp from the crowd... The prince, as the captain of the Qatari equestrian endurance team, successfully rode the horse to the top. The torch was lit, and the hanging giant wheel and astrolabe rotated with courage, excitement, and thrill.

During an equestrian competition, I witnessed a horse that failed to cross an obstacle throw the athlete off and gallop around the field. Fortunately, the athlete was not badly injured. After a brief fall to the ground, she stood up in pain, waved to her beloved horse, and tried to calm it down so that they could walk it out of the field. Probably due to guilt or indescribably complicated feelings, the horse couldn't calm down and forgive itself. It was excited and furious, and it even jumped out of the wall of the arena after running several laps. The sports arena is not like a stage for theatrical performances: there is no lip-syncing or pre-recording. Even if the athletes are well-trained and have experienced hundreds of competitions, what happened at that moment is actually impossible for others to know. The result is cold and cruel, and no one can wear the crown for good.

What made Doha different from the other Asian Games was that it treated the journalists exceptionally well. "Breakfasts were covered by the hotel, and the organizing committee provided a free meal voucher per day. After the queen's visit, she sponsored another meal with her own money, so the second half of the trip was completely free." A journalist who was working in the media center recalled, "It cannot be ruled out that Qatar did this to publicize the Asian Games, including responding to possible public opinion in advance. Anyway, it was goodwill, and the journalists appreciated it. That was effective communication."

Among the Chinese team's 165 gold medals at the Doha Asian Games, one was claimed by a superstar in world athletics: the men's 110-meter hurdles champion Liu Xiang. It was right after the 2004 Athens Olympics, and he was in high spirits. His teammate, Shi Dongpeng, was also in the games. A few years later, I took my daughter, who was in the first grade of primary school, to the Bird's Nest to expect Liu Xiang to make another victory at the 2008 Beijing Olympics. We were saddened that he withdrew due to injuries, but we cheered for Shi Dongpeng and many others.

At the Khalifa International Stadium in the early morning of September 29, 2019, Liang Rui finished the women's 50-kilometer race walk at the World Athletics Championships, securing the first gold medal for the Chinese team and presenting a gift to the 70th birthday of New China. In the early morning of October 2, Xie Zhenye won the 7th place in the men's 200-meter in 20.14 seconds, setting the best Chinese record in international sprint competitions.

When some athletes get old, new athletes grow; that is the law of nature and competitive sports. What we have to do is learn to love, accept, and salute. We love their dazzling brilliance when they reach the top and accept their unwillingness, helplessness, and even despair when they don't make it. We hope they will feel our hearts and stay calm and resilient all the time.

2019 World Athletics Championships (Khalifa International Stadium)

In its journey to adopt sport as its national strategy, Qatar has spared no effort to maintain aggressive momentum. The country's hands-on experience of hosting the AFC Asian Cup in 1988 and 2011 paved the way for its bid to host the 2022 FIFA World Cup, and the success in 2022 has inspired many countries. I had a brief look at Qatar's eight model sports facilities (one of them was the iconic Lusail Stadium) at the 2019 International Horticultural Exhibition in Beijing. Years later, I realized that all eight venues were located within a 21-mile radius of central Doha and that seven were temporarily constructed. The significance of the "Doha City-Based World Cup" lies in the mode and possibilities it creates, which may motivate more countries and cities to work harder to bring the World Cup and competitions to their home soil.

From the Asian Games to the Asian Cup, from the World Athletics Championships to the FIFA World Cup, Doha has been busy for 16 years presenting wonderful events to Asia and the world, which not only greatly promoted the country's international influence but also ignited the fire of desire for international competitions in the Middle East and West Asia.

Stadium 974

Official Fan Festival

International Broadcast Center

Cultural Symbols and the Desire for Diversity

Doha continues to win the hosting rights for the 2030 Asian Games. Like a spinning top, it is impossible to stop. Just as it ignored the feelings of the United States and its neighbor Saudi Arabia when bidding for the 2022 World Cup, the city was too busy bidding for its second Asian Games and did not care much about its rival Riyadh.

The emblem of the 2030 Doha Asian Games consists of four staggered semicircular kaleidoscopic patterns. At first glance, it seems not to be about sports but more like a casual blend of tour posters and city landmarks. When I look at it again, I am not so sure, because in addition to the recognizable "Desert Rose" and the Museum of Islamic Art, the

The emblem of the 2030 Doha Asian Games

other two semicircles with modern and traditional designs may also be related to sports or venues.

This emblem, which has not been exhaustively interpreted visually, might be Qatar's imagination and a new invitation to Asia and the world.

The National Museum of Qatar, as known as the Desert Rose, was the work of Pritzker Prize winner Jean Nouvel. The French architect completed the overall construction with large, curved, and overlapped disks, inspired by the mineral crystals that resemble roses unique to the desert region. At the same time, through the design of the flow of visitors, the narrative of history, industry, and space, especially Qatar's status in the world, unfolds.

"Desert Rose"

The Museum of Islamic Art was designed by I.M. Pei, the top-notch Chinese-born architect, in his 90s. Its understated limestone exterior walls, clever geometry, and the blue ocean create a strong appeal. Yet on the seat screens of Qatar Airlines, the image was a distant view of the artificial island where the museum sits. The two curved windows on the rectangular facade at the top were like mysterious eyes behind a mask, reminding me that there are endless treasures to explore.

It is said that architecture is frozen music, but the music of sports events is a different type. It is straightforward, passionate, and stimulates a chorus easily, and screams and shouts are common.

Part of "Desert Rose"

Just steal your destiny

Right from the hands of fate

Reach for the cup of life

Cause your name is on it

Do you really want it...(yeah)

Do you really want it...(yeah)

Here we go! Ale, ale, ale

Go, go, go! Ale, ale, ale

Tonight's the night

We're gonna celebrate

The cup of life! Ale, ale, ale

The theme song of the 1998 France FIFA World Cup, *The Cup of Life*, is probably one of the most popular songs in the world. I can't remember the songs after that, probably because there are too many raps make it difficult to sing, or I am just getting old. Doha sent a plane to South Korea to pick up world-class boy band members to sing in the opening performance and invited the girl group for publicity. These gestures, from the perspective of young people, are sincere and trendy. Thanks to the bombarded soundtracks, I came to remember the line "this what we do, how we do" of the *Dreamers*.

The emblem of the 2022 World Cup is incredible. The curved and interlocked pattern resembles "infinity" and "8". It looks like a white trophy from a distance, and is decorated with burgundy red Arabic motifs. The 3D rotation symbolizes the infinite possibilities of football and expresses good wishes for the long-term prosperity of the World Cup.

The emblem and mascot of the 2022 World Cup

Qatar did not immerse itself in the carnival of the World Cup for too long before beginning to brainstorm for the future.

The significance of the 2030 Doha Asian Games is that they coincide with the National Vision 2030. Qatar has been trying to get rid of its dependence on oil and gas and find a diversified development path. These activities and foreign exchange have succeeded in fueling the country's tourism, business, and education.

My former colleagues went to Doha for the 2022 World Cup. They could not be prouder to see so many "made in China" facilities or items that made the event possible. At Lusail Stadium (the Diamond of the Desert), Al Janoub Stadium, and other stadiums, they witnessed the penalty shootouts and the final. As veteran reporters and passionate fans,

Corniche

International Broadcast Center Service Desk

Exterior view of Lusail Stadium

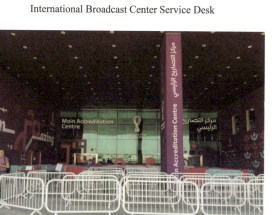

Main Accreditation Center

they delivered a number of quality articles. I was at home, watching the competition and looking up the materials from the China-Arab States Forum on Radio and Television Cooperation held in Hangzhou earlier. At some point, I felt that all the dots of Doha—its past, present, and future—were connected into one.

Martin Cooper and the "mobile" people

"手机的诞生是为了实现一个梦想，即所有的个人通信将实现真正的可移动；手机号码应该代表一个人而不是一个地方。"

Mr. Martin Cooper and IIT alumni

This is a real-life scenario.

An old lady stood in front of a "Zhejiang Mobile" (China Mobile Zhejiang Company) store, looking up at the four huge blue Chinese characters, and asked in a puzzled look: "How can Zhejiang be mobile? Is Zhejiang moving to somewhere?"

Not long ago I finished reading the Chinese translation of Martin Cooper's *Cutting the Cord: The Cell Phone Has Transformed Humanity*. It reminded me of the old lady who I thought was absurd and ignorant. Now I find her so cute and humorous. For whatever reason, ignorant or hilarious, she unconsciously mentioned a critical high-frequency word in Martin's book—MOBILE.

Martin Cooper says, human is to be mobile by nature.

My first encounter with Martin originated from a mobile experience.

It was late June 2005 when I was studying at Illinois Institute of Technology (IIT), Chicago, USA.

One summer afternoon, before I stepped into a half-opened door of a lecture hall, I didn't know a heavyweight entrepreneurial innovation forum was in progress. Moving forward through the middle passage, I couldn't find a vacant seat immediately. While the principal was walking toward the center stage, I had no choice but to head forward to find a seat as soon as possible. Since I didn't find a seat along the way, I just walked and walked until I reached the first row of the lecture hall.

It was the distance from the entrance to the front row that made me meet one of the most outstanding alumni of IIT—Martin Cooper.

While the principal started speaking, I sat down, looked around, and found four gentlemen sitting there and I was the fifth person in the front row. A gentleman in a plaid shirt nodded at me with a smile, which greatly eased my nervousness and embarrassment. So I gave him a smile back, and then looked to the other side. A familiar image came into sight, and it was Ed Kaplan, the chair and co-founder of Zebra Technologies (a Global 500 company) whom I had visited with my classmate before. Since I already knew he was an alumnus of IIT, I realized this was an invited presentation of four IIT alumni innovators, and my guess was proved by a poster next to the stage. Due to this unintended mistake, I accidentally sat next to them. For a moment my heart was pounding, but I quickly transformed the restlessness and excitement into superficial calm and focused on listening.

During the coffee break, Mr. Plaid Shirt sitting next to me has become my acquaintance. When gently asked, I told him I was coming to IIT from China to learn public administration. He exchanged business card with me, which corroborated the introduction in the poster. I couldn't be sure that Mr. Plaid Shirt is Martin Cooper, the life trustee of IIT, renowned electrical engineer of Motorola, and the inventor of the mobile

Mr. Martin Cooper making a speech

Mr. Martin Cooper and the author

phone. His name was not only figured in IIT's history, but also crowned in the long history of technological invention and the industrial revolution.

Being grateful, I asked if he could give me a chance to interview him. With the same smile, he said he would love to share with me the story of mobile phone. I said since there were too many technical terms in this area, I had to do some homework to make our interview smooth. He indicated he would wait and turn up as promised.

A few days later, I saw Mr. Cooper again in the lobby of a hotel downtown. He still wore the same plaid shirt, perhaps to help me recognize him easily, or maybe he just favored that shirt. Who knows?

The moment recorded by the camera is now juxtaposed with the *Cutting the Cord*. At that time I had the confidence to wear sleeveless dress to show my upper arm, neck and shoulder. The photo with Cooper is one of the very few paper photos. I still keep it in file and a friend of mine, who sent me the book, saw the picture and that's why he picked up the book in the Sisyphe bookstore, which turned out to be the last one on the bookshelf. He said to me though he had worked in the Finance Department of Motorola China for many years, he wasn't as lucky as me to have a personal conversation with Mr. Cooper.

"Thank you, Mr. Cooper. It's you who made my connection with my family possible across the ocean." Since I was afraid that it would be difficult to talk about scientific topics in English, this introduction seemed appropriate.

Mr. Cooper obviously got my true feelings. To an overseas student who had been separated from the family for a whole year, the importance of mobile phone is self-evident. Classmates mainly used MSN to communicate, while I spent quite some time making phone calls with my family and friends sitting in the corridor alone during the night.

"Hi, Vicky! Mobile phones were originally invented because people are mobile. It is impossible for us to walk around with a landline. No matter how long the phone line is, it is too short compared to the distance a person needs to move. Now that you're here, away from your family, you understand better what I'm talking about, right?"

I "hummed" to show that I understood. Literally speaking, at least at the beginning, I did understand, not to mention that I had already listened to his speech. But years later, after I quickly read his book *Cutting the Cord*, I realized that I didn't understand it all.

In Mr.Cooper's first round of dialogue, at least the following information was emphasized and implied, namely, "man on the move" or "mobile man", "limits of traditional telephone", and "radio makes mobile phone possible". I reckoned he must pay tribute to Marconi (Italian inventor), the pioneer of wireless communication and the Nobel Prize winner in physics, Paul Galvin, the founder of Motorola, and Bob Galvin, the "second generation" of the founder's family. There was Motorola's culture of inspiring innovation and not being afraid of failure, but I couldn't remember the details at that time.

"So besides the wireless, what else, Mr. Cooper, made you the inventor of the world's first hand-held portable cellular telephone?"

"It's not me but many people. Vicky, I'm just the conceiver of the mobile phone, and of course some people call me the prophet. It's the whole team that made it happen." Mr. Cooper's eyes shone with sincerity, "As for success, to a large extent, it depends on good luck, daring to dream and perseverance."

I was not convinced though as Cooper took it so lightly that luck was the reason, but when he said "luck", we all recalled the famous and real story of "Titanic" in 1912, which was portrayed in Hollywood blockbusters of love at first sight and love until death. Moreover, if it were not for the long-distance international Morse code distress signal (SOS) sent by two telegraphers of Marconi on board, more than 700 lives that survived the cruise couldn't have been saved at all.

Marconi's vision of practical wireless was unexpectedly tested during a devastating shipwreck, leading him to see the enormous potential of wireless communications to reshape the way people connect and communicate. What Cooper had to do was to continue to explore along the line opened up by the pioneers.

Investigating the life experience of the inventor Cooper, we found that he was originally born and raised in a "mobile" home. Cooper's parents were both Ukrainian. Ignoring all the twists and turns and turmoils they experienced, they immigrated to Canada and the United States successively. Cooper successfully obtained American citizenship because he was born in the United States, but his parents and brothers did not have such an easy time in this matter. His parents made a living by running a grocery store, similar to the French female writer Annie Ernaux who won the Nobel Prize in Literature in 2022. But unlike Annie Ernaux who was condescendingly called the "grocery store girl" and who sharply described class barriers in a literary way, Cooper seemed to have no sensitive troubles in this regard. He focused on his parents' super ability to sell and maintain customer relationships. This gene has also become the "entrepreneurial spirit" rooted in his heart.

After entering the IIT, in order to reduce the financial burden of his parents, Cooper joined the US Navy and became a submarine officer. This unique experience cultivated his ability to "act immediately without hesitation".

In Cooper's mind, thinking slows him down. Therefore, He was bold, fast and affirmative when choosing careers or solving technological problems.

A research engineer in the teletype company was Cooper's first job, but within a year he accepted Motorola's offer. Motorola was founded in 1928. The headquarters building was located on Augusta Avenue in Chicago. During the golden stage of the company's development, Cooper joined the company. At the same time, the company foresightedly bought the patent rights of any inventions invented by Cooper during his tenure at a symbolic price of one dollar. This deal, which might look extremely uneconomical in hindsight, made Cooper feel grateful, since it allowed him to be with a group of talented professionals, who collided and inspired each other. Besides, he could learn excellent management and strong market development abilities from them.

It can almost be said that throughout his career at Motorola, Cooper, often dreamed of the future and "creating dreams" for the future, or preparing and fighting for this "dream" in his heart. That is, based on human needs for mobility and freedom of communication, he envisioned a portable wireless communication device. With it, people could communicate seamlessly with anyone from anywhere. What has Cooper been through for this change in communication and the future of a better world?

"The line is not straight," Cooper said, "in many cases, especially when threatened by monopoly industries, it strays."

Historically, the Bell System (consisting of AT&T and some affiliates, Bell Labs, and Western Electric) had long held a government-regulated monopoly on telecommunications. From birth to popularization and commercialization, mobile phones had gone through 10 years of continuous investment, research and development, struggle, persuasion and endeavor.

Perhaps most of us will clearly remember the outstanding contributions of some well-known laboratories or companies in the field of specific scientific and technological inventions and manufacturing when doing world history exam questions. Without this cross-cultural dialogue with Cooper, I would not really understand when a kind of progress is focused on defending the special interests that come with it, traditional monopoly industries can be self-contained and go to great lengths to prevent the birth of new things.

So when Martin Cooper held the "brick", named DynaTAC and

developed by himself and his team, walking south from the New York Hilton and strolling down Sixth Avenue on April 3, 1973, his first call wasn't to his "pre-entrepreneur" Mom, nor his wife, or even his own office, but to Dr. Joel at competitor AT&T. DynaTAC was the first in the world since then, deemed as the ancestor of billions of mobile phones. It was so big that people born in the 1970s and before remember that its common name was "Big Brother".

"Hello, who's this?"

"Hi, Joel. This is Martin Cooper."

"Hi, Martin." said Joel doubtfully.

"Joel, I'm calling you on my cell phone. This is a real cell phone, a personal, portable, hand-held cellular phone."

Cooper said those were the best words he could think of, and there was a silence on the other end of the line. Cooper thought Joel might be gritting his teeth. Because for so long anything new was an addition to the wired phone system in the "eyes" of the Bell system, and Cooper and Motorola broke Bell's driving logic with the wireless system and the freedom it entailed.

Joel's position at AT&T was equivalent to Cooper's position at Motorola. He was an engineer in charge of the cellular network communication project. Although he was angry, he didn't think that the call Cooper gave him was so great, at least he didn't have enough predictions that it would revolutionize the way people live in the future. He was furious, perhaps first because it took only about three months for a competitor to develop the phone first. Although the Bell System did not wish to reveal in any way to the public that they had a monopoly idea, in 1972 they settled on their attitude towards the mobile phone — if someone had to do it, it should be them, because they were the phone company, and they had to have full control to do it. But now Motorola and Cooper have taken the lead, throwing a "brick" mobile phone in front of the world.

The topic naturally turned to Mr. Cooper's third keyword "persistency", more precisely, to the continuous cooperation and competition between Motorola and Bell System.

"This road of competition and cooperation begins in New Jersey, winds in Chicago, and ends in the capital, Washington." Mr. Cooper said.

In the context of the conversation at the time, I couldn't digest so much information for a while, but Cooper's narration made me feel that he was so sober that he held a completely pragmatic attitude towards competition and cooperation. Cooper and Motorola actually adopted such a strategy: not only to get a share of the cooperation, but also to secretly work hard to stand out from the encirclement and win by surprise.

This allowed me to try to capture a series of situations that could be followed—

In the fall of 1959, in an all-glass building at Bell Laboratories in suburban New Jersey, Cooper fully felt the arrogance of his opponents as they emphasized terms such as "telephone" and "surveillance" for wired telephony.

Returning from New Jersey to Motorola headquarters in Chicago, Cooper, was still angry, and he convinced the executives that they must participate in the IMTS (Mobile Wireless Telephone) project whether they like it or not.

A few years later, Bell Labs chose Motorola to develop the wireless portion of the IMTS project, then to the fixed wireless base station business, and later to expand IMTS to the new 450MHz frequency (an "UHF band" as opposed to "Very High-Frequency Band").

In 1960, the Chicago Police Department was in a deep crisis of public confidence, and Mayor Richard J. Daley hired a new superintendent (chief) named Wilson. Wilson needed a portable handheld two-way walkie-talkie that could be used both in police cars and on foot patrols, and kept in touch with the communication center at all times. Motorola was successfully "asked for this favor".

Motorola created the first viable cellular communication system in the United States in response to a request from the Chicago Police Department.

A heavily armed police officer with a baton, handcuffs, flashlight, gun, and spare ammo on his belt said while he was issuing a ticket to Cooper, "Look, I've got this new thing you invented (a new hand-held Transceiver HT-220)". So Cooper began to conceive of smaller, lighter, and portable wireless devices.

Motorola and AT&T once again met unexpectedly. Around the use of cellular communication technology, the two companies with different histories, concepts, and under the guidance of different historical views and values launched an all-out war for the future of communications in the capital Washington, DC.

   ...

Going back to that summer night in Chicago in 2005, if my conversation with Cooper was still going on, we would have talked about the FCC, and talked about government regulation. Before that, Cooper would first brief me the knowledge about the wireless spectrum in a super simple way. Its public property attributes, and a kind of capacity that can be infinitely doubled through the efforts of technicians and engineers, so it will never be exhausted as a resource.

"The wireless spectrum is a public property." This was Cooper's motto, but also his belief. AT&T didn't want that, and it had been working to gain a monopoly on the cellular spectrum, not just in the landline phone system, but into the land mobile business and all air-to-ground communications. It wanted to take the whole "cake", in Cooper's words.

The FCC had long held a highly unreasonable partiality toward AT&T, but it was not without merit. It had taken early steps to prevent

AT&T from becoming a monopoly, although those measures had been very limited. In the hearing held by the FCC in May 1973, Motorola's active role in promoting technological progress was highlighted. Cooper eloquently denied AT&T's excessive desire to occupy the wireless spectrum. He offended the chairman of the world's largest communication company, but won a possible future for mobile phones and personal communications, as well as the FCC's public policy (opening and sharing wireless spectrum).

That conversation with Cooper partially changed my spare time arrangement at IIT. Thanks to the social network built by mobile phones, my classmates and I had the opportunity to participate in the New Year reception hosted by Mayor Daley for Asian Americans and some Chinese in Chicago. We visited the Chicago Police Department to try to find out if there was any trace left by the old chief who had "questions"(raised customer needs) for Motorola. In front of the Gateway Arch, a landmark in St. Louis, we paid tribute to the same designer who designed the glass building at Bell Labs in New Jersey. In early July 2005, we visited Zebra Technologies again and were eager to have an in-depth exchange with Ed Kaplan.

The author visited the Chicago Police Department

Mr. Richard Michael Daley, Mayor of Chicago, and the author

Mr. Ed Kaplan, the then Chairman of Zebra Technologies and the author

298

The Motorola mobile phones collected by the author's friend

"We always have to go out to have a chance."

This is another reading of mobility of the friend who gave me *Cutting the Cord*. A child who believed that dreams can come true and was born in a poor family, who emerged from Motorola to become the CFO of another top global joint venture company, to him, "keep going" was the only secret.

On that rather short summer night in Chicago, Mr. Cooper and I could not have communicated so profoundly. Memory and reading have been intertwined, entangled and enlightening each other. Speed reading the progress of mobile phones and the Internet, at the end of the story, both Motorola and Cooper ushered in a happy ending like a fairy tale. The dream of the future of personal communication has become a myth in the real world.

So many people in this world—so many mobile phones!

"The interconnection between people has nothing to do with location." This is Cooper's another statement after "people are mobile".

As I write this, I really want to call Mr. Cooper and tell him that after so many years, I still miss him sincerely. Obviously, I have lost his business card, from Motorola to later Ericsson and Nokia to generations of iPhone and Huawei, the constant replacement of mobile phones made it impossible for me to find that string of precious numbers. In the permanent maintenance of human emotions, technology also shows its pale side. After all, functional storage cannot replace careful memory.

The original manuscript from Mr. Martin Cooper to the author

Today, especially in the few years since COVID-19 has spread around the world, the relationship between humans and mobile phones has ushered in a permanent change. We can stay out of the country for several years, but we can't live without mobile phones for a day. Learning, education, medical care, payment and telecommuting… mobile phones have become a part of our lives and even our bodies.

"The portable phone industry is still in its early stage, and we are just beginning to understand the important value of human-machine communication," predicted Martin Cooper, "If we combine mobile phones and artificial intelligence technology, there is a possibility of a hybrid of human-machine integration in the future, that is, the new humans in versions 2.0 and even 3.0..."

As the "father of mobile phones", Martin Cooper once again left us thinking about the "future". Having left Motorola long ago to start his own company, he inherited the courage and wisdom from his mother who was the proprietress of the grocery store, selling his "ideas" and "dreams" to the world as always.

> "我们只需不断学习，不断前行，这是我们唯一的生活方式。"
>
> ——马丁·库珀

> "The cell phone was created to fulfill a dream that all personal communication would be truly mobile.
> A phone number should identify a person not a place."

Postscript

From bones to souls

Witnessing *Cities of Sporting Events* from its conceptualization to its completion, I was deeply touched by the challenge of writing. For one thing, with the Asian Games approaching, even the most magnificent ideas require to be written down word by word. For another, no matter how urgent it is, the narrative still demands precision, and the words still deserve to carry their flavor. Therefore, after months of intensive writing, the book presented in front of the readers may still lack composure, but it is already refreshing enough.

How should we write about "events" ? When browsing social media, it is not difficult to find encyclopedic introductions to the Asian Games and corresponding series of reports, and sports journalists may have long been combing through the past and present of these events. This book does the same but also tries to go further. For example, might the hands-on experience of art and aesthetics reinvigorate the emblems, mascots, and promotional videos that dwell in the corner of museums? Or, for example, could the observation of and participation in the world give a sense of presence to the moments in front of and behind the scenes?

As for how to write about "cities", it seems to be a more complicated question. Throughout history and modern times, many excellent travelogues, movies, geological writing, and even social science research have provided their answers. Facing such a melting pot of rich cultural repertoire, knowledge and insights, this book is both humble and ambitious. The film of Manila, which seals the laughter and tears of female migrant workers, is gradually rendered visible through sociologist Pei-chia Lan's contemplation of gender, class, and national boundaries. "Sleepless in Jakarta" kicks off with a motorcycle, where decades ago, Anderson, a young political scientist, also rode a motorcycle down the streets with trepidation and enthusiasm. Abbas and Wong Kar-wai are probably both windows into a particular mountain village or highway, and *Hiroshima mon amour* and *Sovjetistan* may have both touched on people's hidden concerns about drastic social changes and their inner nuclear explosions. Walking through the streets of Lausanne, will the imaginary and real-life encounters remind us of the Nesbit who got off the train at Lausanne station in *Strangers of Cambridge*, or John Berger's mesmerizing sentence, "We travelled from bone to bone, from continent to continent"?

In the way that only a diverse range of genres can absorb such a diverse collection of resources, I believe that this book is equally open to diverse interpretations. To some extent, it can be news reports, work logs, movie reviews, and book reviews, but also smart experimental writing, and earnest introductions to other works. Hopefully, these sincere words will satisfy or further pique the curiosity of the reader. Following the clues contained in the book, we can arrive at places that may be far beyond our expectations.

CHEN Jiahe

Sciences Po

Acknowledgments

A hand-writing letter from a friend arrived when the book was completed.

"Writing is like wild geese crossing the boundless sky, and shadows sinking into the chilly water. The wild geese leave no traces, and the water holds no shadows."

Though the geese pass by silently, the sky affords them unlimited space to soar, while remembering the elegant trajectories of their travels.

The shadow and the water, though as elusive as a phantom dream, like the flower in the mirror and the moon in the lake, achieve mutual recognition and rediscovery by mirroring each other.

The author and their works, the person who writes and the person who reads, are in this kind of detached yet intimate, carefree yet mutually fulfilling relationship.

I would like to express my gratitude to Zhejiang Education Publishing House, especially to the publisher, Mr. Zhou Jun, and all editors and proofreaders.

I would also like to thank relevant units and all the experts, friends, colleagues, family members and readers who have supported me and contributed to this book.

图书在版编目（ＣＩＰ）数据

赛事之城 / 周澍著. -- 杭州 ： 浙江教育出版社，
2023.9
ISBN 978-7-5722-6498-6

Ⅰ．①赛… Ⅱ．①周… Ⅲ．①亚洲运动会－历史－青
少年读物 Ⅳ．①G811.23-49

中国国家版本馆CIP数据核字(2023)第159922号

赛事之城

周　澍　著

策　　　划：王水明　王文韬　Vicky
责任编辑：王方家
美术编辑：韩　波
责任校对：姚　璐
责任印务：陈　沁
封面插图：常　青
封面设计：张　文　邓陈波　志　华
装帧设计：商亚东　李小忠　王　蓓　Caleb
　　　　　朱晓卿　应单旻　Bob　林蔚颖

出版发行：浙江教育出版社（杭州市天目山路40号）
制　　版：杭州海洋电脑制版印刷有限公司
印　　刷：浙江省邮电印刷股份有限公司
版　　次：2023年9月第1版
印　　次：2023年9月第1次印刷
开　　本：787mm×1092mm　1/16
印　　张：21
插　　页：4
字　　数：420 000
书　　号：ISBN 978-7-5722-6498-6
定　　价：128.00元